P9-CKJ-231

NO

PATHFINDERS OF THE WORLD MISSIONARY CRUSADE

Pathfinders of the World Missionary Crusade

by

SHERWOOD EDDY

ABINGDON-COKESBURY PRESS

New York • Nashville

PATHFINDERS OF THE WORLD MISSIONARY CRUSADE

COPYRIGHT, MCMXLV
BY WHITMORE & STONE

All rights in this book are reserved. No part of the
text may be reproduced in any form without written permission of the publishers, except brief quotations used
in connection with reviews in magazines or newspapers.

K

Printed in the United States of America

14,960

FOREWORD

FOR the last fifty years I have been engaged in traveling work. Though I never sought or planned it, my work—by a fortunate accident, or providence—has taken me through most of the world's great mission fields. After fifteen years among the students and masses of India, I spent the next decade and a half doing student evangelistic work across Asia—from China, Japan, and the Philippines, through the Near East to Turkey, Palestine, Iraq, Egypt, and then to czarist and later to Soviet Russia.

I began in India in traveling work among the colleges, speaking to high-caste Hindu and Mohammedan students, both of whom were at that period standing in an almost unbroken phalanx against what seemed to them the hostile invasion of Christianity. Later, while not abandoning the high castes, I turned my attention chiefly to the poor and the outcastes, to the common people who "heard Jesus gladly." To do this I had to learn the Tamil language; and then I devoted most of my time, with Indian fellow workers, to the Indian Christians, that they might undertake the evangelization of their own people, which they could do far more effectively than any foreigner. To acquire and to master the vernacular, I took a mission station out among the masses in the heart of the area occupied by the United Church of South India, which included Congregational, Dutch Reformed, Basel Reformed, and Free Church and Established Church of Scotland missions.

In retrospect, I find I have spent half a century along the far-flung battle line of missions. I was one of the first of sixteen thousand student volunteers who were swept into what seemed to us nothing less than a missionary crusade. We were considered fanatical by some, and we made numerous mistakes which we ourselves came to realize later in bitter experience. Many sacrificed early plans and ambitions for wealth, power, prestige or pleasure, to go to some distant country about which they knew little save its abysmal need. Not wholly unlike the unity of Christendom achieved during the Middle Ages was the feeling of these student volunteer missionaries that they were one team, working for one world, under one Captain. We felt much as Wordsworth did about the French Revolution—which he doubtless idealized as we did our crusade:

> Bliss was it in that dawn to be alive,
> But to be young was very Heaven!

As I look back upon it now, I see that the greatest privilege of my life has been to be a part—however small or unworthy—of this great movement, to live with and work among those who were in the front lines of this missionary crusade. I have come into contact with many of the sixteen thousand volunteer missionaries, watching them at their work and living in their homes. They were as human, and some of them as imperfect, as the Crusaders; but, with all their shortcomings and limitations, they were the finest body of men I have ever known.

I do not attempt to write a complete biographical history of missions, which would require many volumes; I simply take a few typical men and women, drawn about equally from Methodist, Baptist, Presbyterian, Episcopal, Lutheran, and Congregational churches—chiefly the student volunteers of our generation whom I have known—and sketch their later lives and their missionary work. But I cannot ignore entirely the great pioneers who went before us. We emphatically were not

> . . . the first that ever burst
> Into that silent sea.

To make the work of our generation more intelligible, I describe briefly, by way of background, the great pioneers who laid foundations upon which we could build. There were men like William Carey in India, Adoniram Judson in Burma, and Robert Morrison in China. I do not confine myself in this volume to those who worked in foreign fields, but pass on to the work of the often more important nationals and members of the younger churches who led the missionary crusade in their own land. I write of men like Bishop Azariah, Bishop Abraham of the ancient Syrian Church, and K. T. Paul, in India; Chang Po-ling, Wu Yi-fang, and James Y. C. Yen, in China.

I am indebted to my friends who have read portions of the manuscript and who have made many helpful criticisms and suggestions, especially to Kenneth Latourette, T. H. P. Sailer, Daniel J. Fleming, Ruth Rouse, and Charles H. Fahs; and to H. A. Popley of Erode, South India, who has helped me collect valuable material on Indian missionaries and national leaders.

I have tried to make this a book which would have been of value to me as a student, or as a volunteer, sent as I was to the field with little knowledge of missions and very inadequate preparation, or as a missionary when I lived in an isolated section far from a railway in South India; also, a book that might prove helpful to a pastor in preparation for a missionary sermon or to a layman who wished to know of the lives of some of the great pathfinders of the present world missionary crusade.

SHERWOOD EDDY

CONTENTS

9

CONTENTS

1

MISSIONS AS A CRUSADE

THE original Crusades were fervid but fanatical movements that sometimes degenerated into sordid affairs of slaughter and lust. They consisted of a series of campaigns undertaken by the Christians of western Europe for two centuries, from 1096 to 1291, for the recovery of the Holy Land from the Moslems. They derived their name from the cross worn as a badge by the crusaders. At the heart of the movement was the symbol and sacrifice of the cross and the belief that true crusaders were fellow workers with God. These early Crusades were a strange mixture of good and evil. At their best they represented a surge of the religious revival then sweeping western Europe. They included an important chapter in the interaction of the East and West, affording a meeting point and mutual modification of Orient and Occident, as do modern missions. They were conceived as "holy wars" or "pilgrims' progresses" toward Christ's sepulcher, under the ideas of an age that was dominated by otherwordliness. There was at least a nucleus that was good in the heart of medieval chivalry, of pilgrimage, and of penance, though gross evils and supersitions followed in their train. Although the cross was for many but an amulet, a talisman, or a material symbol like those employed by witchcraft, for others it was a symbol of the love of God as Father manifest in the sacrificial death of Christ as Lord and Saviour, calling his disciples to follow in his steps. In this best sense I would think of missions as a crusade and recall the lives of the great pathfinders and crusaders who led this movement in ancient and in modern times.

We find today no spiritual meaning in the material possession of an empty tomb, won by slaughter and bloodshed accompanied by hatred and lust. But connected with the early efforts to rescue Christ's sepulcher, beneath the preaching of Peter the

Hermit and the dedication of the best of the crusaders, was the attempt at a diffusion of Christianity over the whole of the known world. The ends were noble, though they were often betrayed and morally defeated by the use of unworthy means.

Looking back across the nineteen centuries, we can see that missions have advanced in great waves, like the movement of the ocean rising to the gravitational pull of the sun and moon, at the high tides of the spiritual life of the church. Professor Kenneth Latourette—himself one of the student volunteers of the "Yale band"—in his monumental *A History of the Expansion of Christianity* sees three or four great periods of advance in the world mission of Christianity.

The first period covered the five centuries that were occupied chiefly in the winning of the Roman Empire. By the year 500 the majority of the population of the Empire had become professedly Christian, and Christianity had begun to spread beyond the Empire into Asia. In the second period of missionary expansion, which covered roughly from 500 to 1500, Christianity won the adherence of the peoples of northern Europe and made its entrance into Persia, India, and China. Among the first conquests of this period were the conversions of the peoples of Italy, Spain, Gaul, Ireland, Scotland, Wales, England, and of the Saxons and Scandinavians. We may take the third period in the extension of Christianity to be from 1500 to 1800. It was introduced by the age of geographical discoveries which carried Europeans into the Americas and throughout Asia. We take the fourth period of missionary expansion as covering the nineteenth century—"the great century"—and the opening of the twentieth, down to the present. In this period Christianity, attaining its widest geographical extent, embraced about a third of the world's population. European peoples, the first to be equipped with the mechanical appliances of the great age of scientific discoveries and thus the first to become industrialized and powerful, penetrated every corner of the globe as the bearers both of their religion and of Western civilization. The West had experienced a fresh religious awakening in the Protestant Reformation in northern Europe and in several Roman Catholic lands. There was a phenomenal increase of the white population of the globe, and through the influence of the churches these peoples were gradually kindled with the passion to share their religious privileges with all men.

In the present period of missionary expansion Christian educators introduced Western forms of life into Oriental lands, and with this introduction went all the creative—and disruptive —influences of modern science. Missionaries reduced several hundred languages to writing and began the creation of a literature in each. They were frequently pioneers of Western medicine and of European and American humanitarian movements. Their work resulted in scores of reform movements which gradually put an end to many ancient abuses and religious superstitions. They challenged the evils of slavery, poverty, illiteracy, disease and pestilence, as well as unnecessary suffering from famine, flood, natural calamities, political corruption, and tyrannical misgovernment. Most modern missionaries were as unwilling as they were unable to isolate religion, to confine it to a separate, watertight compartment of life. Instead, they found religion to be the throbbing center of all individual and social human existence. These Western peoples had, moreover, a faculty of organization which inevitably influenced all phases of living. Unprecedented wealth coupled with the missionary enthusiasm of the times developed a new spirit of giving which resulted in the sending out of by far the largest number of professional missionaries of any period in history. In 1928 there were some sixty thousand foreign missionaries, Protestants and Catholics being about equal in number. The nineteenth was not only "the great century," it was also the missionary century.

Always Christianity is missionary to just the extent that it is truly Christian. The word "missionary," from the Latin, is the same as the word "apostle" from the Greek, both meaning "one sent." Christians believe that Jesus was sent by the Father not only to the lost sheep of the house of Israel but to all mankind. Jesus Christ in turn sent the Twelve upon their mission of proclaiming the Kingdom of God upon earth. So every true Christian is not only one who is saved but also one who is sent

13

to the rest of mankind. Christianity has meaning for none unless it is for all. Each believer bears the responsibility for the universality of his religion. The apostolic methods were preaching, teaching, and healing to make men whole; and they inevitably resulted not only in the making of new men but also in the creation of a new social order. As the great Alexander Duff pointed out, the object of missions was to share in the divine purpose of creating the spiritual universe and to carry forward the whole message and scheme of redemption for all mankind. No Christian can rightly say he does not believe in missions, for that would imply that he does not believe in his own religion. Christians should look upon the whole non-Christian world as the "prodigal son" of humanity and believe that it is the duty of true Christians to call this prodigal humanity home to God and to share with them their treasure—the gift of the Father's love.

THE EARLIEST MISSIONARIES

The book of Acts is the first flaming missionary report of a world crusade. The Twelve that followed Jesus through Galilee, chosen for fellowship and training that he might send them forth to preach and to make men whole—spiritually, mentally, and physically—were typical representatives of all the missionary movements that were to follow, down to the present. The Apostle Paul was for all time the ideal pioneer missionary. He continued in his great work even though, with his dozen fellow evangelists, he was beaten, stoned, and persecuted through the cities of the Roman world, from Thessalonica to Rome, where he was beheaded. Everywhere cities in uproar cried: "These that have turned the world upside down are come hither also!"

From the first the new religion was contagious. Pliny as a governor in Asia Minor might well complain to Trajan that "the infection has spread not only through the cities but into the villages and country districts." Justin Martyr could claim: "There is not a single race of human beings—barbarians, Greeks, nomads, or herdsmen living in tents—where prayers in the name of Jesus the crucified are not offered up." Tertullian, as a pagan lawyer, proud of his Stoic learning, when he saw Christians martyred in the amphitheater and witnessed their victory over the universal fear of death, and their transformed lives, wrote: "Every man who witnesses this great endurance is struck with some misgiving. He is set on fire to look into it to find the cause of it. When he has learned the truth, at once he follows it himself." Tertullian himself became a link in the continuous chain of living witnesses who constituted a "new race of men." He then wrote: "We are but of yesterday. Yet we have filled all the places you frequent—cities, lodging houses, villages, townships, markets, the camp itself, the tribes, town councils, the palace, the senate, and the forum. . . . No race now lies outside God, the gospel flashing over all the earth and to the world's boundaries." Eusebius claimed great churches of tens of thousands of men: "In Rome itself, in Alexandria, in Antioch, in all Egypt, in Libya, in Europe, in Asia, and among all nations. I am compelled to confess that they could not otherwise have undertaken this enterprise, than by a divine power which exceeds that of men." This new race outthought the pagans, they outlived them, they outdied them. Finally over wide areas of the earth there was left not a single worshiper of "the great goddess Diana," of Apollo or Venus, of Baal or Dagon, of Isis or Serapis, of Thor or Wodin, or of the Druids of ancient Britain.

The first great missionary college was at Alexandria. It was presided over from about 180 to 200 by Pantaenus, the "Sicilian bee," who was a convert from Stoicism. From Alexandria, Christian teachers and evangelists went forth to Africa, Arabia, and the Near East, while Pantaenus himself was sent as a missionary to "India," though that name included a more vast and vague geographical area than at present. Clement of Alexandria and Origen succeeded Pantaenus and maintained Alexandria as a missionary center till their work reached its climax in Augustine, the greatest of the Latin Fathers, in the fifth century.

THE CONVERSION OF EUROPE

The finest elements in European civilization we owe to Christian missions. Ulfilas (311?-381) became the apostle of Christianity to the Teutonic Gothic tribes. He designed the Gothic alphabet for his half-savage people and, through his translation of the Scriptures into the Gothic language, raised a barbarian tongue to the dignity of a literary language, thereby becoming the father of Teutonic literature. Ulfilas, sent as missionary bishop from the Greek Church of Constantinople, worked for forty years for his own Gothic people and among the Visigoths beyond the Danube. The Goths then carried the Bible of Ulfilas all over Italy and Spain. Chrysostom (345?-407), most eloquent of the Church Fathers, was a force for missions and founded a missionary college at Constantinople to continue and to extend the work of Ulfilas by training Goths and other converts to work for the conversion of their own people. So humanizing and civilizing was the work of Ulfilas, Chrysostom, and their successors that Augustine almost forgave the Visigoths and Vandals because of the charity and clemency which characterized conquerors like Alaric in the first sack of Rome, in 410. The great Benedict established his monastery and missionary order in Italy about 529; and this was followed by other monastic missionary orders, by which Europe was largely evangelized.

St. Patrick (389?-461?), the patron saint of Ireland, made his country famous as the "Isle of Saints" and the "University of the West." He sent learned teachers to pagan areas of Britain, France, and Italy. Patrick was educated as a Christian in Britain or France until the age of sixteen, when he was carried away to Ireland by a band of wild Irish marauders and held in bondage for six years, after which he escaped. While he was in Britain the call came to him to return to Ireland as a missionary. After a long nonviolent crusade he won over the worshipers of the Druids, overthrew famous idols, and founded a church and monastery at Armagh, becoming its saintly bishop. He left us, in his Hymn of St. Patrick, a rude chant which sings the faith by which he lived:

16

>Christ as a light,
>Illumine and guide me!
>Christ as a shield, o'ershadow and cover me!
>Christ be under me, Christ be over me!
>Christ be beside me
>On left hand and right!
>Christ be before me, behind me, about me!
>Christ this day be within and without me!

For a third of a century Patrick evangelized Ireland, winning over whole heathen Celtic tribes. He established schools from which missionaries were sent forth for four centuries after his death. He introduced a higher civilization among the rude Celts, until Ireland became the chief center of missionary impulse. Irish monasteries became centers of scholarship and of deep religious life, and their missionaries had a large share in the conversion of the peoples of England and Scotland in the sixth and seventh centuries.

Columba was one of many youths of noble birth whom Patrick and his successors attracted to the missionary calling. He built the monastery which grew into the city of Londonderry, and founded a missionary school of the prophets. Finally, in 562, at the age of forty-two, endowed with marked gifts of leadership and eloquence, he left Ireland with twelve compainons and set out for Scotland "for the love of Christ." He labored so successfully for the conversion of the heathen Picts and savage Scots that the descendants of his converts in North Britain and Scotland finally became a great missionary people who enriched the world. Columba's Scottish followers, known for the next four centuries all over Europe, were characterized by pure gospel teaching and discipline, sound learning, and Christlike zeal. The Columban Church, established in Northumbria by King Oswald in 635, was the means of the conversion and transformation of the rude Angles there.

Pope Gregory the Great, unable as a Benedictine monk to fulfill his early wish to go as a missionary to Britain, sent Augustine, with forty associates, to Canterbury in 596 to attempt a new conquest of Britain by Rome. The high priest of Odin was the first to pull down the chief pagan temple near Canterbury. The conversion of the Anglo-Saxons from paganism to Christianity required about a century. But almost from the first the English Christians, like the Irish and Scots, were a great missionary people and early sent their evangelists to Denmark, Norway, and Sweden. Celtic and English Christians also undertook the evangelization of pagan Teutonic peoples.

The great English Boniface of Devonshire (680?-755) had the missionary impulse to elevate savage races in Europe to the blessings of Christian civilization. He refused the office of abbot in England and asked to be sent to preach in Germany. As he and his Saxon monks labored with herculean might to convert the Teutonic pagan tribes from their animistic beliefs and from the practice of human sacrifice, he was sustained by the prayers of English Christians in Canterbury and York. He wrote to the clergy in England for help: "Have pity on the pagan Saxons, for they themselves were used to say, 'We are of the same flesh and bone.'" Many men and women left the cultured English monasteries and nunneries for the hardships of the German forests, and there won converts and founded industrial and agricultural schools among the rude and ignorant tribes of Germany. After Boniface had founded many bishoprics in Germany, he reorganized the Church of Bavaria. With the desire to see the conversion of East Friesland, the aged saint of seventy-five joyfully met a missionary martyr's death from the heathen ancestors of the Dutch. Teutonic Europe has long commemorated the death, on June 5, 755, of the great Englishman Boniface, regarding him as the father both of its religion and of its civilization.

Anschar, a courageous Christian of Saxon stock, was called in 826 to carry the Christian message to the fierce sea kings of Jutland and Sweden. He opened schools and, as perhaps the first medical missionary, founded a hospital to heal the sick. The Scandinavians finally left their impotent gods and savage superstitions and embraced the Christian faith and its new way of life. Under the Christian King Canute, the church was firmly established in Denmark. In 1016 Canute the Great, having married an English wife, became king of England. He forbade the rites of heathenism there, and sent missionaries to the north to complete the conversion of the Scandinavians. Norway and western Lapland were the last parts of pagan Europe to become Christian.

Constantine (827-69), or Cyril as he was later called, and his brother Methodius (826-85), two prominent citizens of Thessalonica, were sent from Constantinople to evangelize the Slavic peoples. They devised a Slavonic alphabet and translated the Scriptures for these illiterate tribes. After the death of Cyril, Methodius and his followers labored in Moravia, Bulgaria, and elsewhere in the Balkan Peninsula; and all the Slavic countries within the fold of the Eastern Church are indebted to these men, who take rank among the greatest of missionaries. Their followers carried the gospel to the Poles, and Byzantine Christianity was finally introduced into Russia. King Vladimir was baptized at Kiev about 988, and the pagan idols of the Slavs were sunk in the Dnieper River. Under the bitterness of the yoke of their Mongol conquerors, the Christian Church became to the Russians the symbol of unity, patriotism, and hope, as well as of spiritual life. Though their religion was at first external and superficial, peasant and noble alike took pride in the names "Orthodox" and "Christian," and this land of wild Slavic tribes became in time "Holy Russia." With a sense of a divine world destiny the Russians felt themselves to be the successors of the Byzantine Empire, and proud Moscow became the "third Rome."

The flame of evangelism, kindled by reading the record of the early Twelve in the Gospels, leaped up again in Francis of Assisi (1182-1226). He went out with his twelve "little brothers of the poor," who strove to carry the good news not only throughout Italy and Europe but also to the Saracens and Moors, and to the ends of the earth.

Raymond Lull (1235?-1315), a young Spanish nobleman, was the first missionary who sought to give his whole life to the Mohammedans. After the failure of the Crusades in an age of

19

violence, as a philosopher, scholar, and poet, he determined "by love, by prayer, by proclaiming the word of truth rather than by force of arms" to bring the Saracens within God's kingdom of love. Selling all that he had, he sought—five centuries before William Carey—to awaken the church to its missionary responsibility. After preaching Christianity in Tunis for a year, he was imprisoned and then expelled from the country. He then sought to establish missionary colleges for the propagation of the gospel to Moslems and other non-Christians. Again facing the threat of death, he returned to preach to the Moslems in North Africa, and was once more imprisoned for six months and then expelled. With ardor unabated, in his seventy-eighth year he crossed to North Africa a third time; and while preaching there he was stoned to death outside the city walls of Bugia. His life motto was: "He who loves not lives not; he who lives by the Life cannot die."

John Wycliffe (1320?-1384), "the morning star of the Reformation," also had the crusading missionary spirit. His return to a pure apostolic gospel and his translation of the vernacular Bible, open to every common man, who thus had immediate access to God, made him the spiritual father of John Huss, Jerome of Prague, and the missionary Moravian Church. Wycliffe's work led also to the emigration of the Pilgrims to Plymouth Rock and the new world. Wycliffe trained and sent out his Oxford students and other poor preachers over the length and breadth of England, as his spiritual children John Wesley and General Booth later sent their lay preachers over Britain and America. The reformers Luther, Melanchthon, Zwingli, and Calvin purified the religious movement in northern Europe and cleared the way of abuses and error, in order that the church might resume its task for the evangelization of the world, though Luther and the others never had time to widen their vision to the missionary horizon.

In 1528 in Paris, Ignatius of Loyola shared the rooms of Pierre Favre and Francis Xavier. Together they laid plans to take the vows of poverty and chastity and to go to the Holy Land as missionaries. The movement they inaurgurated, like

20

that of the Wesleys and Whitefield two centuries later, was to be of far-reaching consequences. In 1534 these three, with four others, in the crypt of the church of St. Mary in Paris, dedicated themselves to form the Society of Jesus. They not only worked for the much-needed reforms of the Counter Reformation within the Catholic Church but also carried their blazing evangel across Asia, until Xavier finally lay dead on the island of Sanzian at the gates of fast-closed China. If we can overlook his reprehensible methods, his great decade in Asia, from 1542 to 1552, reads as an epic. With all his faults, he towered head and shoulders above all other Europeans in Eastern Asia in his day.

During the Reformation, Erasmus in his *Art of Preaching* had made a passionate plea for missions to the heathen. Although Leibnitz, the German philosopher, sought to rouse the Protestant churches to send missionaries to the non-Christian world, his purpose was not realized until the Pietists of Germany, led by the great Francke, sent out the first Protestant missionaries under the Danish-Halle mission to India. Ziegenbalg and Plutschau went to Tranquebar, South India, in 1705; and the great Christian Freidrich Schwartz in 1750 founded powerful churches in Tanjore and Tinnevelly.

The Pietist missions of the Moravians and of the Danish-Halle missions in India were contemporary with John Wesley (1703-91). Spiritual life had leaped to flame in the Holy Club, meeting in Wesley's room in Lincoln College, Oxford. The evangelical revival of the eighteenth century, that followed in the wake of the work of Wesley, Whitefield, and Jonathan Edwards in Great Britain and America, resulted not only in the Methodist Church, with its millions of members, but also in a world-wide movement for missions. Every one of these movements was spiritually powerful both at home and abroad. The "Great Awakening," in Virginia and from Georgia to New England, under Whitefield and Jonathan Edwards, contributed directly not only to the rapidly multiplying membership of the popular churches and to the religious life of the colonies but also to the movement for popular education, to the rise of

21

Whitworth College Library
Spokane, Washington

political democracy, and to the social revolution which transformed the colonies and ultimately stimulated missions at home and abroad. Wesley and the evangelical revival were preparing the way for William Carey and the great century of world-wide missions.

WILLIAM CAREY

It is impossible fully to understand the work of the missionaries of our own generation without becoming aware of the foundations laid by the great pioneers. One of these pioneers was William Carey. When a group of young Indian leaders met to organize their own indigenous National Missionary Society, on December 25, 1905, they asked to be allowed to work in the great library of William Carey at Serampore, as the most fitting and historic spot in which to draft their new constitution. As I met with these men, we looked with wonder and awe at the great tomes about us in the library—dictionaries, grammars, and translations of the Scriptures in forty languages and dialects of India and Central Asia.[1] Our wonder increased when we learned that while Carey himself had received a total of only three thousand dollars from the Baptist Missionary Society, he, together with his fellow workers Marshman and Ward, the great trio, had earned or contributed the enormous sum of four hundred and fifty thousand dollars toward the expense of translation and printing, and buildings for their college, schools, and churches, and their scientific and humanitarian work in Serampore.

We had to stoop to get down to the small crutches which bore the feeble frame of Carey at the age of seventy. It was an inspiration to recall to ourselves the mighty works of this frail pioneer —shoe-maker, scholar, and saint—who had preached the gospel, mastered languages, labored as one of India's first foreign scientists, and reared the magnificent buildings of the Serampore College and other institutions covering the five acres about us.

[1] George Smith in his *Life of William Carey* lists thirty-six Bible translations which Carey and his colleagues made with their own hands, or which they revised and edited, or corrected and printed for others on the Serampore Press under the care of William Ward.

It seemed to us so catholic and colossal that it furnished the complete type of the great work of missions we were all as one great team called to extend throughout Asia.

As we looked upon these great memorials, Carey's life seemed to pass before us in rapid panorama, like a moving picture. We recalled how he had been apprenticed to a shoemaker in England at the age of fourteen, converted as an outcast dissenting Baptist at eighteen, and ordained at twenty-six. At Hackleton, Carey's sign read: "Second-Hand Shoes Bought and Sold." Since his salary as a minister was never more than seventy-five dollars a year, he was forced to sustain himself by shoemaking for twelve years, as indeed he was compelled to support himself all the rest of his life by his own labors. In imagination we could see this humble cobbler at his bench, with a map of the world, which he himself had made, hung upon the wall before him, and a book ever open at his side. While at his work, he devoured Captain Cook's *Voyages*, mastered Latin, Greek, and Hebrew without a teacher, and then Dutch and French. He taught school by day and worked in leather at night—as the Apostle Paul worked at his tents. He preached on Sunday, walking from one to sixteen miles to his impoverished charges.

In 1792 Carey published his remarkable *Enquiry into the Obligations of Christians for the Conversion of the Heathens*, which is still perhaps the greatest missionary treatise in the English language. Praying daily at his cobbler's bench for all the non-Christians and slaves of the earth, in season and out of season he laid upon the conscience of his humble Baptist fellow ministers the duty of forming the first English organization for missions to the whole human race. He also devised a simple plan for its support—the raising of a penny a week from every Christian member. In 1792, after nine years of waiting, he preached his great sermon on "Expect Great Things from God: Attempt Great Things for God." As a result, twelve village pastors, moved by Carey's passion, met in a back parlor and became the successors of the apostles by the organization of the Baptist Missionary Society, with sixty-five dollars in the treasury. Thus through one humble shoemaker, or cobbler as he called himself, Almighty God was laying the burden of missions upon the whole Christian Church.

In 1793, at the age of thirty-two, after surmounting incredible obstacles, Carey reached India by the only ship that would carry him—a Danish vessel bound for the Danish settlement at Serampore, fifteen miles from Calcutta. The lucrative East India Company at that time considered "the sending out of missionaries into our Eastern possessions to be the maddest, most extravagant, most costly, most indefensible project which has ever been suggested by a moonstruck fanatic. Such a scheme is pernicious, imprudent, useless, harmful, dangerous, profitless, fantastic. It strikes against all reason and sound policy, it brings the peace and safety of our possessions into peril." Certainly the East India Company did not believe in foreign missions! Bengal, at the time, with its more than seventy million inhabitants, was probably the most strategic province in all Asia for the propagation of the gospel as well as an area of maximum human need. When Carey, Marshman, and Ward as fellow workers combined their talents, the mission party, including ten adults and nine children, planned to support themselves by means of a neighboring indigo factory at Kidderpore. They had all things in common, and the whole company lived on some five hundred dollars a year. Their revised agreement, which was read thrice a year at all stations of the mission, concluded with these noble words: "Finally let us give ourselves unreservedly to this glorious crusade. Let us never think that our time, our gifts, our strength, our families, or even the clothes we wear, are our own. Let us sanctify them all to God and His cause."

Later Carey's chief source of income was from his appointment by the governor general, Lord Wellsley, as professor in three languages—Bengali, Marathi, and Sanskrit, all of which he spoke "with fluency and correctness"—in the government college at Fort William, near Calcutta, for training the young British rulers of India. Here for thirty years he influenced some of the governors and other able men of the Bengal Civil Service as well as those of South and West India.

After seven years Carey baptized his first convert, and the

Bible was published in Bengali. Christians from as far away as Philadelphia contributed some five thousand dollars to help make possible Carey's press and its output of two hundred and twelve thousand copies of the Scriptures in some forty languages.

Carey was persecuted and vilified both in Britain and in India; his wife was insane for about fourteen years; he buried one child after another in tropical Bengal; his priceless printing establishment, the labor of years, was burned to the ground in a day, with the loss of irreplaceable books and translations; and there were heartbreaking altercations with his missionary society.

Carey was not a thinker, he laid claim only to the humble gift of plodding; but his labors were titanic. It was his daily habit to begin each morning by reading a chapter of the Bible, first in English and then in the vernaculars, which soon numbered six. In his aim to translate the Bible, with his fellow workers, into all the languages and principal vernaculars of India and Eastern Asia, he was more ambitious than his great precursor Wycliffe, or than Martin Luther; yet at one time he wrote, "Indolence is my prevailing sin"! When Carey began work in Calcutta the Bengali language had no printed and very little written literature. He wrote that he was engaged in supervising translations in twenty-seven languages at one time and finally rejoiced in the arrival of William Yates as his prospective linguistic successor. In 1818 he issued the first newspaper ever printed in any Oriental language.

If almost every great reform in the first instance is the work of one man, Carey's herculean task was to arouse the Christian Church till it acknowledged the duty of the evangelization of the world. Dr. George Smith points out that in the first third of the nineteenth century we have as the himalayan result of Carey's work the following achievements: (1) the first—complete or partial—translations of the Bible printed in forty languages and dialects of India, China, and Central Asia, at a cost of some four hundred thousand dollars; (2) the first prose work and vernacular newspaper in Bengali; (3) the first printing press (on an organized scale) , paper mill, and steam engine ever seen in India; (4) the first Christian primary school in North India; (5) the first efforts to educate Indian girls and women; (6) the first college to train Indian ministers and to Christianize educated Hindus; (7) the first medical mission and the introduction of Eastern medical science to the Orient; (8) the establishment and maintenance of at least thirty separate large mission stations; (9) the first society for the improvement of Indian and European agriculture and horticulture in India; (10) the first people's savings bank in the land; (11) the first translations into English of the great Sanskrit epics, the *Ramayana* and *Mahabharata;* (12) the first translation of the Bible into Sanskrit; and (13) the baptism of the first Hindu Protestant convert—in North India in 1800. Today there is in India a Christian community of over six million, and Christianity is still growing—much more rapidly than any of the non-Christian religions. In the opinion of Dr. George Smith, Carey educated Great Britain and America to rise to the great trust of jointly creating a Christianized India and a series of self-governing Christian nations in Southern and Eastern Asia.

While Carey appreciated in large measure and eagerly translated and printed the great religious books of Hinduism, he found that at the end of the eighteenth century the indigenous religion had sunk to its lowest depths. From the time he saw a shrieking widow burned against her will on her husband's funeral pyre, he set himself courageously to arouse the callous conscience of the governments of India and Britain to prevent the murder of innocents by widow burning, female infanticide, and voluntary drowning, all of which were then common. By 1829, after Carey's repeated memorials and long agitation, Lord Bentick at last had legislation passed prohibiting *sati,* or widow burning; and the abolition of other flagrant evils followed. Carey maintained that from 1757 to 1827 Christian Britain was responsible for the known immolation of at least seventy thousand Hindu widows. He was also moved to moral indignation by the cruel practices connected with the idolatry of Jagannath; and his righteous soul burned at the lucrative and licentious temple prostitution, like that which the prophets had fought throughout the Old Testament. His Christian concern for the multitudes of lepers and for the nine million slaves in India at that time at last aroused several of the British rulers to action.

Since Portugal and Holland, which had held India as a lucrative possession for some centuries, had done nothing of importance in the scientific exploration of India, Carey was in his element. Sanskrit was rediscovered, and the old Vedic and epic literature was brought to light. The flora and fauna of the tropic belt were classified. In 1801 Lord Wellesley had erected a college for the training of candidates for the civil and military services in a three years' obligatory course. The indispensable Carey, as the greatest living student of Bengali and a master of Sanskrit and of Marathi, was paid six thousand dollars a year and set free—for scientific as well as for religious activities.

Printing was still in its infancy. With the aid of Ward, a master printer, the Serampore giants built a magnificent printing house, with their own paper mill and type foundry. Here type for many of the tongues of India and Eastern Asia was first cast. Brilliant scholars like Colebrooke sent their works to Serampore to be printed. The Marshmans founded a school for children of educated parents, from the most prominent families downward, that maintained its high reputation until 1837. When the public press was practically nonexistent, this Serampore group in 1818 founded a Bengali newspaper, the *News-Mirror,* and an English magazine, the *Friend of India,* both of which were widely influential in humane reforms for fifty-seven years. Serampore became a shrine, and governors general and the most distinguished men held it an honor to consult Carey.

At the same time, the Serampore brethren were founding mission stations in a score of great centers in eastern Asia, where many missionary societies are now working most intensively. The Serampore giants earned and spent $75,000 to erect a fine college, to which the king of Denmark granted the right of conferring degrees, as was done in European universities.

Carey was the founder, in 1820, of the Agricultural and Horticultural Society of India, which formed the model for the Royal Agricultural Society of England, founded in 1838. As an erudite botanist, he studied scientifically the fauna and flora of India as his one permitted recreation. He was the pioneer of many practical agricultural and economic plans which Sam Higginbotham fulfilled and surpassed a century later in his work in British India and the Indian States. He was the first in the Orient to advocate scientific forestry and a system of people's savings bank. By 1821 Carey and his fellow workers had founded 26 Christian churches and 126 Indian schools, with 10,000 pupils.

As results of Carey's early letters and labors, the London Missionary Society was established in 1795, the Netherlands Missionary Society in 1797, the American Board in 1810, and the American Baptist Missionary Union in 1814. In response to Carey's call Henry Martyn, the brilliant senior wrangler of Cambridge, was sent to India by the great Charles Simeon. Soon the Church Missionary Society and the Society for the Propagation of the Gospel were sending a steady stream of missionaries from the Church of England to India and the world. The Religious Tract Society, founded in 1799, and the British and Foreign Bible Society, handmaids of the missionary enterprise, resulted indirectly from Carey's work; and soon almost the whole Christian world was effectively organized to carry out the "great commission" which had been laid upon the conscience of this humble shoemaker.

Among those who visited Carey in his last illness was the brilliant young Scotch missionary Alexander Duff, who praised the aged veteran's great work. Carey feebly replied: "Mr. Duff, you have been speaking of Dr. Carey, Dr. Carey; when I am gone, say nothing about Dr. Carey—speak about Dr. Carey's Saviour." On the morning of June 9, 1834, William Carey passed quietly into the larger life beyond. His tombstone bears the only inscription which he permitted:

WILLIAM CAREY, BORN AUGUST 17, 1761
DIED JUNE 9, 1834
A WRETCHED, POOR, AND HELPLESS WORM
ON THY KIND ARMS I FALL

Carey died so poor that his books had to be sold to meet a modest need of a few hundred dollars for his son, yet the three families who are buried with him had contributed to the cause of God £90,000 from their own earnings. In the light of all the facts, is it too much to look upon this humble, self-educated cobbler as not only the father of Protestant missions but also the greatest missionary since the Apostle Paul? He was the great exemplar for the world pathfinders of our modern missionary crusade. Within little more than a century Christendom had become largely animated by his spirit; the Word of Life had been translated into almost every tongue and carried to the ends of the earth. Thousands had forsaken all to follow Christ, and missions and the bringing in of the Kingdom of God on earth had become the great enterprise of the church.

ADONIRAM JUDSON

A marble tablet in the Baptist meeting house in Malden, Massachusetts, bears this inscription:

REV. ADONIRAM JUDSON
BORN AUGUST 9, 1788
DIED APRIL 12, 1850
MALDEN, HIS BIRTHPLACE
THE OCEAN, HIS SEPULCHRE
CONVERTED BURMANS, AND
THE BURMAN BIBLE, HIS MONUMENT
HIS RECORD IS ON HIGH

Young Adoniram was a precocious student, able to read at three, brilliant at twelve, and at nineteen graduating as valedictorian from the college that was later Brown University. With an overweening ambition to be an orator, writer, or statesman, he fell a victim to the French infidelity of the period and became a skeptic. He was ambitious to enter the law and politics, or the stage, as a field for his dramatic gifts. He was sobered, however, by the sudden death of a skeptic student friend; and after experiencing conversion he joined the church, at the age of twenty-one. Entering Andover Theological Seminary to prepare for the ministry, he felt an overwhelming call to become a foreign missionary; and, after joining with Samuel Mills and the Williams Haystack group, he became obsessed with the project of arousing the American churches to the responsibility of foreign missions.

In 1810 Judson wrote a paper, which was signed by the student missionary group at Andover, asking the General Association of Congregational Ministers, which was meeting at Bradford, Massachusetts, whether the students might expect patronage and support from a missionary society in this country or should commit themselves to the direction of a European society. Judson and his colleagues made a profound impression upon the association, and the next day a resolution was passed recommending the formation of an American board of commissioners for foreign missions.

In 1812 Judson sailed for Calcutta in the hope of working in British India. During the long voyage he studied the question of baptism in preparation for his anticipated meeting with Carey in his home in Serampore. Much against his will, he was forced by his conscience to become a Baptist; and on landing in Serampore he and his wife were baptized by Carey's associate, the Reverend William Ward. This providentially led to the founding by Baptists in America of the Baptist Society for the Propagation of the Gospel in India and Other Foreign Parts.

The Judsons were immediately ordered out of India by the British government, but as a last resort they were permitted to embark in a "crazy old vessel" that took them to Rangoon. They had just buried their first child at sea; and after a year and a half of wandering as exiles and refugees, flooded Rangoon appeared to them as a nightmare. It seemed little better than a neglected swamp, with its surrounding jungles abounding in venomous reptiles, insects, and wild animals. Burma was under an autocratic monarch who exercised the power of torture, and of life and death, over the people; and her government was rife with corruption.

With terrific concentration, Judson settled down to master

the Burmese language in all its intricacies. Seven years after leaving America he baptized his first convert, in spite of the fact that every Christian had to face the possibility of persecution and perhaps of death. For the missionaries there was also at times the danger of confiscation of property, imprisonment, and torture and death in their most shocking forms. Judson was advised to appeal directly to the king, "the lord of life and death," for permission to preach. He appeared in Ava before "the golden feet" to see "the golden face" of the haughty king, but when the monarch read the first sentence of Judson's tract—that there is one eternal God—he dashed it to the ground and said with reference to the missionary's sacred books, "Take them away." Judson learned that the type of Hinayana, or Southern Buddhism, which dominated the king and his abject subjects taught officially that there was no God to save, no soul to be saved, and no sin to be saved from.

When war broke out between England and Burma, Judson was imprisoned for twenty-one months under indescribable conditions. He was seized, with six other foreigners, and thrown into the death prison at Ava for the first eleven months—for nine months bound with three pairs of fetters and for two months with five pairs. From Ava the prisoners were removed to another prison ten miles away. They were roped together two by two and driven under the lash, by the king's slaves. Such were the agonies of the journey that one of the foreigners died on the road. Judson's bare feet became solid blisters, and finally all the skin came off. He walked on in agony over sand and gravel which were like burning coals of fire, and when they crossed a river he was tempted in desperation to throw himself into the cooling water. All believed they were going to a horrible death. It was true that the king intended to offer these foreigners as a human sacrifice to insure victory, but this was providentially prevented.

Judson was thirty-six when he was imprisoned, and his constitution had long been weakened by malignant malaria. A hundred prisoners—Europeans and Burmese criminals, men and women indiscriminately—were thrown into a loathsome black

31

hole about forty feet long and thirty feet wide under the stifling heat of the summer sun, with the temperature often over 110 degrees. The prisoners lay in long rows with their feet made fast in the stocks, or strung up on long poles. The prison had not been cleaned in years, and putrid remains of animal refuse covered the floor. As the prisoners lay in their filth, without sanitary arrangements, the stench was indescribable; and the whole place was crawling with vermin. The five pairs of fetters which Judson wore weighed some fourteen pounds, and he carried their scars to his dying day. To prevent their possible escape at night, the jailors strung the prisoners up on long bamboo poles with their feet hoisted to a painful height which barely allowed their shoulders to rest on the ground.

Judson's brilliant mind was fettered as well as his body. His esthetic sensitiveness and his passion for neatness and order made his imprisonment a continuous martyrdom. He was morally outraged by the coarse language of the criminals and their shrieks of anguish under frightful torture. The jailors noisily sharpened their knives for beheading the prisoners, and the roar of a hungry lioness in her cage convinced them of the fate that awaited some, while there were rumors that others were to be burned alive at the head of the Burman army to secure victory. At three o'clock each afternoon there was a period of silence when the jailors entered to take out their victims for torture or execution.

Judson was harassed also by the easily imagined sufferings of his helpless wife. During his imprisonment she gave birth to her baby, without the benefit of medical care, and when able to walk she carried the child in her arms as she sought permission to take food to the imprisoned missionaries. She nursed her Burmese girls through smallpox, and then caught the loathsome disease herself. Mrs. Judson lay helpless for a month, with scarcely a drop of milk for her wailing baby. After the attack of smallpox she was seized by the usually fatal spotted fever, which raged for seventeen days. Her head and feet were covered with blisters, and her hair had to be shaved. In her moments of consciousness she still clung to the promise, "Call upon me in the day of trouble: I will deliver thee, and thou shalt glorify me." She wrote: "I became quite composed, fully assured that my prayers would be answered." Judson himself courageously endured his sufferings, believing that he could see the hand of God in letting this sunken and degraded country be subdued by an empire which at the worst was yet the most enlightened and tolerant in the world. He believed that the British would guarantee religious liberty and permit Christian education, which might some day prepare Burma for final enlightened self-government.

After the defeat of the Burmese armies Judson was taken from prison as an interpreter in negotiating peace between the British and the Burmese. He could at last give thanks, after a year and a half of suffering, that the missionaries were free from the oppressive yoke of Burmese tyranny, and that they had secured the blessing of religious liberty for his beloved people.

During twenty years of interrupted work Judson completed his translation of the entire Bible, published tracts, prepared a grammar, and almost completed his monumental English-Burmese dictionary. At the time of his death the Burmese church had a membership of seven thousand, and Judson had the oversight of 163 missionaries, Burmese pastors, and assistants. Like Paul, Judson was in a unique way called to suffer for Christ. He had lost two gifted wives and several children in different parts of the world. As he himself lay dying, while taking a sea voyage as his only hope of recovery, he exclaimed: "Oh, no man ever left the world with more inviting prospects, with brighter hopes, with warmer feelings!" He died at sea without a friend, and his wasted body was buried without a prayer; but his triumphant and unconquered spirit had entered the abundant life beyond.

The life of Judson was vividly brought before those who met to form the National Missionary Society by the two representatives from Burma. These young men wanted to take up their cross for the evangelization of the world, to fill up on their part, as Judson had done, what was lacking of the afflictions of Christ.

ROBERT MORRISON

As the son of a farm laborer in England, the man who was to become the foremost Western Chinese scholar of his day had few advantages in his youth. Like Carey, Morrison was a plodder, an indefatigable worker. He began to prepare for the ministry; but for his field of work he asked only for the place of greatest need, and this seemed to be in non-Christian lands. His prayer was that "God would station him in that part of the field where the difficulties are the greatest, and to all human appearances the most insurmountable." This prayer was abundantly answered in China, the field upon which the London Missionary Society decided when Morrison offered his services. To equip himself for his work, Morrison went to London, where he studied medicine and Chinese. He found in the British Museum a Chinese translation of the Bible, and he discovered a young Chinese scholar whom he induced to share his lodgings in order to help him in speaking and writing the language.

In 1807 Morrison started for China; but owing to the hostility of the East India Company, which allowed no missionaries on its ships, he was compelled, providentially, to go by way of New York. The American ship owner was amused at the thought of any man going to China to convert it, and said, "And so, Mr. Morrison, you really expect you will make an impression on the idolatry of the great Chinese Empire?" Morrison replied, characteristically, "No, sir, but I expect God will." In Washington, James Madison, then secretary of state, gave Morrison a letter of introduction to the American consul in Canton, requesting his aid for the missionary.

When Morrison arrived in China, the first Protestant missionary to that country, it was considered the impregnable Gibraltar of the non-Christian world, the hardest mission field on earth. Morrison was forbidden to preach in public, and he was able to speak of his religion only behind locked doors, to three or four men in his employ. He was beaten and driven out in turn from Canton and Macao, and he labored for seven years without a convert. He was persecuted alike by the Chinese of Canton and by the Roman Catholics of Macao. He faced the almost daily fear of arrest, lifelong petty annoyance, constant opposition, recurring periods of ill-health and heartbreaking discouragements; yet his labors were monumental. Gladstone said of Morrison, "Hercules never undertook such a task."

Patiently Morrison won a few friends and supporters. The American consul in Canton gave him a room in his house. Since an imperial edict made it a crime to publish Christian books, to gain protection for his work Morrison accepted a post as translator for the East India Company at a salary of $2,500; and the company later helped him, as its agent, in the publication of his works. As a literary pathfinder, Morrison began work on a Chinese vocabulary, then a grammar, a huge dictionary, and the translation of the Scriptures. In 1823 he published his great *Chinese Dictionary,* which was almost an encyclopedia, in six massive volumes, at a cost of sixty thousand dollars. It had required almost sixteen years of labor, and in its preparation Morrison had consulted some ten thousand Chinese volumes. This work made Morrison famous. Finally he published his translation of the Bible.

In 1813, six years after he landed, Morrison was joined by the able William Milne, but Milne was driven by the bigotry of the time to settle in Malacca, where he could found an Anglo-Chinese college. In answer to Morrison's appeals for workers in China the American Board sent E. C. Bridgman, and later S. Wells Williams, who became a great Chinese scholar, writing the first monumental work about China for the American public, *The Middle Kingdom.* Williams so mastered not only Chinese but Japanese that he was taken as the official interpreter for Commodore Perry's expedition to Japan, which succeeded in opening that hermit nation in 1854.

S. Wells Williams was one of two Protestant missionaries who, with three Chinese Christians, made up the entire membership of the Protestant Church in China in that early day. When Morrison died in 1834, Williams must have been a man of prophetic faith to have declared: "The dawn of China's regeneration was breaking as his eyes closed on the scene of his labors. . . . His name, like that of Carey, Marshman, Judson, and Martyn, belongs to the heroic age of missions. . . . His work was the work of a wise master-builder, and future generations in the Church of God in China will ever find reason to bless Him for the labor and example of Robert Morrison."

2

THE MODERN STUDENT MISSIONARY MOVEMENT

I HAVE condensed into a single chapter a brief glance at the first nineteen centuries of missions because I wish to concentrate upon the great pathfinders of our own day and generation, especially upon outstanding members of the Student Volunteer Movement. I shall consider in this chapter the beginnings of the missionary movement in America that sprang from the students of the Williams Haystack and Andover in 1810 and 1812; then the Student Volunteer Movement for Foreign Missions that originated in the first student conference under D. L. Moody in 1886, and finally, as typically of many others, the first Student Volunteer Band at Yale, and especially what the men of the classes of 1892 and of 1898 accomplished abroad. Perhaps the volunteer bands at Princeton, Oberlin, or Northwestern University accomplished as much or more, but I present the group I knew best, whose work I personally observed in the Far East.

SAMUEL J. MILLS AND THE WILLIAMS HAYSTACK

The spirit of the God of Elisha fell upon Samuel J. Mills while he was in the field at the plow upon his farm in Connecticut in 1802. This call to preach the gospel to the non-Christian world came as the climax of a long spiritual struggle. Mills went to Williams College, as Mark Hopkins said, to kindle a fire, just as Martin Luther and William Carey had done in their day. Williams had only just been founded—in 1793, the time of the French Revolution and the year of the ordination of William Carey to the work of missions. Mills entered Williams as an obscure freshman in 1806. Never brilliant, a man of but one talent, Mills dedicated all his power to a single task and concentrated upon a single cause. And, as President

37

Griffin of Williams said, by the influence of a revival in college Mills was able so to diffuse his spirit through his inner circle that he raised Williams College to the distinction of being the birthplace of American missions.

Mills became the center of a small group that met frequently for prayer in a grove of maples near the college. One day, as a thunderstorm was coming up, five of them took refuge under a haystack—and there they came to the climax of their bold proposal to launch a missionary movement in America, which finally developed into a project to send missionaries to Asia. Mills said, "We can do it if we will." In 1808 the Williams group organized the Society of Brethren, the first foreign missionary society in America whose members proposed to go themselves to work for the "heathen," as non-Christians were called. The Brethren united the fire of the Holy Club at Oxford and Loyola's Society of Jesus; yet, because of the almost universal opposition to an idea so bold as missions, the organization was kept secret. A later member of the Society of Brethren was Royal Wilder, the father of Robert Wilder, the founder of the Student Volunteer Movement.

On leaving Williams in 1810, the group separated and went deliberately to other institutions, like Yale and Andover, to kindle missionary fires there. Andover Seminary was then a new institution which was itself the outcome not only of theological controversy but of missionary zeal. Here the Williams men were joined by the brilliant Adoniram Judson, who became the natural leader and spokesman of the group as they proceeded to organize the Society of Inquiry on the Subject of Missions, which has continued in existence to this day. After more than a year of prayer and counsel, Judson, Mills, Nott, and Newell offered themselves to the General Assembly of Massachusetts of the Congregational Churches to attempt a world mission. As a result of this offering of youth for service, the Board of Commissioners for Foreign Missions was founded to carry the gospel to other lands.

In 1812 Judson, Hall, Newell, Nott, and Rice were ordained as missionaries in the old Tabernacle Church of Salem, Massachusetts. While these men were to go abroad, Mills was charged by his colleagues with the important task of calling the young men in the colleges and theological seminaries "to sound the alarm of war" for a world-wide missionary crusade. In the same year Judson and his brilliant wife, and Mr. and Mrs. Newell, sailed for Calcutta; but upon their expulsion from India they were finally led to Burma. Hall and Nott were driven to Bombay to open a mission in Western India; Hiram Bingham and Asa Thurston sailed for the Sandwich Islands; then China, Turkey, and a score of other lands were occupied.

The foreign missionary enterprise immediately quickened the home missionary endeavor; and it became a world movement with the motto, "Save America to save the world." In the same year that Judson sailed for Calcutta, Mills and an associate undertook a hazardous missionary journey to New Orleans, and then started on horseback to pioneer through the Louisiana Purchase—which included all or parts of fifteen states—when this territory was almost an unknown country to Protestantism. Mills found that he did not have to go abroad to find the "heathen." In the western wilderness of his own country there was an appalling scarcity of Bibles, of religious services, of Sabbath observance, and of other marks of a Christian civilization. President Theodore Roosevelt later pointed out that it was such missionary work in the conquest of the continent which prevented the American pioneers from sinking perilously near the level of the savagery against which they had to contend. Mills's first missionary journey on horseback, through the uncharted wilderness, took over a year and covered some three thousand miles. In this and subsequent journeys he traversed nearly every state and territory in the Union. Mills appealed for half a million Bibles, he formed Bible societies in various regions, and finally rejoiced in the organization of the American Bible Society in 1816. Mills never even contemplated marriage, but devoted himself to his single missionary task with monastic zeal. Toward the end of his life there was laid heavily upon his heart the evangelization of the Negro slaves in America and of the Dark Continent beyond. Mills finally reached Africa, but he

39

died of tuberculosis in 1818, at the age of thirty-five, in connection with his journey to the Dark Continent. So ended the life of the man who was in a real sense the pioneer of American missions.

ROBERT WILDER AND THE
STUDENT VOLUNTEER MOVEMENT

No national student movement had followed the "haystack band," and the state of religious life in the colleges and churches was low. Three quarters of a century later, however, in 1886, the time was ripe for a great missionary uprising among students. In many periods, great creative religious ideas have germinated in the hearts of young men. "It is a holy sight," said Disraeli, "to see a nation saved by its youth." In the last quarter of the nineteenth century in America the tinder for flaming youth was furnished by the Student Christian Movement, and the unexpected leader was Dwight L. Moody, the great evangelist of the century. Moody was at first an inarticulate layman who had left his boot and shoe business when seized by the passion for evangelism. As president and general secretary of the Chicago Young Men's Christian Association, he had organized evangelistic work in the godless city of Chicago, and, when war began in 1861, among the soldiers of the Northern armies in the field during the War Between the States. In 1873 Moody had gone to England as an unknown man. Within six months he had become "the strongest religious force in the country." Upon his return to America, when the students besought Moody to address them, his great campaigns in Yale and Princeton opened the American colleges, as Oxford and Cambridge had been opened in England. The greatest universities of the Anglo-Saxon world were moved for Christ as they had never been before. Moody preached the gospel to more people than any other man who had ever lived. Though a simple, unlettered man himself, this mighty human dynamo was used of God directly, and indirectly in the student conferences which he led, to thrust forth thousands of Christian workers into Anglo-Saxon countries and into all mission fields.

Robert Wilder was the missionary par excellence of our generation; in his heart the crusading fire burned with purest flame. As John R. Mott says in the introduction to Wilder's life, written by his daughter, Ruth Wilder Braisted: "The life and work of Robert Wilder is a convincing demonstration of what God can do with a life placed at his disposal and dominated with the world-wide vision and purpose of Jesus Christ. Through him the Spirit of God accomplished a work the influence of which touched every land." Wilder was a fine illustration of Moody's saying: "The world has not seen what God could do through a young man thoroughly consecrated." Although the time was ripe and the occasion ideal, humanly speaking, the Student Volunteer Movement would not have come into being without Robert Wilder. The movement was the result of Wilder's vision, Moody's spiritual drive, and Mott's organizing genius. It was fitting that Wilder should be the founder of the Volunteer Movement in America, Great Britain, and other lands, for his was a missionary family to the third and fourth generation.

In 1846 Robert Wilder's father, Royal G. Wilder, was one of four missionaries who sailed for India under the American Board, in an old ice ship. In 1852, as a pioneer, he entered the Indian state of Kolhapur in Western India and became "the incarnate conscience" for its four million inhabitants. In the face of fierce Brahman opposition he opened a school for a dozen boys, and his wife opened a school for girls. His son, Robert Wilder, was born in India in 1863. As a child Robert studied and attained a thorough knowledge of Marathi. In his own home and in the palace of the maharaja, he became the playmate of the young raja, Shivajirao, with whom he wrestled, raced on horseback, and played duets on the piano. Very early, religion became a simple and vivid reality to him, without any violent conversion, or journey into a far country as a prodigal. At the age of ten, with his twelve-year-old sister, Robert Wilder joined the church and later taught a Sunday school class of Marathi children. He wrote: "When I joined the church I made up my mind, God permitting, to become a foreign missionary.

41

It seemed to me there was nothing else to do, since the need abroad was so much greater than that in America."

When Robert was fourteen his father, broken in health after thirty years of service in India, returned to America with his family to make their home in Princeton. In 1878 he began the first volume of the *Missionary Review of the World,* which he continued successfully for a decade, until he passed on the editorship to Arthur T. Pierson.

As a boy in his teens Robert Wilder was sensitive and shy, without playmates of his own age; and he felt he could never speak in public; but his sister Grace took him in hand and showed him that *nothing* was impossible if one had a bold faith. Later he won prizes in oratory in his freshman, junior, and senior years in college, and he became an effective speaker in the leading countries of Europe and Asia.

In 1881 Wilder entered Princeton. He had never been strong physically; his childhood, spent on the hot plains of India, had impaired his health. He was an ambitious and conscientious student in Princeton, but he was so frail that he broke down after a short term of service in each task that he undertook. Providentially, however, this led to his service as a world missionary in a score of lands. He was apparently intended to launch movements that others were able to carry to completion. In Princeton he excelled in Greek and philosophy and had such an aptitude for languages that in later life he could use ten or twelve with ease. He took his B.A. and M.A. degrees and was later elected a member of Phi Beta Kappa.

Although he maintained a high scholastic rating in college, immediately upon his entry he threw himself into Christian work and put through a successful campaign to have every saloon in the borough of Princeton closed. He became a teacher and later superintendent of the Sunday school; but chiefly he concentrated on the student Christian association, known as the Philadelphian Society, which he served as president and secretary. In 1883, in his junior year, he organized the Princeton Foreign Missionary Society, for small daily prayer groups to pray and work for the conversion of non-Christian classmates, until a flame of revival swept Princeton. He sought to challenge the Christian students with the missionary declaration, "We are willing and desirous, God permitting, to become foreign missionaries." The Princeton volunteers also adopted as their watchword, "The evangelization of the world in this generation."

In his senior year Wilder broke under the strain of overwork, and he took a year as a cowboy on a ranch in Nebraska to recover his health. Even on the ranch, he held meetings and established a cowboy missionary society! Wilder returned to Princeton to graduate, and in 1886 he attended the epochmaking student conference at Mount Hermon. Dwight L. Moody held but one platform meeting a day, but Wilder began to form a group of young men who were concerned about missions. They fanned to flame the missionary interest until it became the major issue of the whole conference.

Wilder proposed to Moody to have a "Meeting of the Ten Nations," and when this meeting was held, Wilder spoke first with a plea for India, the land of his birth, and was then followed by nationals of other countries. Wilder's aggressive challenge was not "Why should you go?" but "Why should you not go?" After this meeting John R. Mott spent many an hour in prayer and in "conclusive thinking," until he signed the declaration of purpose to become a foreign missionary. In Mott's view, that meeting "may occupy as significant a place in the history of the Christian Church as did the Williams haystack prayer meeting." In a room in the Mount Hermon boys' school there is a plaque which reads: "In this room in the month of July, 1886, during the first international student conference the Student Volunteer Movement had its origin, and one hundred young men signified their willingness and desire, God permitting, to become foreign missionaries." In the list of volunteers appears Mott's name; it is characteristic that on this list he specifies his field as "the world."

After this memorable conference the group, eager to make the movement nation wide, selected Wilder and John Forman to carry the missionary challenge through the colleges of North

America during the following year. Within that time some two thousand men and women volunteered. Wilder's contributions to the volunteer movement seem to have been: (1) the volunteer declaration: "It is my purpose, God permitting, to become a foreign missionary"; (2) the volunteer band, which united groups in hundreds of colleges in a genuine self-propagating student missionary movement; (3) the vision and passion of enlisting students of all nations and races in a missionary crusade; and (4) the immediacy of the watchword, "The Evangelization of the World in This Generation." One who reads the lives of the early student leaders in America and Britain will see what a powerful motive this watchword was in their lives. After a decade of experience, however, it was dropped by all the volunteer movements outside of North America. In 1888 fifty leading volunteers met at Northfield, Massachusetts; and to avoid many obvious dangers in this zealous crusade, they definitely organized the Student Volunteer Movement for Foreign Missions, with John R. Mott—who had just graduated from Cornell and who was one of the first hundred volunteers —as chairman and executive leader, a post which he held for thirty years with wise sanity and statesmanship. Young volunteers as traveling secretaries carried the torch of the crusade through the colleges. When, in 1891, Wilder sailed for India to work among students under the Presbyterian Board, on an undenominational basis, President McCosh of Princeton wrote: "I know no young man who has done so much good in America in calling young men to the work of God in the missionary fields."

Wilder broke his journey to India by visiting England, upon the invitation of British students, where he attended the great Keswick Convention in 1891. There he reached, among others, a young Scottish student named Donald Fraser. Fraser told me personally that he went to Keswick as a scoffer and drew caricatures of the speakers in the opening meetings, until finally, under an agony of conviction that fell upon him that he was a lost soul, he made his peace with God. On the last day he crept inside the crowded tent and stood behind the platform to hear

Wilder's missionary appeal. He was moved so deeply that then and there he dedicated himself to the mission field. He became the leader of the Student Volunteer Missionary Union of Great Britain and Ireland, which was organized in 1892, following Wilder's tour of the British universities. After distinguished service as a missionary in South Africa, Donald Fraser became secretary of the Missionary Society of the Free Church of Scotland, and the leader of the missionary movement in Scotland.

When the movement in the British Isles had been organized, Wilder went on to kindle the missionary flame in Norway, Sweden, and Denmark. Later, the students of these countries organized the Student Volunteer Movement in Northern Lands. In the beauty of Norway, Wilder met his future wife, Helene Olsson, a member of a large and influential family. After they were married they built Norheim, their northern home, to which Wilder often returned to recuperate from his frequent breakdowns.

On arrival in India, Wilder began student work in Calcutta in 1893, which continued for eighteen months; and in 1895 he moved to Poona, the bigoted center of orthodox Brahmanism of Western India. When the first Brahman convert in eighteen years was baptized, a storm of persecution broke upon all the missionary workers. From 1897 to 1899 Wilder was called to America to work among the theological seminaries of thirty denominations, and then he renewed his contacts with the students of Scandinavia and Great Britain. In 1900 he returned to India as college secretary of the Y.M.C.A., and then for a time as national secretary of that organization. In 1902, after two years under the tropic sun, he suffered a nervous breakdown and went for rest to Norheim; but he was soon speaking again among the Scandinavian colleges. In 1904 he was asked to become a secretary of the British Student Christian Movement, which had grown from the Student Volunteer Union he had organized twelve years before. He spent the next eleven happy years in Britain, in turn as traveling secretary in the colleges, London secretary, secretary of the Student Volunteer Missionary Union, and evangelistic secretary. Princeton had left its stamp upon Wilder, and he was a little too painfully orthodox and conservative to be fully one with the modern youth of Britain; but all were tolerant, seeking "unity in essentials, diversity in nonessentials."

In 1913 and 1914 Wilder was again on the move in a new task, as the representative of the World's Student Christian Federation in Lands Without National Organizations. During these two years he did fruitful work among the colleges of Germany, Hungary, Austria, Czechoslovakia, Poland, Finland, Sweden, Denmark, Holland, Italy, and all the Balkan states. In 1916 he returned to America, working as senior secretary of the Religious Work Department of the Y.M.C.A. In 1919 he succeeded Fennell P. Turner as general secretary of the Student Volunteer Movement, which he had originally organized three decades before. In 1922 we find Wilder in China at the conference of the World's Student Christian Federation, and in 1927 he went for six years to Cairo as executive secretary of the Christian Council for Western Asia and Northern Africa. At the age of sixty-five, when others were retiring, Wilder was just beginning a fresh work in a field which extended from Persia in the east, to Morocco in the west, and from the Balkans and Turkey in the north, to Arabia, Abyssinia, and the Sudan in the south. It was an especial joy for him to work in the Bible lands of the Near East.

After revisiting the British universities for the last time, and holding evangelistic meetings in Paris, Robert Wilder returned to his beautiful home in Norway, where, in his supremely happy family life, it seemed that his spirit was more radiant than ever, and spiritual realities were more vivid to him. He wrote his last letter to Mott out of a deep friendship of more than fifty years, and at the age of seventy-five passed quietly over to the "land of great distances." The marble stone that marks his grave in Norway bears the simple inscription: "The path of the just is as a shining light, that shineth more and more unto the perfect day."

The high tides of the student Christian movement were reached in the international conventions held once each student generation of approximately four years.[1] These "volunteer" conventions literally marked epochs both in the missionary and in the religious life of the colleges of North America, and they affected the churches as well. In 1902 the Young People's Missionary Movement endeavored to carry the missionary spirit to the youth of the churches, and later this evolved into the Missionary Education Movement. The volunteer movement was also one of the potent factors leading to the launching of the Laymen's Missionary Movement in 1906. A young layman, John B. Sleman of Washington, D. C., got his vision and caught the spirit of this missionary crusade at the convention of the Student Volunteer Missionary Movement in Nashville, Tennessee, in 1906. At the interdenominational meeting to commemorate the Williams College haystack prayer meeting, November 13-14, 1906, in the Fifth Avenue Presbyterian Church in New York City, a group of laymen organized the Laymen's Missionary Movement in North America; later it was reproduced in a dozen other countries. The income of the mission boards the year it was organized in 1906 was $8,980,488; but by 1924, partly as a result of increased lay interest and giving, their receipts reached $45,272,293. During this period the number of Protestant foreign missionaries increased from 5,708 to 16,-754. Many laymen first learned the joy of sacrificial giving through this movement.

Just as the volunteering of Carey led to the formation of the first missionary societies in Great Britain, and as the offering of students at Williams and Andover led to the formation of the American Board and the Baptist Missionary Society, so student volunteers of all denominations meeting in conventions and working together have initiated forward missionary movements, both at the home base and on the foreign field, and have promoted the movement for co-operation and unity among some two hundred divided segments of Protestantism. Most

[1] The dates and cities of the student volunteer conventions are as follows: 1891, Cleveland; 1894, Detroit; 1898, Cleveland; 1902, Toronto; 1906, Nashville; 1910, Rochester; 1914, Kansas City; 1920, Des Moines; 1924, Indianapolis; 1928, Detroit; 1932, Buffalo; 1935, Indianapolis; 1939, Toronto; 1943, Wooster, Ohio.

of the leaders who launched the student Christian movements in America, Europe, and Asia were student volunteers.

HORACE PITKIN AND THE FIRST YALE VOLUNTEER BAND

I was far from any thought of joining the Yale volunteer band during my college course, but I recognized its members as the spiritual leaders in college. I had all my plans made for going into business, and I had chosen the line in which I thought the most money was to be made—the lumber business, which Mott also intended to enter after Cornell. Like most of the men in college, I heard no missionary call; for, with self-centered plans and ambitions thundering in our ears, we were simply not within calling distance.

Horace Pitkin was the first man of the group in Yale to make his decision to become a missionary. He had come from Litchfield County in Connecticut, through Samuel Mills, the birthplace of American missions. It was the county that produced Harriet Beecher Stowe, Henry Ward Beecher, and a notable group of Christian workers. Born in a well-to-do Yale family, a descendant of Elihu Yale, Pitkin was educated at Exeter, Yale, and Union Theological Seminary. When he entered college in 1888, he at once became a teacher in the Bethany Mission Sunday School, and then its superintendent; he plunged into the Grand Avenue slum mission, and the boys' club in New Haven. At his first Northfield conference, on classic Round Top in 1889, as he heard the claims of the vast non-Christian world, he became convinced of the greater need and larger spiritual opportunity abroad, and he signed the simple volunteer declaration to become a foreign missionary. He now had a new purpose in life and he believed that his cause was the greatest in the world. No crusader ever girded on his armor to capture the Holy Sepulcher, no knight ever sought the Holy Grail, with a holier fire burning in his heart. The saying of Mackay of Uganda became more true of Pitkin than it did of Mackay himself: "I must be more terribly in earnest where I am, knowing I must so soon go elsewhere."

48

Pitkin won his roommate, D. T. Huntington, who later became Bishop Huntington of China and who testified that the greatest blessing of his course in Yale was rooming with this most consecrated man in college, who was "always doing with his might whatever his hand found to do." There were better scholars and greater athletes, but no man in Yale had so great a power of translating his faith into action. He made a high scholastic rating, barely missing Phi Beta Kappa because of his absorption in his primary missionary task. He was on the Yale Glee Club, and editor of the Yale *Courant*. His life was cheerful, full of wit and fun, but from the moment of his signing the volunteer declaration to the hour of his martyrdom in China he was consumed by a single passion. He sought first the Kingdom of God; and whether all other things were added or lost, he counted them but refuse. His life was contagious and had multiplied itself many fold before he left college. He began as an obscure freshman, but he so aided others to do conclusive thinking regarding their life work that before he left college he had raised up a volunteer band of twenty-four, some of them the strongest men in college. He began almost alone among the two thousand students there at the time, but it was largely his work that led on to the founding of Yale-in-China and made Yale for all time a great missionary college. He could have written on the flyleaf of his daily used New Testament, as did John Wesley: "Live today!" I have known many greater missionaries but never a greater student volunteer. He was the living embodiment of Bonar's hymn:

> Time worketh:
>   Let me work too;
> Time undoeth:
>   Let me do.
> Busy as time my work I ply,
> Till I rest in the rest of Eternity.

Pitkin's work ultimately led his classmate Harry Luce to go to China as an educator and E. C. Lobenstine as secretary of the China Christian Council, and his classmate Frank Keller, to attempt to open up Hunan, with its twenty-one million inhabitants, the last closed province that then allowed no single Protestant missionary to live and preach within its border. Pitkin also inspired Norman Whittemore to join a group of men for the evangelization of Korea, and led many others to enter various mission fields.

I was thrown even more closely with Pitkin when we entered Union Theological Seminary as classmates. Here he was toiling night and day for the missionary cause, recruiting men and raising money. Although I professed to be willing to go to the mission field, I noticed that no one else decided to go or to give to the cause because of my professed willingness. When another volunteer, who was a classmate, died suddenly, I faced the question of my immediate duty and went to Pitkin's room to pray with him for guidance and then to my own room for silent prayer. No man wants to make a mistake in the matter of the supreme choice of his life work. No man wants to throw his life away. The air seemed to clear when I realized that all I had to do for the rest of my life was to find and to do the will of God. After long thought and much prayer I saw that it was my plain duty to form the definite purpose of becoming a foreign missionary. From that moment my life was focused upon what seemed to me the greatest work in the world. I too felt I must be a crusader. I was jarred broad awake: my studies meant more, and even athletics had a new meaning. When I would box every afternoon with Pitkin and when we would run our daily mile in the gym or the open air, we would say, "This will carry us another mile in China." Henry Luce, who was then my roommate, also reached his independent decision; and then the three of us began to work together on the great crusade. China was the goal, the lodestar, the great magnet that drew us all in those days.

Pitkin, Luce, and I, all classmates and all roommates at different periods, began to work as a team, one for all and all for one. That first year we witnessed a "missionary revival" in Union Theological Seminary. Pitkin went out through the churches and young people's societies and raised $5,000 for missions, as he had done in Yale. Then John R. Mott as chairman of the movement assigned the three of us to work in the colleges of New York and New England over week ends, and the next year we were all called as traveling secretaries of the Student Volunteer Movement for Foreign Missions. The volunteer movement could afford to support only one man, but Pitkin, who then had an income of $3,000 a year, always put into his work all that he had—life, time, and money—so for the first time three men and one woman, Mrs. H. B. Sharman, entered the colleges in 1894-95 as secretaries. Each of us sought a hundred men and women who would go to the foreign field. Pitkin, in the colleges of the Middle West, secured more volunteers than any of us. A student at Mount Holyoke said that Pitkin spoke twice on Sunday and turned the college upside down. With his wife, Letitia Thomas, of Mount Holyoke, he started for his field in China in 1896.

Pitkin went to China at his own expense, and was assigned to the American Board Mission in Paoting, near Peiping. This was the period of the collapse of the reform movement and the bitter anti-foreign reaction under the old dowager empress. Pitkin wrote of the spread throughout his province of secret societies whose members were drilling to develop magic spells to make them bulletproof, and proclaiming their slogan: "Death to the Foreigners." He had just passed his second language examination when he wrote a round-robin letter to a group of us Yale men, on April 27, 1900:

We're getting rumors of war here all right. You know of the Boxer Sword Society to root out all foreign devils and exterminate their religion. . . . We are surrounded. Fifteen miles from here the Boxers are assembling in great numbers. They are bound to sack a Roman Catholic station near by, then another, and then Paoting. At present the city sends fifteen soldiers a night for our guard. It's after midnight. . . . The Lord be with you all, boys. He has been very good to me and I thank him.

On June 2, 1900, Pitkin wrote his last letter to American friends in Peiping:

51

It may be the beginning of the end. [All the Roman Catholics near by had been killed.] God rules and somehow his Kingdom must be brought about in China. We may not be left to see the end. It's a grand cause to die in. Jesus shall reign, but we do hope a long life may be for us in this world. . . . "I had fainted, unless I had believed to see the goodness of the Lord in the land of the living." I know I shall up there. Down here may he help me also to see it. . . . God leads, thank God he does. We can't go out to fight. We have no soldiers to trust. We must sit still, do our work, and take quietly what is sent us. And it will be but a short time till we can know definitely whether we can serve him better above or not. We can't be sure of a single day's life. Work and pray for us.

HORACE TRACY PITKIN

The edict of the dowager empress on June 23, 1900, led to the murder of foreigners. On June 28 Pitkin's beloved Chinese colleague, Pastor Meng, was dragged to the temple and beheaded. On June 30 a mob attacked the mission premises and began burning, looting, and killing. Pitkin prayed with his Chinese teacher, and wrote some last letters to his wife and buried them in two places. To the faithful letter carrier, Laoman, before he escaped over the wall, he gave this verbal message: "If all the letters are destroyed, tell my wife that God was with me at the last, and his peace was my consolation. Tell her to send our little son to Yale and that it is my hope that when he is twenty-five he will come to China as a missionary."

On July 1 the American Board compound was attacked. General Feng, later called "The Christian General," was a young soldier stationed at the gate of the mission compound, ostensibly to protect the missionaries but actually to see that every one was murdered—that not one should escape. Feng told me personally that the first awakening of his conscience came when he saw Miss Morrell come out from the mission compound and face the Boxer mob, offering to lay down her life if they would spare the women and children inside. Ashamed, the crowd slunk away, but the next day a fresh mob stormed the gate. While Pitkin was endeavoring to defend Miss Morrell and Miss Gould, he was beheaded and the two ladies were bound, taken to the temple, and put to death. Pitkin's head was offered at the shrine of the Boxer's god, while his body was thrown outside the city wall in a pit with nine Chinese Christians. When it was later discovered, his hands were lifted as in prayer, expressive of the attitude of his life.

Fourteen years later, in 1914, when I was asked to visit Paoting in a nation-wide evangelistic campaign, three thousand students came pouring out to attend the first meeting. Many of these men stood for nearly two hours during the address, while several hundred were turned away from the doors for lack of room. We gave three addresses without a break, and at the close spoke of the cross of Christ. We could find no better illustration of that cross than the death of Pitkin himself, for there were men in that audience who had seen those martyrs die. When I came to the story of the cross and of Pitkin's death the interpreter broke down under deep emotion and stood silent, unable to speak. It is considered a shameful disgrace for a Chinese to weep in public. The audience bowed their heads in sympathy and in shame. Many were in tears. When, after a pause, we quietly gave the invitation, some decided for Christ and many became honest inquirers. More than ten thousand Christian books were sold in a single day in that city where Pitkin had been martyred. Two hundred and fifty-eight missionaries and some thirty thousand Chinese Christians had laid down their lives in the Boxer Uprising, some of them with incredible heroism. Over and over again in China the cross of Christ proved to be the power of God unto salvation, especially when it is reincarnated in the lives of his followers.

Robert Speer in closing his account of the life of Horace Pitkin thus aptly quotes Bunyan's Valiant-for-Truth: "My sword I give to him that shall succeed me in my pilgrimage, and my courage and skill to him that can get it. My marks and scars I carry with me, to be a witness for me that I have fought His battles who will now be my rewarder. . . . So he passed over, and all the trumpets sounded for him on the other side."

HENRY LUCE AND THE EDUCATORS

In many ways the long life of Henry Winters Luce, the educator, was in contrast to the short life of Horace Pitkin, the martyr.[2] With widely differing gifts, no two men alike, missionaries are a team who supplement each other. Both Luce and Pitkin were of the Class of '92 at Yale, and the sons of both were in the same class in Yale in 1920—Henry Luce, later publisher of *Life, Time,* and *Fortune,* and young Horace Pitkin. Henry W. Luce, the father, was editor in chief of the Yale *Courant,* with Horace Pitkin as a fellow editor, and Henry R. Luce, the son, of whom his father was always proud, was an editor of the Yale *News* while in college.

Luce and I were roommates in both Union and Princeton seminaries. In our senior year, anticipating the staggering weight of responsibility of being ambassadors for Christ in the revolutionary Orient, we followed the practice of the "morning watch" and daily set our alarm clock for five in the morning. After a cup of cocoa made on our gas jet, we began with an hour of Bible study, followed by an hour of private prayer, each in his own room. These two hours laid the spiritual foundations of our lives abroad, which were to be subjected to far greater strain than we could then anticipate. Luce's year of study in the life of Christ furnished the preparation for his teaching and textbooks on this subject later in China.

Coming from Yale and Union, we had both learned the necessity of the application of science to religion, and the principles of historic criticism, from Professor William Rainey Harper while at Yale. When the trio—Pitkin, Luce, and I—met the leaders of the Student Volunteer Movement, we flatly refused to teach the old hell-fire appeal to fear, of so many millions of "heathen" going every hour into "Christless graves." We later saw with sorrow the greathearted Cambridge oarsman Stanley Smith expelled from the China Inland Mission because he could not believe in and preach a Molochlike God who in-

[2] I am indebted to the well-written life of Luce by B. A. Garside, which was kindly furnished to me in manuscript. It is probably to be published under the title *First the Kingdom.*

54

sisted upon eternal punishment. This issue of fundamentalism versus modernism was a problem we had to face in China and India, where it is more acute than it is in free America. We came to the conclusion that the mission boards must send both conservatives and liberals to the mission fields, for both were represented in the Early Church, in the New Testament, and throughout the centuries. But we also believed that the boards should send only the best men abroad, tolerant men who would be able to co-operate with others. Extreme radicals and reactionaries—nontheistic humanists on the one hand and intolerant fundamentalists on the other—can hardly present a united front and work together harmoniously on the same team.

In 1897 Luce reached his station in Tengchow, North China, in Shantung, the sacred province of Confucius. Here the pioneers John L. Nevius, Hunter Corbett, and Calvin Mateer had labored not only to evangelize the masses but to raise up an educated Chinese leadership that could carry on the self-propagating and in time self-supporting work of missions. Luce was shocked at the death of Horace Pitkin in 1900, and escaped with his family on a Chinese gunboat. From the first he gave himself to the cause of Christian education, helping to found two union universities. He was called alike to teaching and to administration, to literary and financial work, the last of which he found immeasurably the hardest of all. Luce was a pioneer in recognizing that missionary education must be conceived in broader terms than merely those of a small church school. Missionary institutions had to become the pathfinders for the education of all China by government and private agencies. Luce had his early training under the great educator Calvin Mateer, but it was Luce who saw the importance of moving the college from Tengchow to Weihsien, a strategically located city in the center of the Christian communities of the "sacred province" of Shantung. This small college, however, did not satisfy him. He felt the need of a real university under Christian auspices, and he was largely instrumental in moving the college to the capital at Tsinan and in securing the co-operation of other missionary societies interested in higher education. This led to the formation of the Shantung Christian University, which is now supported by eight mission boards and is one of the leading and most fruitful Christian institutions in all China.

Luce was next called to the vice-presidency of Yenching University, and he devoted the best years of his life to helping the president, J. Leighton Stuart, to build that institution into the leading Christian university in China. When he went to America to raise money, Luce met the remarkable and saintly Christian, Madame McCormick. Observing that Luce was tired and ill, Madame McCormick put him to bed in her son's room, received Luce's family into her home, and for sixteen years generously and wisely gave her princely gifts to the union colleges. Luce declined the attractive call to be the first president of the new Yale-in-China, and later of the Hangchow Christian College, and concentrated all his efforts on Yenching.

Luce was the chief means of raising the greater part of the first million dollars for Yenching, which was supplemented by gifts of several millions from the Hall estate of $14,000,000, a fortune founded on Hall's discovery of the electrolytic process of the aluminum industry. Luce was one of the first who conceived the idea of combining Chinese architecture with the best scientific experience of Western architecture. He helped to secure, to build the new buildings of the union colleges, the great architect Henry Murphy of Yale, who was swept off his feet by the majesty and beauty of the architecture of the Forbidden City in Peiping. Luce was deeply impressed when he finally went over that wonderful campus at Yenching—one of the most beautiful in the world, with a score of buildings which his work had helped to make possible, each a triumph of architectural genius, combining Oriental beauty with Western scientific and industrial efficiency. On a little island at the heart of the campus is the Luce Pavilion, bearing his Chinese name, which means "one who seeks righteousness."

The key to Luce's whole life is found in the passage "Seek ye first the kingdom of God." Luce sought that kingdom first, last, and always. To an unusual degree his mind was active, vigorous, and buoyant to the very end. When he returned to

America, he threw himself with great energy into the developing of a series of "Interpretive Institutes" as summer schools at Silver Bay, Lake George, at Auburn, Princeton, and at the University of Chicago. Here he was an inspiring and contagious teacher. One prominent minister said he was the greatest teacher he had ever known. Another spoke of the inner radiance of his character showing in "the most Christian face I ever saw." Luce made his students world-minded.

The last shock of Luce's life was Japan's attack at Pearl Harbor, December 7, 1941. He passed away quietly in his sleep that same night; but he lives on in the beautiful buildings of the great union colleges at Tsinan and Peiping, in his books all over China, in the lives of thousands of his students, and in the growing understanding of all races that "under Heaven there is but one family." He was a worthy member of the great crusade. He had hitched his wagon to a star. The tablet dedicated to him summed up his life and that of many another Christian educator:

IN MEMORY OF
HENRY WINTERS LUCE
1868-1941
SEEKER AFTER THE KINGDOM OF GOD
DREAMER WHO MADE HIS DREAM A REALITY
FRIEND AND SERVANT OF CHINA
INTERPRETER OF THE WEST TO THE EAST
AND OF THE EAST TO THE WEST

FRANK KELLER AND THE OPENING OF HUNAN

Frank Keller, with other student volunteers, was a member of a group in Yale that met each week to study how to win men for Christ. (That work required more moral courage in Yale in 1891 than it did later on in China or India!) Several of the spiritual leaders of Yale were even then turning to China as their goal, as the land of the greatest need and opportunity. But the hardest field, the inner fortress of China, was the conservative and ever antiforeign province of Hunan. About the size of England and Scotland combined, with a population of twenty-seven million, this virile province that had produced such proud scholars and statesmen had more successfully closed its doors against the Christian gospel than had any province in all China. When, in 1893, in consultation with three members of the Yale band, we issued a pamphlet called "The Supreme Decision of the Christian Student," we challenged men to enter and occupy this most fast-closed province in China.

For thirty years Protestant pioneers had been knocking vainly at Hunan's iron-barred portals. Adventurous missionaries had passed through the province; but, when they had tried to gain a foothold there, they had been roughly handled, or mobbed, or driven out. Continuously after 1875, backed by the prayers of Hudson Taylor, courageous workers of the China Inland Mission had repeatedly entered, only to be evicted. The officials, literati, and gentry sowed suspicion, fear, and hate in the hearts of the common people, spreading the wildest rumors concerning the "foreign devils" and their nefarious designs. For eight years Adam Dorward, having turned from closed Tibet, traversed the province and broke his heart trying to gain a permanent base in Hunan; but he was repeatedly cast out as the offscouring of the earth. His life was constantly threatened, he often was mobbed, and his iron constitution finally became undermined and he died of dysentery in 1888. The people of several towns collected money to buy swords, knives, flags, and uniforms to resist every attempt of Protestant missionaries to enter the province. After the Yangtze riots of 1891 the province was more firmly closed than ever.

On October 26, 1898, we were proud to have our classmate Frank Keller, of Yale '92, who had completed his medical training for China, enter Hunan as medical missionary and evangelist under the China Inland Mission. When people there began to attend his services, his life was threatened. In 1899 he escaped with his life when a mob looted his landlord's shop and gave Keller a "house warming," as he modestly described it, destroying some two thousand dollars worth of property. Keller slowly began to win confidence by generously releasing the official from all claims for damages to his property, by saving the life of the wife of the magistrate's son through his medical skill, and by successfully treating wounded Chinese soldiers. In 1899, as the Boxer crisis approached, Keller escaped a riot in which the London mission and Roman Catholic stations were destroyed and three Italian priests were killed and their bodies horribly mutilated and burned. In another center where the city was placarded, Keller was struck, he was followed by crowds shouting to beat and kill him, and he finally was driven out, pelted by stones. In 1900, when the empress dowager's message to kill all foreigners arrived, the magistrate's son, whose wife Keller had saved, called him to the yamen and told him of a plot to kill him. Keller knew that his classmate Pitkin had just fallen in Paoting, and he told the magistrate that it did not matter to him where he died, and that he would leave at once in order to save the magistrate and his son from death. He fled at midnight, but for two weeks, with riot and disorder on every hand, he had to pass through fierce crowds heaping curses and threats of immediate death upon him.

Within six months, after the storm had passed that had left several hundred foreigners and several tens of thousands of Chinese Christians slain, Keller returned to Hunan. In 1901 he finally opened Changsha, the capital city and key to the province, the first foreigner to gain a permanent foothold within the walls of that proud city. It was the cleanest and one of the best built of the cities of China. It could point to the tablet of the Great Yu, who had lived two hundred years before the traditional date of Abraham. Hunan's ancient Confucian college antedated Oxford and Cambridge; and it was proud of its long roll of officials, scholars, and famous statesmen who had saved China from the foreigner and had led the entire country in stubbornly excluding foreign trade and foreign religion. Keller rented large premises and won his way for evangelistic work by his medical ministry. His troubles were not ended, however, for in 1902, when the people attributed an outbreak of cholera to foreigners poisoning the wells to destroy the population, two of his fellow workers, Bruce and Lowis, were murdered.

In 1903 a conference was held in Changsha by thirty-two missionaries from twelve societies to co-ordinate their work throughout the province. In the China Inland Mission, Keller now had seven foreign and twelve Chinese fellow workers, with eleven chapels. He reported: "During our residence in Changsha thousands have heard the gospel, twenty-four have been baptized in our mission alone, and five Chinese evangelists have gone out from our training classes to serve with acceptance in other missions." The governor of Hunan donated $1,500 toward Keller's hospital within the walls of Changsha. Dr. Harlan P. Beach, a veteran Yale missionary, upon visiting the city wrote that the officials and persons of rank had now become friendly and even attended classes and services, and that he had never seen such a thorough acquaintance with the letter and power of the Scripture in converts of only a few years' standing. He concluded: "The missionaries give themselves to the people with a Christlike abandon at all hours of the day, and the 'church in the house' is made like a large Christian family, where all are welcome, reminding the visitor of the halcyon days of the early Apostolic Church."

In June, 1905, Dr. Hudson Taylor, the founder and head of the China Inland Mission, closed his great career as the pathfinder to Inland China in a thanksgiving service in Changsha as Frank Keller's guest in this last citadel of the proud and exclusive Middle Kingdom. Just forty years before, in 1865, on the sands at Brighton, he had entered his claim for the first twenty-four workers—two for each of the provinces of Inland China. He could well say: "Now lettest thou thy servant depart in peace, . . . for mine eyes have seen thy salvation, which thou hast prepared before the face of *all people.*" Here was the place he would have chosen to die.

In 1914 I visited Changsha, at the invitation of Chinese leaders and missionaries, in order to hold evangelistic meetings for the students and gentry. Twenty years before I had written of the challenge of this fast-closed province to student volunteers to enter the province. So complete was the change of attitude that we now came to the city in answer to a telegram from fifteen

Confucian principals of schools and colleges, inviting us to address their students. As we left the river steamer and entered the great gates of the ancient walled city, we saw the posters announcing the evangelistic meetings on the very notice boards where a few years before had hung the decree: "Kill the foreign devils who have come to make medicine out of the eyes of your children whom they have kidnapped." Fourteen—or even four—years before, we ourselves might have been driven out. We realized that the generous hearing accorded to the message, and the results of the meetings, were due to those who had sown the seed, who had borne the burden and heat of the day, the very lachet of whose shoes we were unworthy to unloose; and they were due to an almost complete change of attitude and of atmosphere in China as a whole.

As we came to the opening meeting, there was a young missionary acting as gatekeeper who had first entered the city on Thanksgiving Day, 1898. Driven out himself from the city gate by the officials, he had come back a week later by another gate, only again to be forced out and driven down the river. The next year when he returned, he was again attacked by the crowd, swung by his queue, beaten and driven from the city by an angry mob shouting, "Kill the foreigner!" At the meetings in 1914 he opened the gates to let in the throngs of modern students, who almost fought to get tickets of admission. The meetings were held in a great pavilion erected near the Confucian temple, in the grounds granted by the governor himself. Three thousand students were admitted by ticket, the governor's band attended and the governor's hearty message of greeting in approval of the meetings was read to the students by the leading government college president, who was in the chair. At the close of the meeting the band played "God be with you till we meet again."

I shall never forget the scene on the second day. After plain speaking on the bribery, graft, and dishonesty of the officials and merchants, and the immorality of students as the cause of China's present weakness, we had expected a falling off in the attendance. Instead, the doors had to be closed nearly half

61

an hour before the time of the lecture; for over three thousand students were crowded into the hall, and five hundred were gathered outside in an overflow meeting addressed by one of the missionaries. The question in every heart was, "What can save our country?" Our subject on this day was "The Hope of China." We asked the students if they possessed anything that could save their country and make honest officials, merchants, and students; but they were silent. For an hour we laid before them the claims of Jesus Christ in the challenge of his teaching to the mind, the appeal of his character to the heart, the offer of his power for the will. We tried to show that he was able to solve China's social problems, to meet the test of universality in a gospel valid for all men, and to give the dynamic of progress which China so desperately needed, in that he brings us to God, the ultimate power of the universe. Some eight hundred of these men came out the next day, in spite of the rain and the distractions of a Chinese feast day, to be assigned to Bible classes. We shall see how the Christian community has been steadily multiplying in Hunan through missionary evangelistic, educational, and medical work.

EDWARD H. HUME AND YALE-IN-CHINA

Yale is bound to China by a hundred ties. Samuel Wells Williams (1812-84) responded to the appeal of Robert Morrison and went out to join him in 1833, becoming himself a Chinese scholar. In 1844 he wrote the first monumental work on China for the American public, *The Middle Kingdom*. In 1853 he served as Commodore Perry's interpreter in Japanese on the expedition that was to open up Japan which was then, like Korea, a "hermit nation," and later served as secretary of the American Legation in Peiping. After forty-three years of service in China he returned to America and settled in New Haven, where he occupied the chair of Chinese language and literature. When he was succeeded by his son, Professor Frederick W. Williams, Yale became a center for Chinese studies.

In 1839 S. R. Brown, Yale '32, opened the Morrison school

in Macao, which was later removed to Hong Kong. When Brown broke down and was compelled to return to America, in 1847, he offered to take with him one or two Chinese boys in order that they might complete their education in America. Yung Wing, a boy of twelve, was the first to get on his feet, eager to go. After spending eight years in America, Yung graduated from Yale in the class of 1854. Taking a B.A. degree, he was the first Chinese to earn a degree from any American university. When he returned to China he was looked upon with suspicion because of his foreign education, and nearly all of his proposed reforms were thwarted by the reactionaries. Finally he was able to lay his plans before the great viceroy Tsêng Kuofan, China's greatest statesman of the nineteenth century, who rescued his country from the Taiping rebellion. The viceroy, assisted later by his younger colleagues Li Hung-chang and Chang Chih-tung, finally decided to send 120 carefully selected Chinese students to study in America in the care of Yung Wing, who was commissioner of the Chinese Educational Commission, and later associate Chinese minister to Washington. In 1872 Yung Wing took the first contingent of these men, established a large Chinese headquarters in Hartford, and placed these students two by two in the best homes in New England, to prepare them to enter Yale and other colleges. Nine years later, in 1881, the same reactionary element that led to the Boxer Uprising recalled these promising students to China. In spite of their incomplete education and the early prejudice against them, several of them attained a high place among Chinese officials and statesmen of the New Republic thirty years later.

There were two great missionary classes in Yale in our generation: the Class of 1892, the class of Pitkin, Luce, Keller, Bishop Huntington, Lasell, and Whittemore, who rendered distinguished service in China and the Far East; and the Class of 1898, that produced the "Yale Band," composed of Brownell Gage, Laurence Thurston, Charles Vickrey, A. B. Williams, and Brewer Eddy. They toured the country speaking on behalf of missions, and several of them finally helped in the founding of Yale-in-China.[3] This was a bold project, the idea of which was suggested by the Cambridge University Mission in Delhi and the Oxford University Mission in Calcutta. After the Yale pioneers had surveyed the field, the province of Hunan was chosen because of its great leadership in literature, government, and military skill, and because there was no institution of higher learning in the Western sense in this long-closed province. The capital Changsha was selected as a site because of the hearty invitation of the first Hunan missionary conference in June, 1903. As Dr. Hume approached Changsha by river, it was symbolical that he found the archway over one of the highways at the entrance to Hunan Province walled up and blocked by the gentry to exclude the still-hated foreigner. With infinite pains, surmounting countless obstacles, and in the face of age-long prejudice, the first school and hospital were begun modestly in rented quarters. It was a day of elation when, in 1906, Dr. Hume could open the "Yale Court of Medicine," where he was to put into practice the teaching of his great professor Sir William Osler. He was warned not to operate for the first two years lest a single fatality might close the doors through fanatical prejudice. Happily, however, he was able painlessly to remove a bullet from the leg of a noted bandit, after "putting him to sleep" with ether. The reputed "miracles" worked by modern Western medicine led the city and province to pour in their sick to the foreign hospital.

A site was at last secured for the permanent and fine buildings of the Yale College of Arts and Sciences, the Middle School, the Medical College, the Hospital, and the School of Nursing.

[3] Yale-in-China came into being from the vision of Arthur Collins Williams, Yale '98, and was carried out by his classmates Laurence Thurston and Brownell Gage, and by Warren Seabury, William Hail, and Edward Hume, Yale '97, the last of whom became the first president. With these men were associated great Chinese colleagues: F. C. Yen, F. L. Chang, Z. Z. Zee, and other Yale men, all on an equal footing with equal salaries. The project was made possible by Yale's generous graduates Edward S. Harkness, '97, Clarence H. Kelsey, '98, Samuel Thorne and Russell Colgate, '96, and many others. Yale-in-China was backed and promoted by President Timothy Dwight, Dean Henry P. Wright, Harlan P. Beach, Anson Phelps Stokes, F. W. Williams, W. Walker, E. B. Reed, and their successors. It had the co-operation and advice of John R. Mott, Robert E. Speer, James L. Barton, and other pioneers.

Rome was not built in a day—nor was Yale in Connecticut or Yale-in-China. Edward H. Hume was wisely chosen as the first president. Hume was the leader of a very able team of Yale men in China, such as Warren Seabury, Brownell Gage, William Hail, and later Kenneth Latourette and Francis Hutchins. They had to begin by building from the ground up an academy that caught the imagination of its students, their parents, members of the gentry, and officials of the province. Prejudice was gradually broken down by both the educational and the medical work. These Yale men were pathfinders in rapidly associating themselves with Chinese colleagues upon an absolutely equal footing in all respects. They were pioneers also in the development of a missionary project into a nationalized, adequately supported government institution. The medical college was the first institution in the history of China to be launched by a Christian mission, maintained for twenty-five years by a joint board, Chinese and Western, and finally transferred to the national government of China, continuing, however, to maintain the same close, friendly relations with Yale-in-China as in the past. The college was temporarily closed when the Communists overran Hunan and drove out all foreigners.

Edward Hume went to China in 1905 and left in 1937. He served as president of Yale-in-China from 1923 to 1927. In 1928 Yali College of Arts and Sciences, under the wise initiative of Edward Hume, joined with four other Christian colleges to form the Central China College at Wuchang. Hume's classmate Edward Harkness generously gave over two hundred thousand dollars to erect the splendid Yale hospital as the center of a modern medical plant. But Hume's ambition for the Kingdom of God reached far beyond Changsha and the twenty millions of Hunan, to the one fifth of the human race in China, a land of poverty, famine, and disease. He gladly acknowledged the achievements of the Chinese in his *Chinese Way in Medicine,* but they had not healed the woes of China. A death rate of fifteen per thousand is high for any country, but far more than twenty-five per thousand were dying in China. Infant mortality was far more than two hundred per thousand births, while the maternal death rate was more than fifteen per thousand births. The great bulk of the population still believed in the old-fashioned practitioners of herbal medicine. About a third of the population was suffering from trachoma, and 8 per cent had pulmonary tuberculosis. There were over a million lepers, and there was always danger of violent outbreaks of cholera, typhus fever, and plague. There was a basic lack of the understanding of germ diseases, sanitation, public health service, preventive medicine, health education, and of hospitals as healing and teaching centers.

When Dr. Hume went to China, neither the provincial government nor the national government, which was still under the conservative Manchus, had any conception of their medical responsibilities nor of the possibilities of such public service. Hume was convinced that medical missions were no mere temporary expedient to open the way for the gospel message, but an integral, co-ordinate, and permanent part of missionary work. Christian hospitals always symbolize the whole gospel, which seeks to make men whole in spirit, mind, and body. Dr. Hume saw that medical missions were a means of breaking down prejudice, of winning confidence, and of securing a friendly atmosphere for the Christian message. He believed in the evangelistic work of medical missions as a practical demonstration of God's love. And he saw the immediate and imperative necessity of training an adequate body of Chinese doctors skilled in modern medicine and with spiritual and sacrificial motivation.

As an example of the value and necessity of medical missions Dr. Hume pointed to Robert Morrison, with his first dispensary, and to the first medical missionary, Peter Parker (1804-88), who opened up prejudiced China at the point of a lancet. After graduation from Yale College and Divinity School and after his medical preparation, Dr. Parker arrived in 1834 in Canton, where he opened an ophthalmic hospital—for there was an appalling amount of trachoma, ophthalmia, and blindness—and later a general hospital. The poor would sleep in the streets to be the first in the morning to cry "Cure me! Save me!" after they learned of the free treatment of disease. As the most delicate and difficult surgical operations were successfully performed, rumor took wings and spread the story that the blind were made to see, the deaf to hear, and the lame to walk. In 1838 Dr. Parker established the Medical Missionary Society in all China. When he was on furlough, he appealed in a personal interview to Daniel Webster, secretary of state, for an American minister plenipotentiary; and Dr. Parker himself served as secretary of the American Legation and later as United States commissioner to China. He was a humble mediator between the Chinese emperor and the American secretary of state. He died at the age of eighty-three, after a long and honored ministry of both healing and mediation. Following in Dr. Parker's steps, Dr. Hume points proudly to an average for the last twenty-five years of three hundred medical missionaries in China, and to over a thousand sent out during the last century, serving in more than two hundred mission hospitals. In 1935 there were 325 foreign doctors, 275 foreign nurses, and 530 Chinese physicians in the service of medical missions. Because of his brilliant record in the Yale hospital, Dr. Hume was asked by the national health administration of the Chinese government to visit the hospitals of China between 1934 and 1937, and to report on the capacity of each institution, government or mission, to meet the overwhelming demands of a devastating war, if and when a Japanese invasion should occur. Holding a double post under the government and the China council of medical missions, Dr. Hume as a consultant sought to do all he could to prepare and enlarge the facilities in both government and mission hospitals to treat the wounded, sick, and famine-stricken during the decade of war and invasion that was to follow. Today Edward Hume is urging the several mission boards to respond with prompt eagerness to the invitation sent by the Chinese government in the summer of 1944, to mission hospitals throughout China, to participate in a unified health program for the nation.

For the last seven years Edward Hume has been serving the world-wide cause of missions. Almost every aspect of his present work bears witness to the bold strides of advance in modern missions in the matter of co-operation and in union effort. Dr. Hume is now the senior secretary of the Christian Medical Council for Overseas Work, with offices at 156 Fifth Avenue, New York City. This council is itself a functional committee of the Foreign Missions Conference of North America, of which Dr. Hume says:

Organized in 1893, the Conference is an association of 122 boards and societies of North America, representing 66 Protestant churches and thirty million Christians, for united planning and action in the Christian World Mission. It seeks to provide an understanding fellowship and medium, in which unified and co-operative plans of action can be realized. The Conference meets annually to confer on issues, to create policies, to eliminate overlapping and waste, and to initiate projects of advance. It touches the life and thought of ten thousand American and Canadian missionaries and their national fellow workers in eighty-one countries. In its ultimate objective and outreach, it serves one billion people, or half the population of the world, to whom our missionaries go. It seeks to unite the members of all churches among all nations in a Christian world service that is both spiritual and practical. It unites and co-ordinates the work of some thirty national councils around the world to form and support the I.M.S. (International Missionary Council), and thus seeks to promote ultimate world brotherhood, which it believes is the spiritual foundation of future organized world peace.

In China, the Christian Medical Council for Overseas Work advocates closer co-operation between the government National Health Administration and Christian hospitals as a basis for better integration of government and mission medical service after the war, urging the continuance of a liaison officer by the Christian forces to secure and maintain more intimate and effective relationships. Raymond B. Fosdick, president of the Rockefeller Foundation, shows that all the world is concerned in health conditions in China, and that whereas in the United States there is one hospital for each 22,500 persons, in China there is but one for each 700,000 persons; and while there is one physician for each 750 people in this country, in China there is only one well-trained physician for each 70,000.

The council is humbly proud of the fact that in China alone, in normal years, mission hospitals treat nearly two hundred thousand inpatients and some three million outpatients a year. But like the five loaves and two fishes, what are these among so many? The 60 government hospitals in China and 235 Protestant mission hospitals, with 15 others, make up a total of only 310 modern hospitals in all China, and are utterly inadequate to heal the sick of the 450 million in China. Probably Dr. Hume in his present position in New York is able to do more to remedy this disparity and to meet China's need as a land of poverty, famine, and disease, than when he was serving in one medical center in China.

In Africa, the Christian Medical Council urges the development of medical education at high levels for Africans, so that as early as possible their doctors may be the colleagues and successors of European and American missionaries. It is exploring the possibilities for the training of African nurses, assistants, and public health workers. In India, it agrees that "Christian higher medical education is the most urgent and most important project for medical missions." It therefore supports the Christian Medical Association of India in its efforts to develop a medical college for men as well as women at Vellore, in connection with the institution begun by Dr. Ida Scudder. The Christian Medical Council co-operates with the medical committees of the national Christian councils of China, Africa, and India, as well as the Near East and Mexico; and it seeks to maintain friendly contacts with missionary doctors and nurses everywhere.

At the home base in North America, Dr. Hume says:

The Council seeks to serve the mission boards by suggesting ways of greater correlation at home and more effective integration with the environment overseas, by relating the medical work to the life of the indigenous churches, to government health programs, and to the growing body of nationals practicing modern medicine. It finds appropriate places for graduate study and hospital experience for furloughed missionaries, and calls annual conferences for the consideration of special problems on the field, such as nursing education, hospital evangelism, and public health programs. For visiting nationals from the various mission fields, it helps to orient doctors and nurses from abroad in courses of study and hospital residencies in North America. For government and civilian agencies, it assembles information regarding tropical diseases and suggests appointments for tropical posts. And to all who believe in the obligation of the Christian World Mission, whether they be societies, churches, physicians, nurses, or individual laymen, the Council rightly appeals for funds to help carry on this Christian ministry of health and healing. With all existing missions the Council seeks to unite the spirit of apostolic Christianity with the most modern efficiency of organization, and thus to bring from its treasures things both new and old.

NORMAN WHITTEMORE AND THE EVANGELIZATION OF KOREA

Norman Clark Whittemore, Yale '92, went to Korea under the Presbyterian board in 1896, when his classmates Pitkin and Luce went to China. Whittemore labored so successfully that there were soon more than five thousand Koreans in his station of Syen Chyun who had turned to Christianity, and thirty thousand in the surrounding district. Few men have ever witnessed such a nearly complete transformation of an entire country within their lifetime as did Norman Whittemore and his fellow workers. Whittemore always insisted that he was only an ordinary "garden variety" of missionary, and he would never tell me anything about himself; but he would tell me everything about the Koreans and their great leaders like Baron Yun Tchi Ho. I will therefore, in effect, let Whittemore tell the story of Korea and the Koreans rather than of his own life.

Korea, "the land of the morning calm," had long tried to exclude all foreigners. In 1592 the great General Hideyoshi of Japan invaded Korea, and by six years of bloody warfare so devastated the land that in some ways it never recovered. This seemed to be typical of Japan's later domination, which Koreans resented because of its forcible Japanization, its unsympathetic and autocratic rule, and its economic discrimination, which developed Korea for Japanese imperialism and the profit of Japanese settlers but often impoverished the Koreans. From that time on Korea tried to maintain herself as "the hermit nation." It was death for a foreigner to land, and there was a record of almost continual persecution of Catholics from before 1800 to 1866. Korea's own government was so corrupt that Korean patriots themselves declared that during the last forty years of its existence it was one of the worst governments in the world. The emperor stole from the rich in the capital, the governors extorted their pound of flesh from the provinces, the mayors and petty officials seized what was left from the poor. If a man was found with a yoke of oxen and a little property, he could be seized for the debts of all his profligate relations, imprisoned until he bought his relief by bribery, or made a "Royal Grave Keeper" and have his property sold to pay for the empty title. Offices were sold to the highest bidder; all effort at reform was stamped out; the patriots were thrown into prison; and patriotism and progress were alike impossible under such a degenerate government. Many indigenous governments from Korea to Turkey were thus corrupt when missionaries came to them. The Japanese hired assassins to kill the Korean queen, they imprisoned the king—and to this day they have held the heir to the throne, Yi Ewa, prisoner, so that they might make him a puppet king if the war was ever lost.

In 1905 Korea became a Japanese protectorate and was occupied as a province of Japan, and a government-general was established in 1910. Marquis Ito as Japan's ablest statesman was sent to Japanize Korea completely and to absorb her people into the Japanese Empire. Two forces now began to discipline and reform Korea. There was the outward iron framework of the harsh Japanese government and the inner spiritual leaven of Christianity. The Japanese government was materially efficient: it developed railways, agriculture, industry, and trade. But it denied all liberties, it often crushed the embittered Koreans, and it enriched the Japanese masters and paid a few Quislings their hire. There was an increase of prostitution, venereal disease, immorality, materialism, and cynicism. Vigorous young Koreans, whether men or women, were apprehended, subjected to protracted third degree examination and intimidation, and frequently imprisoned with the application of torture of a cruelty that surpasses description. Koreans have shown me the wounds and scars on their bare bodies; their mental and spiritual wounds were not so obvious, but they were more serious.

No country ever needed Christianity more than Korea or was more visibly and speedily helped by it. The primitive religions of Korea were on a low level and not as helpful to the people as those in China and Japan. Confucianism was a relatively impotent moral code; Buddhism had become corrupt and had been discredited for three centuries. The real religion of animism and shamanism was rife with superstition and demonolatry, and the Koreans were in imperative moral and religious need of *foreign* missions.

My classmate Norman Whittemore arrived in Korea in 1906, at the beginning of the great revival. The Nevius plan from China for putting full responsibility for both work and finances upon a trained native church was followed by the principal missions, especially the Presbyterian and Methodist. I watched Whittemore and other missionaries develop a complete organization for training both clergy and laity. Bible institutes were attended by tens of thousands of church members. Each Christian was taught to be a living witness and a winner of men. There was no need of street chapels, for each Christian was a kind of walking street chapel. While Korea was notable for its primary evangelistic emphasis, coupled with a strong educational and medical program, few mission fields have so effectively developed their scientific agricultural work for the economic betterment of their poor farmers.

Just before visiting Whittemore I went to Pingyang—or Heijo —once the worst city in all Korea. When Robert Germain Thomas, of the London Missionary Society, came from China with a quantity of Christian Scriptures in 1866 in the ill-fated American schooner *General Sherman,* he and all the crew were killed by the inhabitants of that city. In 1883 the Methodists sent R. S. Maclay from Japan and later H. G. Appenzeller and

W. B. Scranton. In 1884 the Presbyterians sent the first permanent missionary, Horace N. Allen, and later Horace G. Under-
wood and other able men. With the old law of death to the
Christian unrepealed, the first converts were baptized in secret
in 1886; but by 1890 there were over one hundred, and by
1907 there were in Korea a thousand self-supporting churches,
thirty thousand communicants, and a hundred and twenty
thousand adherents. When I attended a church service in Pingyang in 1911, I was amazed at the change that had taken place
in twenty years.

Instead of seven believers there were thirty-three thousand.
In place of one little church, eight by twelve feet square, forty-
two thriving congregations had branched off from the mother
church. Instead of a few children, the whole congregation was
coming in a body to study the Bible. Two hundred Bible training conferences in the station had been attended by ten thousand Christians, some walking from fifty to a hundred miles
to attend. I saw a young Christian student whose diary recorded
thirty-four hundred personal interviews during the year. He
was ministering to a little church without salary. One year the
Christians tried to reach a million souls with the gospel, which
was still "good news" in Korea. After thirteen years' absence,
I found the church in Korea had gained 1,000 per cent. In the
twenty years between 1910 and 1930 over two hundred and
four thousand adults had been baptized by the Methodist and
Presbyterian bodies alone. By 1930 Protestant missions in Korea
had a Christian constituency of half a million,[4] and the church
was as near the combined goal of self-propagation, self-support,
and self-government as any of the younger churches in any
mission land. There was a fine spirit of unity, co-operation,

[4] There were 135 Roman Catholic missionaries with about a hundred thousand members and twice that number as a total constituency. The Methodists
and Presbyterians constituted 90 per cent of the Protestants' 3,300 churches, with
450 missionaries, 594 ordained pastors, 500 Bible women, and 3,000 teachers,
doctors, and nurses in Christian institutions. Korean contributions, out of their
prevailing poverty, were over $700,000 in 1930, and two thirds of the churches
were self-supporting. Until the repressive measures of the Japanese occupation
Korea was breaking a world's record in missions.

and comity in the division of territory among the Protestant missions.

When Norman Whittemore arrived in Syen Chyun in 1897, there was only one Christain and one inquirer in that county seat. When he returned to America on furlough in 1924, twenty-seven years later, the town had a Christian population of five thousand. When Whittemore first toured his province of North Pyung An, there were but four small Christian groups with a hundred Christians; when he came on furlough less than three decades later, there were thirty thousand Christians, and there was a proportionate increase in the rest of Korea. During Whittemore's nearly forty years in the country he witnessed a deep change in the character of the people. He saw a large body of the Koreans turn from gross superstition, the fear of demons and evil spirits, and from ancestor worship, to an ethical monotheism which cast out their previous fears. The population abandoned crude and ineffective methods of curing disease for an intelligent acceptance of the practice of Western medicine and surgery, with many of their young men studying medicine and their young women becoming nurses. Whittemore saw the nation turning toward modern education, from the kindergarten to the college, and learning the lesson of liberty, laying the foundations for a future democracy that could never be satisfied with the corruption of their former monarchy nor the harsh cruelties of Japanese autocracy.

When the Japanese placed a severe brake upon the freedom of the Christian movement, there were two principal manifestations of the unbroken liberty-loving spirit of the Koreans against the Japanese: the splendid endurance of the Koreans shown in the so-called "Conspiracy Case" in 1912, when hundreds of Korean Christians were arrested by the Japanese on the charge of conspiracy to assassinate the governor general; and the Korean Declaration of Independence in 1919. Of thirty-three leaders chosen to sign the declaration, sixteen, or practically half, were Christians. The Japanese ended all freedom of thought in the educational system through their typical insistence on the use of Japanese and the absolute prohibition of the Korean language in all grades from the primary to the university. All Koreans were compelled to attend the shrine ceremonies and bow toward Tokyo, even in connection with the church services. The Japanese occupation will leave its scars, as did the bondage of Israel in Egypt, but its stern discipline will not all have been in vain. The missionaries will be eagerly welcomed back when Korea is free, all the more because they had not been in the position of overseers, for the country had had a self-governing church since 1907, Koreans occupying the positions of moderator and chairman on most of the committees.

I may fittingly close this section by referring, not to my beloved classmate Norman Whittemore, but to a Korean Christian who Whittemore would insist was a far greater man than he, Baron Yun Tchi Ho, the son of an exiled Korean nobleman. Yun was sent by the Korean government to study in Japan, where he learned both Japanese and English. Upon his return to Korea he acted as interpreter for the first American minister to Korea. He soon had to leave Korea because of political troubles; and he went to Shanghai, where he studied in the Anglo-Chinese college and became a Christian. Then he went to America, where he studied in Emory and later in Vanderbilt University. Upon returning to Korea, Baron Yun Tchi Ho held the post of vice-minister of education and was a member of the embassy that attended both the coronation of Czar Nicholas and the diamond jubilee of Queen Victoria. He was editor of the first Korean newspaper, the *Independent*, president of Korea's patriotic Independence Club, and president of the Y.M.C.A. He was governor of one of the thirteen provinces from 1899 to 1903, and then he took a post in the office of foreign affairs. His life was repeatedly in danger as a patriot. He gave of his means to start the Anglo-Korean school, and then an industrial school. I heard him make an outstanding address at the World's Student Christian Federation Conference in Tokyo in 1907, where he spoke fluently in Japanese, English, and Chinese. No Anglo-Saxon and no Japanese present was his equal as a linguist. When in America, he had won a gold medal in an oratorical contest over all his American competitors, and he could thrill any audience in Korea as their beloved and sacrificial patriot. He was unjustly imprisoned by the Japanese for four years, with a hundred other Korean Christians, in the Conspiracy Case of 1912. I found him silent and sad at the garden party in Seoul given by Governor General Viscount Saito (who was himself assassinated in the February mutiny of 1936 by the militarists in Tokyo). Dr. Yun seemed a much greater man than the Governor, who was the best of the Japanese. In his suffering and sacrifice, in his indomitable patriotism, in his Christlike character, in his wide public service, and in his unshaken faith in Korea's future, the Hon. T. H. Yun seemed to be a prophecy and guaranty of that future. He is typical of the great indigenous Christian leaders raised up in every mission field.

OTHER YALE MISSIONARIES

Yale has been honored for a century by a long and almost unbroken line of missionaries. No one of them was held in greater affection than Harlan P. Beach (1854-1933). We regarded him as the father of the Yale and Union Seminary and many other volunteer bands. He went to China in 1883 under the American Board to work in its college at Tungchow, but he was compelled to return to America in 1889 because of his wife's health. In 1895 he became educational secretary of the Student Volunteer Movement, promoting the organization of mission study classes in the colleges and theological seminaries and writing textbooks for them. From 1906 to 1921 he was the first to occupy the chair of missions at Yale, and during this period he was the outstanding scholar and authority in the United States on foreign missions.

Dr. Beach and I were roommates on the Cunard steamer *Cephalonia* on our way to the student volunteer convention at Liverpool. On New Year's morning, 1896, we heard the call ring through the ship, "All hands on deck!" The ship had run upon the rocks, dashing into a precipice at the Southstack Lighthouse near Holyhead, and it rapidly went to the bottom.

I can remember every word spoken by Dr. Beach on that memorable morning as we escaped from the sinking ship in the same lifeboat. When we awoke after the crash, I was on the point of exclaiming: "A few minutes, Dr. Beach, and we'll be in heaven!" but it suddenly occurred to me, the benighted bachelor, that he would be thinking of his wife and his earthly cares, so I silenced my thought and merely muttered to myself: "If we do get ashore I'll need my best Sunday suit to speak at that Liverpool convention. That suit will serve me just as well as any if we go down, and better if we get ashore; so here goes for the Sunday suit!"

Yale men are equally proud of Kenneth Scott Latourette, who is in a sense Professor Beach's successor at Yale. Graduating in the class of 1906, after taking all possible degrees—B.A., M.A., Ph.D.—he toured the American colleges as traveling secretary of the volunteer movement in 1909, and served on the faculty of Yale-in-China from 1910 to 1917. Failing health forced him to return to America, where he has served at Yale since 1921—professor of missions from 1921 to 1927, and of missions and Oriental history since 1927. He has given with distinction series of lectures at Harvard, Princeton, and many other colleges. A real historian, his multiplying scholarly works —especially his *A History of the Expansion of Christianity*, in seven large volumes, which gives missions their rightful place in church history—lead many of us to hope that he is becoming the Harnack of America. And Kenneth Latourette is only one of a long line of Yale missionaries reaching in an unbroken chain from the time of Robert Morrison and S. Wells Williams to the present.

There is not space to record the life and work of all the members of that first Yale band who did a fine job in the Orient. But no account, however brief, can omit Edwin Carlyle Lobenstine, Yale '95, whose statesmanlike work as the secretary of the National Christian Council of all China helped to co-ordinate, unite, and make more efficient the service of all his fellow Protestant missionaries and Chinese workers. I remember him as a boy in my home town of Leavenworth, Kansas, where his

77

father did a thriving business in buffalo hides, brought in by the ton from the Western prairies, where the buffaloes were being rapidly exterminated. As a scholarly student Lobenstine followed Horace Pitkin at Phillips Exeter Academy, Yale, and Union Theological Seminary. For thirty-nine years, 1898 to 1937, he was a missionary in China under the Presbyterian Board. From 1901 to 1911 he was at Hwaiyuen, with two Yale and two Princeton men, working in the North Anwkei Province in church and administrative work. Here he saw the need of practical agricultural training to aid the peasants of his impoverished rural province, and he urged men like Professor Lossing Buck to come to China. Professor Buck served with distinction under the Presbyterian Board at Hsuchow and then in Nanking University, training Chinese leaders technically and in general education to meet the need of the desperately poor peasants. His life and work would make an interesting and profitable addition to this volume, as would that of Sam Higgenbotham in India.

In 1911 and 1912 Lobenstine was engaged, with many other missionaries, as an able organizer in famine relief. He served with ability as the honorary executive secretary of the Central China Famine Relief Committee, and later with the National Flood Relief Commission. His eyes were always lifted, however, to ever-widening horizons. He had long desired to survey China as a whole, and he gladly took six months from his local work when he was asked by John R. Mott, in 1912, to set up regional conferences all over China for missionaries and Chinese leaders.[5] This service with Mott, of organizing regionally and nationally the whole missionary work of China, took Lobenstine twice over the entire country.

He was then asked to serve as secretary of the national Christian conference in Shanghai in 1913, and he was made secretary of the Continuation Committee of that conference. He

[5] A few years before, at the great missionary conference in Shanghai in 1907, there had not been a single Chinese representative present after a whole century of missionary work in that land. A few of the younger men, like Brockman and Lobenstine, resolved that "never again" should such shortsighted neglect be repeated.

became secretary of the permanent National Christian Council of China from 1922 to 1935. Here he had to keep in correspondence with and endeavor to co-ordinate the work of 130 scattered denominational missionary societies. One of the first obvious tasks was to avoid overlapping and wasteful competition among these hitherto largely isolated agencies and to get the leading societies to divide the field and formulate agreements on comity and general principles of mission work. The aim was to coordinate the efforts of Protestant missions and isolated Chinese churches, especially their widely scattered educational and medical work.

Lobenstine and the National Christian Council sought to raise money and to strengthen the work both of the China Christian Education Association and of the Committee on Medical Missions of the Chinese Medical Association. In all this work Lobenstine's able colleague was Cheng Ching-yi, who was the outstanding Christian preacher of China and an acknowledged national leader. The National Christian Council in China now began to bring together for the first time the recognized leaders of all the major missionary societies, Chinese and foreign, so that they could think of China as a whole and formulate common objectives and statesmanlike plans for realizing them. If anyone made the discovery of a new or improved method, such as the pioneer John L. Nevius formerly had of building self-supporting, self-governing, and self-propagating churches on indigenous lines, it was now quickly made available for all through a unified organization and the printed page. The National Christian Council sought to make all missions more alert in recognizing indigenous leadership when it arose, and to provide adequate opportunities for exercising it.

From 1900 to 1920, though Chinese leadership was long overdue, it had been supposed that presidents and head masters of educational institutions must be foreigners. The process of developing Chinese leadership was providentially accelerated by the dire evil of the Communist upheaval of 1926-27. Foreigners were driven by the Communists from Central China, and in Hunan the Reds killed the rich, the landlords, and the conservatives. In 1927 the National Christian Council helped to evacuate from the interior, fifteen hundred missionaries whose lives were in danger. In Nanking and other cities all foreigners were driven out, and colleges were opened or continued under Chinese leadership—a step that should have been taken long before. Partly as a result of the Communist uprising, the Chinese government made regulations that presidents, headmasters, and boards of directors of colleges and middle schools should be predominantly Chinese.

The National Christian Council was first to realize the imperative need of a critical examination of the standards of missionary education made by qualified experts from the West. John D. Rockefeller, Jr., sent two deputations to China to investigate the best methods of aiding education there, in the way the Rockefeller Foundation already had done in the South of the United States. Dr. Ernest DeWitt Burton, Dr. Wallace Buttrick, Bishop Francis McConnell, Dean William F. Russell, President Kenyon L. Butterfield, and President Mary E. Woolley, were among those who served on a commission of experts to make a study of higher educational institutions in China in 1921-22. This was followed by the Layman's Inquiry Commission in 1931-32. Not only were educational standards raised and Chinese leadership developed, but union in educational effort was more widely achieved and stronger union colleges were organized.[6]

Typical of the whole movement for more efficient and united

---

[6] It is a notable result that more than a score of relatively weak and inadequately supported Protestant mission colleges in China have been strengthened by amalgamation so that now they number only thirteen, ten of which are union institutions. The budget in normal years of all these China colleges affiliated together in the Associated Boards for Christian Colleges in China, 150 Fifth Avenue, New York, is $780,000; but in 1943-44, because of wartime emergencies, it was some $2,000,000. The union colleges include Yenching University, near Peiping, of which the chancellor is H. H. Kung and the president, J. Leighton Stuart, and in which five missions are united: Cheeloo, or Shantung Christian University, in which ten mission boards are united; West China Union University, supported by eight mission boards; Ginling College, for women, of which Wu Yi-fang is president, uniting seven bodies; Fukien Christian University, a union of four missions; Hangchow Christian College, of two; Hua Chung, or Central China College, of four; the University of Nanking, four; and the University of Shanghai, three.

effort, a headquarters missions building for the National Christian Council and other united Christian agencies was erected in Shanghai at a cost of $382,000.

Lobenstine became one of the trustees of the Peiping Union Medical College in 1929, and served until 1936, when he became chairman of the China Medical Board in New York, which is endowed by the Rockefeller Foundation.[7] The Peiping Union Medical College has largely stimulated governmental and provincial medical education and furnished a high standard for government hospitals and for the development of scientific medicine and public health in the new China. Lobenstine has reached the conviction that Protestant denominationalism has come to the stage in which a larger degree of integration and union of Protestant churches and their activities is essential to a clear understanding of Christianity and to its effective functioning in China. He believes that narrow, competitive, sectarian denominationalism is out of date in the Orient. He does not believe that two hundred Protestant sects in America can do their best work by each independently propagating its peculiar denominational doctrines in the East. Competition may be the life of trade, but it is not the life of the church. Most of the modern student volunteers who went to foreign fields felt that they were in one spiritual Kingdom of God serving a Master who prayed that they might all be one. To realize the possibilities of Christian statesmanship in the furtherance of this unity has been the dominant purpose of Edwin C. Lobenstine, Edward H. Hume, and their fellow workers.

[7] From 1906 to 1915 this was a union medical missionary institution, but since 1915 it has been a Rockefeller organization. The former staff of missionary doctors has been replaced by a staff of experts, Chinese and foreign, and by physical equipment and financial resources that compare favorably with the best in America. The language of instruction is now Chinese instead of English. The foreigners on the faculty have been reduced from 100 per cent to 48 per cent, and they now number about thirty, while fifty-eight Chinese graduates are employed on the staff. In addition to the large investment in Peiping Union Medical College, the Rockefeller Foundation helped thirty-nine mission hospitals with grants of $1,379,827, and missionary schools with gifts of $2,645,234. In addition, large sums have been given for fellowships and to the International Health Board.

3

PATHFINDERS IN INDIA

I NDIA is a vast subcontinent with a population of approximately four hundred million. A remarkable census has been taken by the government of India each decade for sixty years, beginning in 1881. After long and thorough preparation by several million employees, the census is taken in a single night, between sunset and sunrise. In millions, India's population since the census began has been:

1881	253
1891	287
1901	294
1911	315
1921	318
1931	352
1941	389

This includes 199 million men and 186 million women, 296 million in the provinces of British India and 90 million in the 562 Indian states. The number of Hindus per ten thousand of population has steadily decreased each decade, from 7,432 in 1881 to 6,593 in 1941. Each decade the total number of Mohammedans and Sikhs has slightly increased, the Christians have increased much more, and Protestant Christians most rapidly of all. Between 1901 and 1941 the Christian community gained 127.6 per cent, while in Bishop Azariah's district, in the state of Hyderabad, Christians gained 858.9 per cent. The number of Christians in British India and the states in the 1941 census—6,316,549 out of the total population of 388,997,955—is incomplete in four respects: (1) For the first time, figures for Burma—with a population of seventeen million—are omitted. (2) In 1941 the figures include only *Indian* Christians; European and Anglo-Indian Christians being omitted. (3) The census commissioner reports that tribal Christians are not included—which may number 800,000. (4) Many Hindus have become alarmed at and opposed to the advance of Protestant Christians, especially in the mass movement areas, so that Hindu census takers have eagerly recorded every possible advance of the hill-tribe animists into Hinduism, claiming them as Hindus, and have in some instances, for which I could give chapter and verse, minimized or deflated the Christian statistics. The increase of Protestant Christians is therefore much larger than the census would lead us to believe. A present annual increase of about five million a year would indicate an estimated population of over four hundred million in 1945. There are a dozen major languages, with the Hindustani group reaching over a hundred and twenty millions. There are some two thousand different castes and tribes, and from fifty to sixty million untouchable outcastes—according to which castes are reckoned untouchable. Including the hill-tribe animists, there are eight principal religions in this great religious arena of the world, divided as follows:

Hindus	255,080,505
Moslems	94,389,428
Christians	6,316,549
Sikhs	5,691,447
Jains	1,449,286
Buddhists	232,008
Parsees	114,890
Animist tribes	25,441,489

In the whole of India, Hindus form 65.6 per cent of the total population, Moslems 24.3 per cent, Christians 1.6 per cent, Sikhs 1.5 per cent, Buddhists .06 per cent, and Parsees .03 per cent of the population. Of the entire population, 15 per cent are literate, and nearly 1 per cent know English. There are 15,769,890 scholars in all educational institutions. The government scheme for universal compulsory education would require 1,800,000 teachers at a prohibitive cost rising to one billion dollars a year.

During the fifteen years I lived in India—from 1896 to 1911, before the conclusion of America's experiment in the Philippines—I believed that, with all its faults, the government of India by Great Britain was the finest instance I knew in history of the government of one people by another. I saw Lord Curzon land in Bombay as the last great autocratic viceroy, and then watched India advance toward self-government in five steps, roughly a decade apart, culminating in the Cripps proposals. India has been promised and will certainly achieve self-government after the war, either by evolution, like Canada, or by revolution, like the United States. The path she follows may be determined by British statesmanship, whether it tries to "divide and rule" this land for the welfare of Britain, or to unite all in self-government for the welfare of India. Each of the pathfinders whose lives we shall now briefly study definitely helped to prepare India for her great destiny.

BISHOP THOBURN AND THE MASS MOVEMENTS

My first contact with Bishop Thoburn was at the Northfield Student Conference in 1890. He made a powerful appeal, voicing the needs of India, and mentioning incidentally that very simple Indian workers could be supported for thirty dollars a year, though he made no request for money. Mr. Moody silenced the applause which greeted this address by saying it would be better to support some of Bishop Thoburn's workers than merely to applaud. He said that he and Mr. Sankey would each take one subscription, and that a leader on the platform would be ready to receive others. I was one of a hundred there who gave thirty dollars each, and Bishop Thoburn was left breathless as he received the three thousand dollars contributed on the spot. Perhaps that money meant as much to us who gave as to the men in the field. At the end of the same year, when I was told that the Indian worker supported by my thirty dollars had brought over a hundred men to Christ, I took another subscription, and another, and finally sold the gold case of my watch to support yet one more evangelist. I never dreamed at the time that some day I would have to give my own life to

84

the cause. This was in the first flush of the mass movement work which broke in the North India Methodist field about the time Thoburn was made a bishop—in 1888. He had returned to America to raise funds for this work that was outstripping all possible appropriations from the board.

James Mills Thoburn (1836-1922), of St. Clairsville, Ohio, in his periodic "moments of illumination," as he described them, was called to Christ as a youth, then called to preach, and finally called to India as a missionary in 1859. William Butler had gone to India as the first American Methodist pioneer in 1856, shortly thereafter fleeing for his life during the Indian mutiny of 1857. When Thoburn arrived in India there were fewer than a score of Methodist communicants; when he retired in 1908 there were some two hundred thousand. From the first Thoburn was a pioneer and a trail blazer. He was a fervent evangelist with prophetic foresight, a thoughtful student, a bold administrator, and a worthy follower of the great Carey, who bade men expect great things from God and attempt great things for God. Thoburn was a pioneer in his statesman-like handling of the mass movements which brought a sudden influx of converts from the depressed classes; a pathfinder in opening up work among Indian women through unmarried women missionaries who followed his noble sister, Isabella Thoburn; a pioneer in the expansion of Methodism throughout India, following his utilizing of the tour of the old patriarchal evangelist, William Taylor, and throughout the Orient from the Himalayas to the Philippines; one of the pioneers in the organization of Methodist annual conferences on the foreign field; and a pioneer finally in the lengthening of the cords and the strengthening of the stakes for world-wide Methodism that would have gladdened the heart of John Wesley.

I can bear witness that Thoburn's audiences in America were hushed and then thrilled by this small but impressive man who spoke quietly of a living Christ standing by his side upon the platform. I can remember his every look, and gesture, and word. He was a singular blend of the mystical enthusiast-crusader and the clear-sighted, practical-minded American. Under his leadership Methodism became an army advancing with banners to world conquest. He left ten books and many articles as a record of his thought, but, like Wesley, his chief bequest was his contribution to the world-wide Methodist Church, which today numbers some twenty-five millions.[1]

When Thoburn was elected a bishop in 1888, it was a time of awakening among the depressed classes in North India, following the earlier mass movements in the South. As he faced the staggering problems of this unprecedented movement, Thoburn was reminded of two facts: (1) Jesus had begun his ministry with simple fishermen, and (2) when the disciples of John the Baptist asked Jesus for a sign of his mission and messiahship, he pointed out that "the poor have the gospel preached to them." It was not a new thing for Thoburn to be thrown unsupported upon the illimitable divine resources in order to meet India's need, for as a youth he had gone out to his first charge in Ohio with an assured support of only one hundred dollars a year, having to raise the rest.

Although Thoburn was a pathfinder of the mass movements in North India, he had studied and learned the lessons of the earlier beginnings of these movements in the South. During my early years in India I followed Bishop Thoburn in this study and came into personal contact with four great mass movements in South India, each of which had a manifestly providential spiritual origin. I first visited Cape Comorin, the southern extremity of India, near the village of Mailady, where an untouchable of the Sambavar caste, named Vedamanikam, was moved by the Spirit to seek a personal experience of God. Finding no light in the demon worship of his caste and forbidden access to the temples of Hinduism, he nevertheless left home and family like a Hindu holy man, going on a long pilgrimage to the holy places of India where men of the higher castes were said to have found God. Finally, exhausted in body and mind, in the outer courts of the distant temple of Chidambaram, in a

[1] According to the *Lutheran World Almanac* for 1937, Vol. VIII. See the Appendix to this book for statistics of the different religions and of the principal Christian denominations.

trance or vision Vedamanikam was told by a white-robed figure to return south, where he would be given enlightenment.

When Vedamanikam reached the seat of the first Danish Protestant mission, at Tranquebar,[2] he met a young man named William Tobias Ringletaube. Prussian by birth and Lutheran by training, Ringletaube had arrived in India as an agent of the London Missionary Society, and was seeking God's guidance to a field of labor when the wandering outcaste invited him to his home in Travancore. Upon returning to his village Vedamanikam called together a group of his kinsfolk to seek the Christian way of life. In 1806 Ringletaube arrived in Travancore, obtained from the maharaja permission to establish a mission, and settled in Vedamanikam's village of Mailady. He found a small group, like the Gentiles about Cornelius, prepared to confess Christ. He baptized them and appointed Vedamanikam as their catechist. The eccentric Ringletaube opened schools and built mud huts as chapels. By 1810 he had baptized about four hundred Indians and had built seven chapels. The next year some four hundred Nadars, or Shanars, of a lower Sudra caste, but above the untouchable Sambavars, came for baptism. In 1816, after a decade of labor, Ringletaube finally left Travancore, placing the work in charge of Vedamanikam. The next year a strong missionary, the Reverend Charles Mead of the London Missionary Society, arrived, and three thousand Nadars were baptized and became the predominant body in South Travancore.

As the Christian converts were obviously rising in their standard of life, persecution broke upon them. The high-caste Hindus demanded that they keep Hindu caste laws which forbade low-caste men and women from wearing any cloth above the waist. The high castes were especially indignant at the neat jackets worn by the low-caste women. The outcaste in Travancore was supposed to withdraw himself to a distance of at least

[2] When the first Protestant Danish mission was founded at Tranquebar in 1706, the early missionaries, including the remarkable Christian Friedrich Schwartz, accepted the distinction of caste among their converts in Tranquebar and Trichinopoly. The high castes and low castes in about equal numbers sat on opposite sides of the church in segregated sections.

thirty paces from any Brahman. I have often seen outcastes standing at a distance in the fields, or covering their mouths with their hands, that they might not pollute the air for the holy and dreaded Brahman. The Indian judges ruled against the innovations of the Christians in the courts. Many converts were beaten, thousands were imprisoned; the missionary Charles Mead was attacked, and a plot to assassinate him was reported. At last in 1859, the courageous Christian governor of Madras, Sir Charles Trevelyan,[3] intervened with a proclamation, to which the maharaja gave unwilling assent, allowing members of the lower castes to wear a cloth over the breasts and shoulders. When it was found that the conditions of the outcastes were improved by Christianity, economically, socially, and legally, as well as morally and spiritually, there was a large ingathering. By 1870 there were over 30,000 adherents, and today some 300,000, in South Travancore. I have spoken frequently to over a thousand Christians in the great churches of Nagercoil and South Travancore of the London Missionary Society, and in Scott College, which has trained the leaders for both the churches and government service.

There was also a mass movement just over the border from Travancore in Tinnevelly, in British India, under the Church Missionary Society. As the result of the labors of Lutheran missionaries who visited the region from Tanjore, five thousand Indians were baptized in three months in 1802. This mission work was followed by that of the godly German, Rhenius, and later by some of the finest men of Cambridge University, like Ragland and Walker, spiritual sons of the great Charles Simeon. By 1835 there were ten thousand adherents in Tinnevelly, many of whom were gathered in Christian villages like Mengnana-puram—"The Village of True Wisdom"—which later produced Bishop Azariah, who more than any other man was the founder

[3] Sir Charles Trevelyan made this prophecy regarding the conversion of India: "I believe it will take place at last wholesale, just as our ancestors were converted. The country will have Christian instruction infused into it in every way. . . . Then at last, when society is completely saturated with Christian knowledge and public opinion has taken a decided turn that way, they will come over by thousands."

of the indigenous Indian missionary movement. It was the evidence of transformed lives like these that made Lord Laurence, the viceroy, say: "Notwithstanding all that the English people have done to benefit India, the missionaries have done more than all other agencies combined."

After Travancore and Tinnevelly I visited the Telugu country, the Andhra Desa region north of Madras, which includes the eastern part of Hyderabad State. At Bezwada I saw where T. Y. Darling, an Anglo-Indian worker of the Church Missionary Society, had worked for seven years without a convert. He had long been seeking the high castes, but when he returned one day, discouraged from preaching to them, he heard the voice of a poor outcaste, Venkayya, whom his servant was trying to send away. Venkayya had been the head of the band of robbers, but when his son fell ill and died, and the village goddess proved impotent, a fellow robber told him of the Christian religion. He then composed a prayer which he said every day: "O God! teach me who thou art, show me where thou art, help me to find thee." After three years, he went to Bezwada, where a Brahman told him that if he did not believe in the methods of Hinduism, the missionary on the hill could tell him of the true God. When Mr. Darling told this former robber the good news of God's unspeakable gift, Venkayya said: "This is my God and Savior whom I have long been seeking. Now I have found him and will serve him." He was converted in 1849, and even when blind in his old age he used to sit outside his mud hut and preach Christ to passers-by.

By 1901 there were some thirty thousand Christians in this district, and by 1930 there were 125,000 in the Church of England alone. I worked among these people and also in the churches and colleges of the American United Lutheran Mission near by at Guntur and Rajahmundry. I next visited the Baptist "Lone Star Mission" at Ongole in the Telugu country. In Ellore, under the ministry of my wife's uncle, the Reverend Frederick Alexander of the Church Missionary Society, a Madiga hide dealer had been converted and spoke of Christ to his outcaste kinsman, Yerraguntla Periah. Though quite illiterate, this man Periah was an earnest seeker of the truth who had been spending an hour daily in his devotions. After a long conversation with Alexander, he said, "This religion is true. My soul is satisfied." Though Periah requested baptism, the missionary dared not baptize a man whose home was so far away that he could not give him further instruction; and he referred Periah to the American Baptists near his home.

The Lone Star Mission at Ongole after twenty-eight years had won but thirty converts, and three times it had been on the verge of closing. On his arrival in Ongole, John E. Clough went to the village of this outcaste, Periah, who had been preaching and gathering converts, and baptized twenty-eight people. They were immediately persecuted by the high castes. As a despised Madiga, Periah could persuade no one to teach him to read. He had turned from the serpent and demon worship of his caste and had tried Yoga practice and every available method of Hinduism, but now he found all the pent-up yearning of his heart fulfilled in Christ. As a fervid evangelist he won hundreds to the Christian faith, and Dr. Clough told me much of this remarkable man.

The coming of the outcastes for baptism drove away the Brahman and high-caste inquirers who had been coming to John Clough, and their boys left his school when the three first outcastes arrived. Dr. Clough was sitting alone in his study, discouraged, when he picked up a new Bible from a pile which had just come from the Bible Society. As it opened by chance, he later told me, his eye fell upon the passage in First Corinthians where the Apostle says to the Gentiles that not many wise, or mighty, or noble are called, but that God chose the weak, the base, and the despised to bring to nought the things that are. In the next room, Dr. Clough's wife had opened another new Bible, seemingly by chance, at the very same passage; and she came to him with the remark, "It seems to be God's plan to save the outcaste first." They concluded that God had spoken to them as truly as to Peter and Paul when the call came to the early church to receive the outcaste Gentiles.

In 1877, while millions were perishing in the great famine,

Dr. Clough, a former deputy surveyor, took a contract to dig some three miles of the Buckingham Canal in order to save the lives of thousands who were starving. After the famine was over he consented to receive outcaste believers, and 2,222 were baptized on July 3, 1878, and 3,536 within three days. Altogether, 9,606 were received during the year in a mission that had won twenty-eight converts in the first thirty years.

Within eighty years of the founding of this work in the Telugu country, a million outcaste Malas and Madigas had been won to Christ among all these missions. Every mission had followed the same methods. The missionaries had first sought to reach the high-caste Hindus, but had later turned to the outcastes. They founded a chain of schools, then a high school, and finally a college for training leaders, Christian and non-Christian. These schools, together with churches and a hospital, illustrated and embodied the gospel the missionaries were trying to live and teach. The transformed lives of the truly converted among the lower castes made a powerful witness and apologetic to the higher castes, who, in every region in the South that had long known the gospel, now began to turn to Christianity.

As Bishop Thoburn studied these group or mass movements in the South, he saw that they were at their best the work of the Spirit of God, often advancing, however, in the face of the prejudice of Western missionaries. Thoburn saw that ever since the Reformation, Protestants of the West have been limited or afflicted by an excessive individualism. They have preached and practiced an often selfish individual salvation of a type that was utterly foreign to the prophets of Israel. The religion of Israel was for the whole Jewish people, and Jesus' message of the Kingdom of God had to do with a social whole. In the conversion of Europe also, whole tribes and peoples moved in masses. In India, under the ironbound caste system of orthodox Hinduism, there was no free individual, just as there could be no "masterless men" in the feudal Middle Ages. Hinduism, which has held the heart of India for over two thousand years, knows nothing of any "four freedoms." The outcastes, who are

themselves fettered by caste, have been physically, psychological-
ly, and spiritually oppressed across the centuries, and it was the
Christian religion which first set them free.

B. R. Ambedkar, now minister of labor in the government
of India, former leader of the Independent Labor Party in the
Bombay Legislative Assembly, former principal of the Government Law College in Bombay, and official spokesman for the
depressed classes in the Round Table Conferences held in
London, boldly attacks Hinduism with scathing bitterness born
of unbroken centuries of the suffering of his people. Ambedkar
is a barrister, a Ph.D. from Columbia and Stuttgart universities,
and a Sc.D. from London. He denounces not only the social
oppression and economic slavery of his fellow outcastes but also
the moral character of some of the Hindu gods, finding his authority in the sacred books. He asks frankly how the depressed
classes can achieve moral freedom and spiritual regeneration
through a religion that holds up such licentious beings for worship and so oppresses the outcastes, from the time of the sacred
Laws of Manu to the present. Thoburn saw that India had hun-
gered for a religion of brotherhood and fellowship as well as
for a message of the God and Father of Jesus Christ. The good
news for these myriads of outcastes was: "Ye shall know the
truth, and the truth shall make you free."

As in the case of every other missionary mentioned in this
book, I confess that I am tempted to give perhaps too much
credit to the one pathfinder who led the way. Bishop Thoburn's
achievements would have been utterly impossible had it not
been for hundreds of his fellow workers and successors, foreign
and Indian, who did the great bulk of the work. This would
never have been brought to fruition had it not been for the able
body of men of this generation who followed him, like Bishop
J. Waskom Pickett, who, after a scientific study of six years, tells
the story of the mass movements so effectively.[4] The impor-

[4] In *Christian Mass Movements in India*, 1933, and *Christ's Way to India's
Heart*, 1938, Bishop Pickett shows that a caste is an exclusive, endogenous,
hereditary, corporate group, bound together by the tradition of a common
origin and by a body of common customs. Any caste compelled by poverty and
custom to the occupation of a sweeper, to the eating of carrion, to the handling

tance of these movements is shown by the fact that perhaps eighty per cent of the Christians in India today are the result of them. That is why I have devoted so much space to them in this life of Bishop Thoburn. Mind moves en masse under the caste structure of Hinduism. In general, the people must either come together or not come at all. Bishop Thoburn was the first American missionary in North India who clearly saw this and interpreted the phenomenon to his constituency.

At the semicentennial sermon preached in his own Allegheny College fifty years after he sailed for India, Bishop Thoburn said that when he went to the Orient the membership of the Methodist Church in India was thirteen persons, and fifty years later it included a community of a quarter of a million, with Methodist workers witnessing in forty languages in southern Asia.[5] In Thoburn's first field in India there was not one woman who could read or write, and there was bitter prejudice on the part of the Hindus against the education of women. Thoburn's letter to his sister, written with the quill of a vulture which was nesting above him, brought Isabella Thoburn to the field in 1869 to attempt to educate the women of North India, and led to the founding of the Woman's Foreign Missionary Society. Eight ladies organized the new Methodist Woman's Society to send out the first two missionaries, Isabella Thoburn for education and Dr. Clara A. Swain for medical missions, for the women of India. The arrival of Miss Swain, the first woman doctor, led to the opening of the government medical colleges to women, so that women in large numbers are now practicing medicine all over India, as we shall see in a later chapter concerning the work of Dr. Ida Scudder. The organizing of the W.F.M.S. was chiefly the work of Mrs. William Butler and of Bishop and Mrs. Edwin Parker, when the ladies met in the Tremont Street Church, Boston, on March 23, 1869.

When Miss Thoburn was appointed to Lucknow in 1870, she

of dead bodies or the hides of animals, is naturally counted untouchable and polluting, and there are from fifty to sixty million that thus lie beyond the pale of Hinduism. I am indebted to Bishop Pickett's books in this chapter.

[5] William Henry Crawford, *Thoburn and India*, New York, 1909, p. 38.

started a school with only six girls. From the first she included in her plans Indian, English, and Eurasian—or Anglo-Indian—girls, so that the school was interracial from the start. A Brahman convert, Mrs. Chuckerbutty, and her daughter both became pupils in the boarding school. When the daughter wished to enter college and study medicine, it was found that though there were then a hundred colleges for men in India there was but one, a non-Christian college, for women. So Miss Thoburn was led to open the first Christian college for women in India in 1887, and this was later recognized as a college with a government charter. When Miss Thoburn began, there was no well-established college for women in India. It is a question whether the Brahmo Samaj Bethune College, in Calcutta, or the Isabella Thoburn College was the first college for women in all Asia. The great Alexander Duff, who had founded the first Christian college for men, had said in his day: "You might as well try to scale a wall fifty feet high as to educate the women of India." Isabella Thoburn was the one who scaled that wall. When she took her brilliant graduate and teacher, Miss Lilavati Singh, to speak to amazed audiences in America, Miss Singh often "got beyond the depth of the average Methodist preacher." When President Harrison heard Miss Singh speak at the Ecumenical Missionary Conference in New York in 1900, he said: "If I had given a million dollars to foreign missions, and was assured that no result had come from it all except the evolution of one such woman as that, I should feel amply repaid for my expenditure." But there was not merely one such woman as a product of the college. Miss Singh herself could point to the fact that year after year in the Allahabad University girls from Miss Thoburn's college had stood at the top of the list in the government competitive examinations, and that six hundred women graduates of the Lucknow institution had entered Christian work in India. No statistics, however, can compute the thousands of Christian homes created by the Isabella Thoburn College, for women, and the Lucknow Christian College, for men.

Miss Thoburn not only opened the first Christian college for the higher education of women in India but also led her fellow workers and graduates to instruct some of the forty million women in Zenanas, and the twenty-five million widows of India, a hundred thousand of whom were under ten years of age. To the day she died of cholera, Isabella Thoburn never lost the burden of the need of India's womanhood. After her death this need was voiced by the graduates of her great college. When Lilavati Singh closed her address at Allegheny College at Meadville, Pennsylvania, on the fiftieth anniversary of Bishop Thoburn's going to India, she said: "Each nation has its gift. India's is the gift of an intensely religious nature. Capture it for Jesus Christ, for in the words of Keshub Chunder Sen, 'None but Jesus, none but Jesus, none, I say, but Jesus ever deserved this precious diadem, India; and Jesus shall have it.' "

We have briefly reviewed Thoburn's work as a pathfinder in evangelism, in handling mass movements, in educational and medical work among women. All these together constituted but a fraction of his work, most of which must remain untold. His prophetic insight, his evangelistic zeal, and his Christian statesmanship were evident in all he said and did. And he, being dead, yet speaketh. This is his clarion call to America, to his own generation and to ours: "The signs of the times, the lessons of the past, the indications of the future, the call of providence, the voices which come borne to us on every breeze and from every nation under heaven, all alike bid us lay our plans on a scale worthy of men who expect to conquer a world."

WILLIAM MILLER AND THE CHRISTIAN COLLEGES

It is fitting that after considering Bishop Thoburn and the mass movements we should turn to the educational missions established by Alexander Duff, John Wilson, and William Miller. In 1896, when I reached Madras, my first center for student work, I looked on the work of Dr. Miller and of the Madras Christian College with admiration and almost with awe. To see the significance of the work of William Miller (1838-1923) in perspective, we must recall the work of Alexander Duff (1806-78), the pioneer educator of India. Alexander Duff had been ordained by Scotland's great Thomas Chalmers, whose mantle was later to fall upon him. After winning the highest honors of scholarship in Scotland, Duff went to India in 1829 as a young man of twenty-three, the first missionary to be sent to India by the Established Church of Scotland. He waited upon the aged Carey, three years before Carey's death, to receive his blessing and to discuss a plan for opening a college for English education in Calcutta. Duff had a keen intellect, he was called "the prince of missionaries," and the burning passion of his "torrential eloquence" swept every assembly that he addressed. Yet he was determined to know nothing but Jesus Christ and him crucified.

When Duff arrived in India in 1830, mission work had reached a dead end, and Duff had to face the problem of getting into touch with the influential classes. Scotland was the homeland of higher education, and Duff determined upon the new line of bringing the youth of India under Christian influence by means of schools. As the Mohammedans for four hundred years had made Hindustani the lingua franca among the babel of Indian tongues, Duff and the British rulers saw no possible common language but English as the vehicle for the new civilzation and culture. Duff believed that Indians would be vitalized by the powerful stream of the new learning and life, as his own Gaelic Scots had been. The success of Duff's experiment shaped the future Indian educational system and, to a large extent, foreign missionary work. The Bengalis and other Indians showed an insatiable hunger for English and Western learning. Duff's emphasis on the Bible and Christian teaching made his college a radiating religious influence. Duff remained in Calcutta only a third of a century—1830-35, 1839-50, 1856-63 —yet his labors and influence resulted in such an onrush of Western culture that it began to shatter Hindu conceptions of the universe. Instead of the subtle poison of materialism and skepticism, Duff offered a new spiritual and rational basis of life by which he helped mold the school system of India. The entire Indian civil service was soon thrown open to English-speaking Indians without distinction of race or creed. Christianity became the burning subject of discussion in the highest Indian circles, and Duff's twenty-six distinguished converts and their families furnished the brilliant leaders of the Indian Christian Church.

Hinduism had held the heart of India for more than two thousand years. It contained many spiritual values, it had almost unlimited powers of assimilation, and it could swallow whole and reabsorb a rival religion like Buddhism; but it was sadly lacking in the power of eliminating the grossest evils. When Duff landed in Calcutta *sati,* or widow burning, infanticide, and the choking of the dying with mud from the sacred Ganges, were practiced just as they had been a century before. Duff proceeded deliberately to challenge the whole Brahmanic system. While his predecessors had sought to separate atoms from the mass by individual conversion, Duff proposed "to lay a mine," by the disintegrating effect of modern science and the self-evidencing power of Christianity, that should one day explode and tear up the whole from the lowest depths.

When he boldly founded his college, Duff was loyally supported by Raja Ram Mohan Roy, the founder of the Brahmo Samaj; and the first "explosion" occurred over the first four converts. Duff deeply influenced the liberal reforms of Lord William Bentick and Lord Macaulay, the law member of the government of India, when Macaulay issued his famous "educational minute" of 1834 to make English the medium of higher education in India. Duff foresaw, with Macaulay, that if the study of English literature should give India the desire for freedom, it would be the proudest day in British history. Duff became moderator of the general assembly in Scotland, he toured North America in the interests of missions, and he was passionately concerned in establishing throughout India educational and evangelistic missions based on the home countries of Britain and America.

Following Duff came the great educators John Wilson of the Wilson College, Bombay, and William Miller of the Madras Christian College. The Reverend John Anderson had opened a Christian school in Madras on April 3, 1837, which later became the Madras Christian College. William Miller, born in 1838 in the northernmost county of Scotland, was the son of a wealthy merchant and shipowner, proud of his Viking Scandinavian ancestors. He distinguished himself in his studies in Aberdeen and Edinburgh universities. He arrived in Madras in 1862, a young man of twenty-four, the only missionary of the Free Church of Scotland in that city. He at first zealously engaged in outdoor preaching, congregational work, medical aid, and the education of both boys and girls. In 1863, convinced that only Christian education could train the greatest leaders of India, he began to specialize on the institution that was to become the Madras Christian College. He saw that missions must take up the burden of university education in order to give it a Christian basis; and he devoted the whole of his life, his brilliant talents, his fortune, and his flaming spirit to the fulfillment of this vision.

By 1865 the first class of six students was ready for the matriculation examination, and in 1867 a class was opened to prepare for the B.A. examination. Miller broadened the basis of support to such an extent that a small sectarian institution became a central Christian college for all South India, maintained by the leading missions, including the Anglican, Wesleyan, and Presbyterian bodies. A period of bold and brilliant experimentation placed the college in the front rank of all India, both in scholarship and in character building. For a long time it was not only the largest but the leading Christian college in India. Dr. Miller erected great buildings, chiefly by his own gifts and those of his brother. He gathered around him a group of loyal and able men, British and Indian, whose names became household words, and who were held in deep affection in South India. His dormitories, or college hostels, were the first of their kind in South India. In these he gave the future government officials and members of municipal and local boards training in democracy and in the art of conducting public business. The daily newspaper the Madras *Hindu* testified that it was to the eternal honor of that teacher of genius, Dr. William Miller, that he not only taught India that all education has its roots in the personal relation between teacher and pupil but that he also fired a whole generation of able colleagues with his own infectious enthusiasm. After several decades every one of the four vice-chancellors of the South India universities was a former student of Dr. Miller's. One of them, C. R. Reddy, speaks of Dr. Miller's "building up a grand fellowship of culture and comradeship in noble lives and aspirations with a drive toward larger ideals of individual and national life." The Hindu philosopher Sir S. Radhakrishnan said: "South India's debt to the Madras Christian College is incalculable, and the influence of the college on other faiths has been great." As a bachelor Dr. Miller was practically married to the college. It was his only home. To it he devoted his time, his talents, his fortune, and himself. He loved every little boy in the institution. With awe they heard him address God as Father on their behalf until they felt finally that they must dedicate their whole lives, each according to his light, to the saving of India.

When the college reached the full capacity of its present plant, there were more than seventeen hundred students with some seven hundred in the college classes. Many of these students became closely connected with the destiny of India's one fifth of the human race. There was a loyal body of several thousand alumni, many of whom became national leaders. Some hundreds of these were Christians—among whom, as we shall see, Bishop Azariah stood out as a churchman and K. T. Paul as a Christian statesman. Some of them were doing much to mold both the religious and secular life of India. It would take a volume larger than this to tell the story of the reformers whom Dr. Miller trained—men like Dr. Natarajan, editor of the *Indian Social Reformer*. They challenged alike the abuses of the government of India, the evils in the British connection, and the graft among Indian politicians. With critical faculties trained in this school of the prophets, they saw and exposed both the defects of Western material civilization and those in their Oriental life, and strove with might and main to abolish or remedy these. They deeply resented the grossly unfair picture of Indian life presented in Miss Mayo's *Mother India,* and from the time of the Madras meeting of the Indian National Congress the majority began to vote for complete independence—after having sought dominion status in vain for forty years.

I wish that space permitted quoting at length from the excellent book on William Miller by one of his Hindu graduates, O. Kandaswamy Chetty. He shows that all of Dr. Miller's students and graduates were his beloved "boys" whether in youth or age. Dr. Miller remembered the names of hundreds of students, and even those of their relatives. Each student was a personality in his own right, and all were spiritually free and equal. Mr. Kandaswamy says in substance: Dr. Miller moved among them like a Pied Piper of Hamelin, drawing their minds and hearts after him, attending his every word and movement. Each student was an individual with a distinctive character. His knowledge extended to the family group to which a student belonged, because he felt that the fortunes of the families constituted the welfare of the community and of the nation at large. He did not believe in repressing young wills but rather delighted in guiding them. Dr. Miller said of Indian students that their home training made them either slaves or tyrants, but they should learn to obey with dignity and differ without disrespect. The art of self-government could be learned only by practice.

Subsequent to a commotion among the students on account of an attempted conversion of a Brahman student, Dr. Miller had to make clear the position of the college with regard to its religious aim, which he declared to be "the formation of right principles, of good habits, and a noble character on the lines inculcated and exemplified by Jesus Christ." When he was asked why he did not say straightway that the object of the college was to preach Christ, he said that such a phrase would represent Jesus in the minds of his hearers as the destroyer of other faiths, whereas Jesus was the friend of all that was good, not only in Christianity but in Hinduism, and the enemy of all that was evil both in Christian civilization and in other civilizations. Such volcanic upheavals in the college were rare.

Dr. Miller did not have as many converts as Duff, for there

had been a decided change of moral climate since that earlier day. Indeed, no educational nor evangelistic missionary was baptizing any large number of individual converts among high-caste Hindus or Mohammedans at that time, though some thousands of caste Hindus later joined Christianity as the result of the mass movements. Hinduism was now striving to reform itself; it was more sensitive, more on the defensive. Long inert and stagnant, it was now showing signs of becoming a missionary religion to the extent of taking in the animistic hill tribes and even the outcastes as Hindus. If Dr. Miller had been only a fervid evangelist, he might have baptized a score of converts. They might have worn boots and trousers and joined the religion of the beef-eating foreigner, severed from their national culture and rootage in the soil of India. But Miller did a far greater work in seeking to leaven the whole lump, or mass, even though the leaven was working silently and unseen. He rejoiced to see hundreds of his boys seeking to live in the love of God and their neighbor as builders of the new India and as bold reformers who dared to be "in the right with two or three," as the motto on the masthead of the *Christian College Magazine* proclaimed. The very breadth of Dr. Miller made him inevitably the object of attack. I remember when a very conservative missionary met him at the steamer on his return from furlough and said spontaneously that he was glad to see him back. Later he salved his conscience by writing to Miller to confess to uttering an untruth—he really believed he was doing more harm than good! One of Miller's most brilliant students was K. Natarajan, the very life and soul of the social reform movement in India for several decades. In the *Indian Social Reformer* of October 28, 1944, he writes: "Christian influence has been more marked in the South than elsewhere, chiefly owing to the powerful personality of Dr. William Miller, who may be called the pioneer in the Hindu Renaissance. Differing from the generality of Christian missionaries, Dr. Miller discouraged proselytism, encouraged the retention of national manners, and fostered in thousands of students the habit of independent thinking."

101

Few at any time have had such honors showered upon them as
Dr. Miller. He was the outstanding educator in all India and
helped to shape the government's educational policy. He
valiantly championed the educational work of missions and
won the appreciation and financial aid of the government for
it. His services to the Madras University as a leading member
of its syndicate were notable. For more than a third of a century his influence on the missionary gatherings of India was
weighty. He was a distinguished member of the Madras legislative council and was influential as a public speaker and writer.
In 1896 he was unanimously chosen moderator of the general
assembly of the Free Church of Scotland. On that occasion a
unique address to the general assembly was presented, signed
by more than two thousand Indian leaders and others of Dr.
Miller's admirers. They wrote that this tribute of affection was
to a man "whose services in the cause of higher education, extending over a period of thirty-three years, have never in this
part of the world been surpassed, and who will himself live in
the memory and affection of many a generation to come." Dr.
Miller was honored as the recipient of the distinguished Order
of the Companion of the Indian Empire, and he received the
Kaisar-i-Hind medal. Honorary degrees were conferred by the
universities of Edinburgh and Aberdeen, and he was the first,
and long the only LL.D. so honored by the Madras University.
He was vice-chancellor of Madras University, and even during
his lifetime a statue was erected to him. The gift of devoted
Indians, it was unveiled by the governor of Madras, Lord
Ampthill, the first tribute of the kind ever erected to a Christian missionary. Lord Napier, speaking in the British House of
Lords, could not gild the lily when he said of Miller: "A missionary teacher, known alike for his piety and public zeal, whose
services in the cause of higher education are probably unsur-
passed in India." Long before, the great liberal Viceroy Lord
Ripon had appointed him on the Educational Commission,
which was to draw up the Magna Charta of education for
all India.

Dr. Miller's real monument, of course, is in living men, his "boys" who are building the new India. In an address on "The Place of Christian Education in the Story of the World" Dr. Miller said:

The characteristic aim of the Christian college is to mold character. It aims at sending out men into the world with their whole being so developed that when truth comes before them they will love it, that when duty comes to them they will do it. . . . It aims at making those whom it has trained aware, not as a mere abstract doctrine, but as a fact that bears on every detail of common life, that the world is in the hands of the Living God and that he rules it according to a plan which however dimly apprehended in many of its parts may yet be clearly traced in others—a plan which it is only the wisdom of every rational being to conform to and which it may be our glorious privilege and sufficient joy to take part in and advance.

While some British rulers sought to "divide and rule" India for the welfare of Britain, Dr. Miller always sought to unite all Indians for the welfare of India and the world. In his last message to the college in November, 1922, he said: "The greatest of all needs, if there is to be any real security for social and political welfare, is that there should be a steady growth of heart-felt co-operation and sympathetic mutual understanding between each and every one of the classes and races which at this critical conjuncture are called upon to work for the well-being of India in days to come." He felt that a freer India must be a leader on the march of mankind toward the appointed goal.

In 1907 Dr. Miller left India to reside in Scotland, where he died in 1923, at the age of eighty-five, leaving the bulk of his property to his beloved college. Those who knew him personally, who knew the India of his day, who saw his boys and the character and work of his graduates, believe that here was a truly great educator, like Alexander Duff, like Arnold of Rugby, or like Mark Hopkins. And Duff and Miller were not alone. They left a worthy body of men who are carrying on their work today in the Christian colleges of India under British and American missionary societies. If space permitted I could write the story of some of these colleges, whose histories are as thrilling as that of Dr. Miller's institution. For instance, I could tell the story of the Reverend C. E. Tyndale-Biscoe of Kashmir, a much more colorful and dramatic personality than William Miller. This one man in fifty years has almost transformed an Indian state, through his great college, in training a new leadership for the whole country. He is a tiny creature, five feet four in height, but as hard as nails. He was the greatest coxwain that ever drove his winning Cambridge crews to victory. In the same spirit he has been coaching his Kashmiri crews in sportsmanship and character-building for many decades. So impressive is his own character that even when he was a boy in prep school the great headmaster of St. Paul's School, Dr. Abbott, said he could hardly resist taking off his hat to him every time he passed him. All Kashmir has taken off its hat—or turban—to this great Christian educator. He is only one of a score that are regretfully omitted from this already overcrowded volume.

LARSEN, THE GREAT DANE

L. P. Larsen, perhaps the greatest missionary I have ever known, represented to me the whole body of Scandinavian, Teutonic, and other European missionaries. These Europeans were a living reminder to our sometimes more superficial, yet often imperialistic, Anglo-Saxons that we were only a part, and a humble part, of a great world movement. In Larsen's presence I felt like a crude, uneducated high school youth, yet he was so humble that he was an elder brother to us all. A Danish Lutheran, he represented the original impulse for the evangelization of India from Denmark, which began in 1706, eighty-seven years before William Carey. It may help to give perspective if we recall the nearly two centuries of missionary work of the Danes and Teutons that preceded Larsen.

From the time of the Vikings, who tried repeatedly to conquer England, the people of Denmark had been among the bravest and most progressive in Europe. They early became leaders in education, in democracy, in co-operative organizations, and in Christian missions. Frederick IV, the deeply religious king of Denmark, while still crown prince formed the purpose of sending the gospel to non-Christians in his overseas dominions. He believed in the Lutheran teaching that it was the duty of monarchs to Christianize their non-Christian subjects. In 1706 he launched his first missionary project. As he could find no suitably trained persons in Denmark, he turned to the godly Pietist movement in Germany, under P. J. Spener and under A. H. Francke at Halle. This was two decades before the Pietists under Zinzendorf, and the Moravians at Herrnhut, began to send missionaries. Until about the time of Larsen, Continental missions did not send out university men.

Chosen by Francke, two earnest German Pietists, Bartholomew Ziegenbalg and Heinrich Plutschau, went out as "royal Danish missionaries" to Tranquebar, the seat of the Danish possession in South India. On landing, they were met by the cruel Commander J. C. Hassius, who tried to exclude them from India and threatened them with violence. He had them thrown into prison for several months, and then reviled and persecuted them. Ziegenbalg was frequently prostrated with sickness, and Plutschau broke down under the strain and returned to Germany. With characteristic German linguistic ability, Ziegenbalg mastered Tamil and began to produce works of merit in that language. He preached with zeal, and within a year had gathered thirty-five members of the church. In 1719, at the time of Ziegenbalg's death at the early age of thirty-six, 428 had received baptism. Fifty-seven Danish missionaries went to India between 1706 and 1746, and up to 1806 they had gained 36,790 converts.

As contributions began to flow in from Germany, England, and Denmark, in a work that looked to three bases for support, Ziegenbalg formed the bold plan of extending Christian missions over British South India, and of uniting the universities of Germany, Denmark, and Holland for the accomplishment of this end. Unfortunately, the Germans and Danes permitted caste to continue in the church, the Sudras and pariahs sitting a yard apart and taking the communion separately. This evil of caste was long to curse the church, as it had poisoned Hinduism for centuries. One outcaste convert, Rajanaiken, became the first flaming evangelist to win many other converts; and he was followed by similar leaders of later mass movements in South and afterward in North India.

Proceeding from Tranquebar, work was begun in Madras by Benjamin Schultze and the great linguist Philipp Fabricius (1742-91), who was called the "monk-priest" and the "Christian sannyasi." He made the first translation of the Bible into Tamil, which Larsen was finally to revise and retranslate. Fabricius' contemporary was the great Christian Friedrich Schwartz (1726-98). Under the influence of Professor Francke at Halle, Schwartz volunteered for mission work in India; he studied Tamil and then went to England, which was to support the mission in India under the Society for the Promotion of Christian Knowledge. He settled at Tranquebar in 1750. He was a master of German, English, Danish, Tamil, Greek, and Hebrew. Not as able a man as Larsen a century later, he was nevertheless distinguished by a remarkable "vivacity and purity" of nature. He was a guileless Nathanael, an apostle of love. At Trichinopoly, where he labored for sixteen years, he gained such a strange moral hold over the British garrison that he was called as a British chaplain. As Trichinopoly was the second capital of the Indian ruler, the Nawab of Arcot, Schwartz mastered Hindustani and Persian to reach these people. Meanwhile he preached in season and out of season to Hindus and Moslems in their own languages, and carried on evangelistic work from Madras to Ceylon.

During the chaotic period of warfare between the Indian states and the British, the Maratha raja, Tulsi, invited the universally trusted Schwartz to his capital at Tanjore. Schwartz visited the raja when he was a captive in prison and formed a lifelong friendship for the weak monarch. At his request Schwartz moved to the capital of his state, at Tanjore, for the last twenty years of his life (1778-98). He preached and won converts, high caste and low, in Tanjore, Madura, and Tinnevelly. He won over *kallan,* or robber, congregations and introduced Christian teaching into the English schools of South India.

The English sent Schwartz as their representative to the Maratha chieftain, Haidar Ali, in Mysore. In the wars that followed, all distrusted each other amid hatred, suspicion, intrigue, and violence; but all trusted Schwartz, so that he alone was able to feed the starving population, devastated by warring raids and invasions. The English appointed Schwartz on a governing advisory council of four, where he had wide powers in civil government and a large salary, but like Carey later, he lived the simple life and gave everything away. He was asked by the raja to act as guardian of the young prince Serfoji, the raja's son; and he was responsible for his education. After spending nearly fifty years in India, Schwartz died in 1798, at the age of seventy-two, the revered and beloved "royal priest of Tanjore."

The warrior Haidar Ali said of Schwartz: "Do not send me any of your agents, for I do not trust their words or their treaties; but if you wish me to listen to your proposals send to me the missionary of whose character I have heard so much from everyone; him will I trust and receive. Send me the *Christian.*" The Nawab of the Carnatic issued the order: "Permit the venerable Father Schwartz to pass unhindered, for he is a holy man and means my government no harm." The hymn writer of South India, Bishop Heber, said: "He was really one of the most active and fearless, as he was one of the most successful, missionaries who have appeared since the apostles. His converts were between six and seven thousand." The East India Company, which later so fiercely opposed missions in North India, was so deeply indebted to Schwartz that it erected a monument in his honor. His life was vocal with the testimony that the work of the missionary "is the most honorable and blessed service in which any human being can be employed in this world."

On the monument erected to Schwartz by the grateful Raja Serfoji in the garrison church at Tanjore is the often-cited inscription:

Firm wast thou, humble and wise,
Honest, pure, free from disguise.
Father of orphans, the widow's support,
Comfort in sorrow of every sort.
To the benighted, dispenser of light;
Doing and pointing to that which was right;
Blessing to princes, to people, to me;
May I, my father, be worthy of thee!
Wisheth and prayeth thy Saraboji.

L. P. Larsen arrived in India about a century after the distinguished Schwartz. Though he never had Schwartz's political contacts nor was called to mediate between armies, rulers, and governments, as Schwartz had been, he was a greater character and a more highly educated university man. Lars Peter Larsen was born in Baarse, Denmark, November 8, 1862, and died in Copenhagen June 23, 1940. He did brilliant work at the Harlufsholm School and at the University of Copenhagen. He took his theological degree in 1888; and, after being ordained by Bishop Stain, he arrived in Madras in 1889. He became the first pastor of the Danish Mission Church in Madras, and opened a reading room as a point of contact with Hindus. His fine philosophic mind, his transparent, Christlike character, and his brilliant linguistic gifts fitted him to be an unusually successful worker among students.

When the impressive new stone building of the association, given by John Wanamaker, was erected in Madras, Larsen was called to be student secretary of the Madras Y.M.C.A. in 1898. For the next decade he was largely supported from Denmark, while working under the International Committee in New York. Brilliant scholars like the Danish L. P. Larsen and the English Professor J. N. Farquhar enabled the association to widen its appeal to students through lectures, through personal friendships, and through the production of a whole new body of literature of the highest grade that India had ever known.

Owing to Larsen's close relation to the students in the adjacent Madras Christian College during Dr. Miller's regime, he was frequently asked to take classes and to give courses of lectures there. He became the spiritual friend and counselor of numbers of students, both Hindus and Christians, of the college. His influence was then extended over South India as he traveled and lectured to educated Hindus. He was called to Travancore by the Syrian Christians whom he had helped in Madras, and his ministry to that ancient church was greatly blessed.

In 1910, when the United Theological College was established at Bangalore, Larsen was called as professor of comparative religion and exegesis; he served as principal of the college until 1920. Here he left the deep impress of his character upon the highly trained ministry of the church all over South India. When the need arose of revising and retranslating the whole Tamil Bible, Larsen, as a great Tamil scholar, with a knowledge also of Hebrew and Greek, aided by one Indian assistant, was entrusted with the task. His translation, corresponding to Moffatt's translation of the entire Bible, was adopted as the official revised version. After finishing the translation and publishing a number of books and pamphlets in English, Tamil, and Danish, Larsen retired to Denmark in 1932 and died eight years later after an attack of pneumonia.

There is left in India a splendid body of Lutheran missionaries who are carrying on the work begun by Ziegenbalg, Schwartz, and Larsen. I have witnessed the great work of these men and women in the fine college at Guntur, South India, and all over the land. Larsen was only one of them.

I last saw Larsen in Madura, when he was engaged in Bible translation. We sat out in the moonlight after the work of the day, discussing with a group of missionaries the current problems of India and of the world. I heard Larsen's voice for the last time over the long-distance telephone in Denmark—I think it was in the summer of 1937. I had just returned from Russia, a land in which Larsen was keenly interested, seeing clearly the significance of that great social experiment. But he was even more concerned in asking questions about conditions that we had found in Germany, which was then threatening Denmark and the Low Countries with invasion, as Hitler was becoming daily more ruthless in his trampling march to power. Larsen was fortunately permitted to pass quietly to his reward before the violation of Denmark and the outbreak of World War II.

Larsen's life was not filled with dramatic situations like that of Schwartz. He could not point to a multitude of baptized high-caste converts, nor could any other man of his day in India. He was not an organizer or a statesman. He was simply a great Christian. His life resembled that of his Master in Galilee. His Christlike character was his message. His influence was deep and profound, alike in India and in Denmark, to the very end of his life. I remember how we as missionaries used to sit at the feet of this great master; he was our guru, our rishi, our example. He was a missionary's missionary. He seemed to have lived more, to have suffered more, and to have solved more deeply life's common problems, than the rest of us. There was a touch of sadness, so frequently found among Scandinavians, in his beautiful face, and a nobility in his huge, leonine head. Philosopher, theologian, linguist, saint—Larsen was all of these in one harmonious blend. As a philosopher he had followed the great Kierkegaard by a generation. The volcanic Kierkegaard, with his piercing insights, was perhaps the profoundest psychological interpreter of the religious life since St. Augustine. I do not pretend that Larsen was as great a philosopher as his Danish predecessor. But he seemed to hold the whole of Kierkegaard in solution, to have fought through all his battles and to have come out into a deep peace, deeper than Kierkegaard himself had ever known.

Without consulting an authority Larsen could have given a course on the whole history of philosophy, with profound lucidity, in Danish, English, German, or Tamil. But he was not a technical philosopher. Like Socrates, or rather like Plato, he was a simple lover of wisdom; yet he was a realist. There were areas of life and things which he frankly did not know and which he did not profess to understand. In those areas his childlike faith was like the great mountains; it rose to himalayan heights. He was a profound theologian, completely modern, going all the way to the very end of historical criticism.

He was sure of the real humanity of Jesus and needed no cumbrous Greek concept of two natures to account for him. Larsen was equally sure of the incarnation, broadly interpreted —that in a unique way God was in Christ. Believing in no Molochlike God, punishing innocent victims, in no mechanical transaction at Calvary, no legalistic fictions, Larsen yet believed profoundly in the atonement, that God was in Christ reconciling the world unto himself—but requiring no reconciliation for himself. I never found Larsen interested in the body of the crucified Jesus, or in an empty tomb; but he was a man vitally and fully possessed by the living Christ, who was as real to him as the earthly Jesus of Nazareth.

Perhaps I unconsciously exaggerate or magnify this older man in a kind of hero worship; but, if I do, he is the only man mentioned in this book who has cast a lasting spell upon me. Our world is richer for Larsen's having lived in it awhile. I would like to dream of someday being a little more like this winsome man—this great Dane, Larsen!

CHARLES FREER ANDREWS, "CHRIST'S FAITHFUL APOSTLE"

I first met Charlie Andrews when he was a member of the Cambridge Mission in Delhi, on the staff of St. Stephen's College. He was keen on Indian leadership and went with me to see his own bishop of the Punjab, Dr. Lefroy, about recognizing the newly organized National Missionary Society of India so that they could open an Anglican mission in the Punjab. I later came in contact with leading Hindus and Mohammedans who had been influenced by Andrews' remarkable character, and who called him, after his three initials, C. F. A., "Christ's Faithful Apostle." He seemed to many in North India, as Larsen was in the South, the one foreigner who bore the most striking resemblance to his Master, especially in his Christlike humility and love. One brilliant Hindu editor, who was accused of being a Christian because he had hung a portrait of Jesus at the foot of his bed, where he could see it on waking and retiring, said to me: "I have read little of the Bible, but I have seen Christ in Andrews' life; and I would give anything to be like him."

Andrews had been a notable cricketer in his youth; and he had rowed for Pembroke College, Cambridge, and had coached his college crews. Severe illness as a child, however, and later attacks of malignant malaria, of Asiatic cholera, and of diseases which afflicted the poor among whom he worked, had weakened his constitution; yet he weathered every attack of illness for nearly seventy years, from 1871 to 1940. He spent his youth in the smoky "Black Country," and in the crowded industrial city of Birmingham, where his father was an "Irvingite" pastor looking fervently for the speedy coming of Christ. Through the betrayal of a friend the family was plunged into poverty, and Andrews had to work his way through Cambridge on a scholarship. He had an abnormally sensitive conscience, and a deep experience of conversion gave him a sense of sympathy which compelled him to suffer vicariously with all humanity. I have never known a person with such a capacity for suffering with others. As a child he fled sobbing to his mother when he saw a chicken killed. And he never became sophisticated and hardened like most other men. Like Schweitzer in Africa, he was Christ's suffering servant in India.

Andrews' many years at Cambridge, both as student and as teacher, were ever-deeping years where the fiercest storms of doubt only played a helpful part in driving him back to his first love in Christ. When ordained under his beloved Bishop Westcott, he took a parish among poor shipyard laborers in an industrial village in Durham, and tried to live as they did on ten shillings, or $2.50, a week. He then labored until his health gave out in the Pembroke College Mission in the slums of East London. When his friend Basil Westcott died of cholera in India, Andrews immediately felt that he must take the vacant place; and he arrived in Delhi in 1904 at the age of thirty-three. He went to India to teach, but soon found that he had need to learn more than to teach. His fellowship with Bishop Westcott had instilled this attitude in him, for the Cambridge Mission at Delhi had been founded by the three great Cam-

bridge scholars Lightfoot, Westcott, and Hort, to represent in
India what the school of Clement and Origen at Alexandria
had meant for the early church.

Andrews had always had great intellectual difficulty in sub-
scribing with conviction to all the articles of the Book of
Common Prayer. In India he found that there were two recita-
tions in the services which he could not tolerate without shame
in a Christian church. One was the imprecatory psalms of hatred
and vengeance which had to be recited in the daily service, and
the other was the damnatory clauses at the beginning of the
Athanasian Creed: "Which faith except everyone do keep
whole and undefiled, without doubt he shall perish everlast-
ingly." Andrews felt his whole soul shrink from such crude
dogmatic narrowness in the condemnation of all unbelievers.

In Delhi, Andrews lived in the home of Susil Rudra, a fellow
professor in St. Stephen's College; and here he found the priceless value of an equal Indian friend, through whose eyes he
came to understand India and the Orient. When the English
principal of St. Stephen's College resigned, Andrews refused to
take his place, or to countenance the injustice of denying the
office to Rudra, who was much better qualified than Andrews
and who had been serving for twenty years as vice-principal.
For Andrews, the sovereign character of Christ was the one
golden thread running through the history of mankind, binding
the ages and the races together. He was such a guileless Nathanael himself that he could never seem to see any fault in
others. He so saw what was best in all men and in all religions
that a controversial attitude toward them was repugnant and
impossible for him. He agreed with Gandhi that the bloom of
the rose does not need to proclaim itself loudly to the world;
its perfume is the witness of its own sweetness. All his life
Andrews never strove nor cried aloud in the streets, but the
very fragrance of Christ was diffused through him. Andrews
not only could see Christ in his friend Rudra, a Christian, but
also could feel Christ's presence in a saintly old Mussulman,
Munshi Zaka Ullah, the account of whose life he wrote. The
old Mussulman and Andrews spent long hours together in spir-

itual communion, and the old man loved Andrews as his own son, as did other Moslems, Sikhs, and Hindus.

During one hot season after Andrews had suffered from several attacks of malarial fever, a young Baptist missionary in Delhi, C. B. Young, like a good Samaritan had nursed him back to health. When Young himself fell ill, Andrews offered to take a service for him in his mission church, but was told by his bishop that his license to minister was thereby in danger of being canceled. Andrews felt that in this and every situation he could be nothing less than Christian—that in every such matter he must obey God rather than man. Together with the feeling that he could not impose the Thirty-nine Articles of Religion upon the infant Indian Church, this denominational exclusiveness was one of the things that marked Andrews' parting of the ways with the Cambridge Mission and finally sent him out to a world-wide sphere of work. As his whole life was immovably centered in the reality of God as a loving Father, fully revealed in Christ crucified, arisen, and living, he completely repudiated belief in eternal torment and everlasting punishment, as an utterly pagan conception. Though a devout High-churchman, he was no more orthodox than his Master had been. He never severed his connection with the Anglican communion; but, taking off his clerical collar, he finally decided to leave the Cambridge Mission brotherhood and direct ministerial work under a bishop for the wandering life of a knight errant of the cross for suffering humanity all over the world. He accepted the invitation of the poet Tagore to live at Santiniketan, the "Abode of Peace," in Bengal, as his future spiritual home. Here he lived and taught and went out to minister to India's deepest needs.

Tagore had built up an ashram, a school and a community around it, and then a university centered in that community, conducting a wide range of research and experimentation for the benefit of the teeming villages of Bengal. Here Andrews learned yet more deeply from Tagore the expression of the gospel of the incarnation in ordinary work and ordinary workmen, as representing suffering humanity. The poor of the earth ever seemed to draw Andrews like an irresistible magnet. Tagore opened his heart in friendship, encouraged Andrews to teach in the institution, set him free for repeated journeys in his world-wide mission, and helped him to full expression through writing, especially in his books about the life and work of Gandhi. Andrews' spiritual kinship and friendship with Tagore, Gandhi, and Albert Schweitzer were characteristic of his catholicity.

Andrews' work, coupled with that of Tagore and Santiniketan for the poor of Bengal and with that of Gandhi for the untouchable outcastes of India, finally led to his complete identification with the cause of organized labor in India and his presiding at the Trade Union Congress of all India. From 1920 to 1930 he made the cause of labor his own. Andrews had to say openly that Indian poverty was not the act of God but was largely man made, the fruit of the avarice of Indian landowners and the sloth and ineptitude of British government officials. He took a bold stand for India's right of self-determination and her complete independence if desired, saying that Britain had no right to conquer and rule India against her will. He immersed himself in the abysmal poverty of India, where, according to some British authorities, 217 million people have to subsist on 215 million acres of land, and where the average income of the 400 million of India is $16.80 a year, or four cents a day.[6] Between 1917 and 1924 most of the larger cotton and jute mills repaid their stockholders several times the value of their original stock. In 1919 I myself found jute mills in Bengal publicly declaring dividends of from 200 to 400 per cent a year; yet the peasants employed in the cultivation of jute, saturated with malaria and working waist deep in water, sometimes had their wages reduced from twenty or thirty cents to ten or fifteen cents a day. Such facts Andrews unsparingly proclaimed to the whole British Empire in an effort to awaken its conscience.

[6] See reports of Sir James Grigg made while he was a member of the viceroy's council; Janet Kelman's *Labour in India;* report of the Royal Commission of 1929; Thompson and Garrett's surveys of India's economic conditions; and the writer's *New World of Labor,* pp. 64-66.

Eighty years after slavery had been abolished in the British Empire the system of indentured labor in India still represented an extension of slavery. Labor agents recruited ignorant coolies for indentured service in many lands abroad. Coolies were bound in five-year periods of servitude and often placed under criminal rather than under civil law; they were plunged into debt, and were allowed only forty women—many of whom were public characters—for every hundred men. This inevitably resulted in gross immorality, venereal disease, and an alarming rate of murder and suicide, conditions which were a disgrace to a "Christian" empire. The unconscious greed of Christian stockholders and the imperial politics of Christians who regarded India as their "possession" were largely blind to these evils till "Christ's Faithful Apostle," Andrews, became the conscience of Britain in this matter. He went out to join Gandhi in South Africa, to live and die for these Indian semislaves and to turn the blazing searchlight of outraged love upon this iniquity, as Jesus had turned his upon the money-changers in the temple.

At the close of a meeting conducted by the great Indian patriot Gokhale, in Delhi, Andrews had donated the whole of his life's savings and given up his post at St. Stephen's College for the service for the oppressed Indians in South Africa. At the age of forty-two, when others were seeking security, without taking the formal vows of poverty, chastity, and obedience of the mendicant orders, Andrews was called to join the inner group of those who had left all to follow Him who had not where to lay his head. He had no time to think of a wife or a home of his own, but in a hundredfold measure all homes were now his, especially where they had all things in common, as in the ashram of Gandhi in South Africa, in a school for American Negroes in South Carolina, and among the Quakers at Woodbrooke, England. To these communities in utter humility he could say: "I am a man with immense resources at my command, and I own absolutely nothing. From the night in 1913 when I left everything there came into my life freedom, poverty, and joy. If you would know these things you must tread the same path."

When Andrews stepped ashore at Durban, in South Africa, he met Mr. Gandhi, just released from prison, where his wife and thousands of his followers were still detained. Andrews instinctively made the well-known gesture of India, bending down and touching the feet of the other, to signify that he took the lowest place before the one honored and loved. With the speed of light, this gesture, which typified every act of his life, flashed its meaning to the whole persecuted Indian community—and raised an angry howl of fierce indignation from Europeans in South Africa. Two physically feeble men, Gandhi and Andrews, now set themselves to the superhuman task of uplifting and liberating the colored races and ending forever the cursed system of indentured Indian slavery. All Indians were so aroused that Britain began to fear the loss of her greatest "possession," India. The conscience of the Empire was so moved that the viceroy, Lord Hardinge, presided at a meeting of protest in support of the Indian cause. When the battle seemed almost won, when there was lacking only General Smuts's signature to the draft agreement which was to set Indians free from indentured slavery, Gandhi received a telegram that his wife was dying from her illness contracted in prison. Still he would not leave without General Smuts's signature. Andrews went over at six in the morning and got Smuts to sign the historic document, and Gandhi was then able to hurry to his wife's bedside.

Once the battle to free indentured labor was won in South Africa, the fight for freedom had to be carried to other battlefields. Andrews' journeys took him all over the world—wherever there was slavery, abysmal poverty, or racial prejudice coupled with injustice and degradation. Fiji, where appalling conditions were found; Assam; the West Indies; British Guiana; Trinidad; Kenya; and Bihar at the time of the earthquake—all were visited in turn. This meant endless interviews with officials in high places, confronting them with blue books carefully analyzed and government reports interpreted by an eyewitness who feared not the face of man. It also meant the use of Gandhi's method of *Satyagraha,* or the nonviolent defense of truth, which seemed at its highest to partake of the method of the cross itself. This was expressed also in Andrews' endless service for the untouchables of India; but he recognized with Gandhi that the shame and crime of untouchability must be swept away by Hindus themselves, from within their own religious and social systems. This never seemed to Charlie Andrews impossible. He believed absolutely in "the light which lighteth every man" and appealed to the "divine witness" in all men, not only in saints, Christian and non-Christian, but also in sinners. He seemed to be looking for Christ, or the divine image, in every man—in immoral indentured coolies and in cynical politicians, whether Indian or European. He was a friend of sinners. He trusted them, he believed in them, and he was always ready to live or die for them. To a unique degree he had the mind and embodied the spirit of Christ. With his capacity of creative friendship and brotherhood, Andrews inspired groups to follow his ministry of reconciliation in many lands— not only in India, South Africa, and Britain, but also in Austria, Spain, Norway, Sweden, Italy, France, Denmark, Ireland, Holland, Germany, and the United States. The ministry of hundreds of groups is described by John S. Hoyland in his *C. F. Andrews: Minister of Reconciliation* and by Andrews in his *What I Owe to Christ.*

In 1916 Andrews accompanied the poet Rabindranath Tagore to Japan, where Tagore warned the people of the ominous growth of aggressive nationalism which was destroying the beauty of the true Japanese civilization. The nationalist press warned the Japanese against this "prophet of a defeated nation." On another voyage Andrews and Tagore both visited China, and that country was warned against worshiping the materialism of the West. On Lake Victoria, in Africa, Andrews left the aged and saintly Roman Catholic priests and nuns in tears of gratitude. Andrews describes them as "sustained in radiant joy right on to the end, till their faces shone with the light of another world, through the living presence of Christ with them in their daily labor of love." He was unconsciously telling the secret of the spirit of love incarnated in his own life as Christ's faithful apostle.

Andrews has sometimes been credulous and naïve with men who were far from guileless. And I could name instances where it seemed to me that he used very bad judgment indeed. But I asked Andrews to write his name in my New Testament, just after the name of Gandhi, on my special prayer list, as I look upon him as one of the five most Christlike characters I have ever met. When Andrews passed quietly away in Calcutta, April 4, 1940, Mr. Gandhi had traveled hundreds of miles to be with him, and an Indian college principal who had traveled a thousand miles to be at his bedside found him dying as he had always lived, "surrounded by an atmosphere of love, joy, and inward peace." He was one of our great pathfinders and crusaders. "In God, who is the God not of the dead but of the living, and who lives in all service for the suffering, Andrews' spirit will pass on across the world, serving in humble ways the neediest everywhere."

PANDITA RAMABAI AND AMY CARMICHAEL

When I arrived in India, in 1896, to begin work among men students, the women of India lived in a world apart, often in seclusion behind the veil, or purdah. Two women were able to help me understand the needs of Indian women because they were so completely identified with them: Pandita Ramabai and Amy Wilson Carmichael. Both told me of the census of 1901 which gave the cold statistics of 144 million women, of whom 26 million were widows, or one in every six. But the census could not reveal the hard fate of these Indian widows. Of these widows, 115,285 were under ten years of age; 19,487 under five years; and 1,064 under one year of age. Whatever her age, a widow was forbidden by Hindu custom to remarry. Young Krishna Rao after marrying a widow suffered so greatly from the persecution of the community that he committed suicide. Even of the wives, 2,273,245 were under ten years of age, 243,502 under five, and 10,507 were babies under one year of age. These baby wives live with their parents until about the age of twelve; but if the little boy husband dies the girl is left a widow for life, her head is shaved, and all the curses of widowhood are heaped upon her. If a poor, defenseless widow, who is at the mercy of the men of her household, gives birth to a child, one of three things must happen: the mother must drown herself in the well, or the child must be put out of the way by infanticide, or it must be sold or given to the temple, in a life dedicated to the gods in temple prostitution.

In South India alone there are some twelve thousand temple women dedicated as devadasis or nautch-dancing-girls. The daily *Hindu* of Madras affirms of this custom of temple prostitution: "The demoralization it causes is immense. So long as we allow it to be associated with our temples and places of worship, we offend and degrade our nationality. The loss and misery it has entailed on many a home is indescribable." Tagore added: "It is a canker that eats into the vitals of our national existence and which, if not removed, in time may lead to the degeneracy and decay of the whole race."

These facts I began to realize soon after my arrival in India. The famines of 1896-97 and of 1900 had just carried away five million people and left fifty million hungry. I saw one group of gaunt specters stalk silently in from the dusty road. They had walked seventy-five miles. "Sir," they said, "we have no work, no food, no water. How can we live?" As we drove through the fields they were withered and burned in the sun. The cattle were gone, the streams were dry, the wells often empty. The parched farms were deserted, the villages were quiet, the people silent and gloomy. The glaring heaven seemed brass, and the earth was burned like brick. It was these famines that gave Pandita Ramabai her great opportunity for rescuing starving women and children.

It was at this time that I met this remarkable woman. It was on a summer evening, and I had left my train and made my way across the famine-parched prairie to the hundred acres of Ramabai's School. A great quadrangle of long stone buildings appeared, a striking monument to a woman's faith and to the grace of God. We went inside the quadrangle, past neatly dressed Indian girls, to the garden in the center, laid out with beautiful design so that the decorations of the flower beds in scripture texts spell out the praises of God. It is well that they should praise him here where the desert had been made to blossom as the rose, and human hearts seem to have been delivered from the shame and sorrow of earth to a heavenly purity and joy.

In the evening we sat upon the mud floor and ate supper with Ramabai and the devoted women who were helping her. We had curry and rice, coarse native bread, and milk. But more interesting than the meal was Ramabai herself. Her face was brimful of intelligence and bright with humor, though there was a touch of sadness about it. I could see in her the long past of Hinduism at its best and the bright radiance of her Christianity. The next day was Sunday. We wondered why no breakfast appeared, but found that the girls gave up their morning meal on Sunday to help their starving people. As the hundreds of girls gathered for Sunday worship, neat, clean, womanly, and happy, we could not but be moved at the thought of the past from which they had been rescued: often from widowhood, starvation, sin, or shame; or at best from idolatry. I found Ramabai in the afternoon having a quiet time with her Bible, and from her own lips I learned the story of her life. She said:

In the great famine of '77, when I was a girl, our family was reduced to starvation. We prostrated ourselves before the idols day and night. When our money was gone we began to sell our jewelry, clothes, and cooking utensils. The day came when the last grain of rice was gone. We went into the forest to die there. First my father, then my mother, and then my eldest sister died from starvation. My brother and I continued our sad pilgrimage from the south to the northern boundary of India, and back again to Calcutta. I was often without food for days. Four long years we suffered from scarcity. My memory of the last days of my parents' lives so full of sorrow almost breaks my heart.

In her early life, Pandita Ramabai, as one woman in a million, had received an exceptional education in Sanskrit and other Indian tongues. She could speak six languages. She had read portions of the Scripture, and had been influenced by the great Christian, Nehemiah Goreh; but it was not until her journey to England that she saw the superiority of Christianity over Hinduism and was baptized. She said:

I read the story of George Müller and the China Inland Mission, and I thought, "If others can trust God, why should not I?" In the famine of 1896-97 I saw these girls dying and I felt that I must save them. I said, "I will depend upon God and not on man," and I began to take in these starving girls, keeping them at first under the trees for shelter. I asked God for money for buildings and he sent over $25,000. Already he has sent me five hundred girls, and if God sends them I will take a thousand more.

It was not long until she had more than that number. Here was one Indian woman, in this land of timid women, drawing the plans and superintending the construction of immense buildings; directing a hundred teachers, matrons, and workers; providing a thousand girls with education and industrial training—in sewing and weaving, housework and farming; running a dairy and oil mill; and having them taught cooking and nursing! She told me that God had abundantly supplied all her needs. She said little of her faith but much of God's faithfulness. In her I could see the whole future of a new Indian womanhood.

Soon after meeting Pandita Ramabai I came to know personally another great soul, Amy Wilson Carmichael. She was the adopted daughter of Robert Wilson, long the chairman of the Keswick Convention, so it was natural that she should become a "Keswick missionary." She had gone out from England to Japan as a missionary, about 1894, to work with Barclay Buxton. She told me that she had broken down from nervous prostration during the very first year of her service, suffering, as some foreigners do, from what was called "Japanese head." Ashamed to return home to England under what seemed to her the disgrace of early failure, she asked to be allowed to try the tropics of India, and was sent to Palamcottah, South India.

When I saw her soon after her arrival she was studying the Tamil language. She was a member of the Church of England Zenana Missionary Society, finally stationed far out in Dohnavur, at the southern extremity of India, miles from any railway, living in the home of the Reverend and Mrs. Thomas Walker.

Walker had the mathematical mind of a Cambridge wrangler. He was a brilliant linguist with a remarkable knowledge of Tamil, the hardest language in India. I went for a time to live in his home while studying the language, and then joined him in "missions," as they were called, for the deepening of the spiritual life among Indian Christian workers. I saw much of the remarkable character and work of Miss Carmichael in that godly Christian home. At the end of a hard day's work, all four of us would sit out under the stars in the cool of the evening and discuss everything in heaven or on earth—at least everything that was within the ambit of the Kingdom of God. Walker was a kind of ascetic Christian John the Baptist, who spent hours in prayer when on his missions.

I asked Miss Carmichael one day when and how she had found the secret of her radiant and wonderful life. She told me that years before, in England, she had attended a meeting; but she had forgotten everything that was said. A man led in prayer, and she had forgotten the prayer—save one phrase that changed her whole life forever. When she heard the words "We thank thee, Lord, that thou art *able*," a new meaning leaped from the context of the prayer to her immediate need. If God was "able to make all grace abound"; able to make the weak brother stand; "able to do exceeding abundantly above all that we ask or think"; able and willing to supply all her need, moment by moment, hour by hour, day by day; and if the living Christ could say, "Lo, I am with you alway, even unto the end," then what had she to fear for the rest of her life? At that moment she took a bold step in faith, and then successive steps as she sought to live one day at a time by faith, hope, and love. It seemed that in the twinkling of an eye all her life had been transformed. She had no doubts as to her own continuing sinfulness and need. True saints always feel that they are utterly unworthy. But she seemed to have built up a mighty, indomitable, and continuous faith that enabled her to live the victorious life, the radiant and joyous life of self-forgetfulness and perfect peace. All the promises of God's word she continuously claimed; all the triumph of the life consistently taught for so many decades at the Keswick convention, that meant so much to evangelicals of both the Anglican and the Free churches in Britain and India, were hers. She was the ideal "Keswick missionary."

Frankly, I have included in this book the story of Amy Wilson Carmichael not because of her achievements, though these were notable, but because of the beauty of her character. Here is the point where many a missionary breaks down. Every normal missionary sails with high purpose but as a very imperfect Christian, and he is seldom thoroughly—or even adequately—prepared for the arduous work before him. There often comes a time of crisis early in his experience on the field. Sometimes it is during the trying and humiliating period of language study, or upon the first realization that there are no immediate magic results from the proclamation of his glorious gospel, whether through his own imperfect pronunciation of a foreign tongue or through his ever-imperfect national workers. The young missionary invariably finds that, however high was his youthful purpose, a short ocean voyage does not materially change his character. Indeed, the unfriendly climate, the non-Christian pagan community in their superstition and idolatry, the loneliness of his mission station, possible friction with his fellow workers—with a few of whom he is shut up and cannot escape— or the stress and strain of his new and difficult environment often reveal weaknesses, limitations, and irritations in his own character that he never dreamed he had when in the more favorable circumstances of his home country.

Ideally, a missionary may be a heroic martyr, but he quickly learns only too well that he is no hero. If, as Emerson says, "what you are thunders so that I cannot hear what you say," the missionary may begin to realize that his own character is his weakest point. His religion, his gospel, is all right; his sacred book is incomparably better than the sacred books of the East. Jesus has no parallel, and Christ alone is Saviour. The God and Father of Jesus is infinitely above all the idols and gods of polytheism, and above the conceptions of the "higher Hinduism," or the new Buddhism, or any other religion. But if his Master's character was Jesus' message, and if the missionary's own life must embody and interpret—or misinterpret—his gospel, what if he fall downs at this crucial point? What if his preaching is but "sounding brass"?

It was just here that Miss Carmichael was a blessing to all who came into intimate and understanding contact with her radiant life. Yet no life outside a monastery was more isolated from the outside world. Far from any railway, in a distant spot in the tropics reached by bullock cart traveling at two miles an hour and visited by few, without a single furlough in fifty years to bring her in contact with her home constituency, in a sense her life partook of some of the limitations of her Lord, and of those who had taken the vows of poverty, chastity, and obedience. Jesus himself had lived an almost hidden life, less than three years in public, in an obscure Roman province in Gentile-polluted Galilee, in a village of such ill repute that men could ask, "Can there any good thing come out of Nazareth?" And Amy Carmichael, like her Master, was a prophet in her own country. Her very Indian dress, which brought her near to her beloved Tamil people, seemed to separate her from her foreign fellow workers when she went very occasionally to the hills for desperately needed rest.

I have mentioned before that I lived in the same home with Miss Carmichael in Dohnavur in the Tinnevelly district while I was studying Tamil. After fifty years of travel—from 1894 to 1944—and after meeting a large proportion of the leading missionaries all over the world, and of the Christian workers of America and Europe, I can say that Amy Wilson Carmichael was the most Christlike character I ever met, and that her life was the most fragrant, the most joyfully sacrificial, that I ever knew. This does not mean, of course, that her work was the most fruitful, or that I agreed completely with her theology;

indeed, some of her convictions were for me quite impossible.

In 1901 Miss Carmichael felt it laid upon her heart to seek to rescue the beautiful children who were being dedicated to the gods for a life of temple prostitution. This whole practice of temple prostitution by hosts of young women, who are "married to the gods" and servants of the gods, is a characteristic and lasting blot upon Hinduism. I regret that conditions are still the same as described in the first government census report (1901) written after I arrived in India, where it is frankly acknowledged:

The servants of the gods, who subsist by dancing and music and the practice of "the oldest profession in the world" are partly recruited by admissions and even purchases from other classes. . . . The rise of the Caste and its euphemistic name seem to date from the ninth and tenth centuries. Inscriptions show that in A.D. 1004 the great Temple at Tanjore had attached to it four hundred women of the Temple, who lived in free quarters in the four streets round it.

As a meritorious act, the parents give or sell the child to the temple while it is a babe. When eight or nine years of age, it is taken to the temple and married to the god before the idol. The child's "husband" is at first one of the temple priests. She is early taught sensuous poetry, singing, and dancing, to make her more attractive to her future wide clientele than the illiterate Hindu housewives are to their husbands.

For fifty years Miss Carmichael has fought fearlessly to expose and abolish this deep-seated evil. All her efforts and those of her fellow workers and the Christian community only seem to drive it farther underground. Hinduism, with all its noble qualities and sacred books and saints like Gandhi, *will not* abolish this thousand-year-old evil, against which the Hebrew prophets fought for so many centuries. It is one of the things that make Christian missions and missionaries like Miss Carmichael imperative for India from a Christian point of view. The number of children about to be dedicated who were rescued by Miss Carmichael now runs into several thousands.

Others have been stirred by seeing what it has been possible for Miss Carmichael to do and have undertaken the same kind of work. There are now, in 1945, over eight hundred children in her three homes. Each institution is at once a Christian home, a school, and a center for character building. Each is permeated by the personal touch of the workers who have caught Miss Carmichael's spirit, and by a deeply spiritual atmosphere where love reigns and every psychological character problem yields ultimately to a solution suggested by love.

The law of the land regarding temple prostitution has been reformed, but the evil goes on as of old. By a skillful evasion of the law and by a deep denial of morality the evil is simply driven deeper underground. Babies are still bought both for the temples and for cinema purposes. Both boys and girls are wanted, and the Indian cinema is almost as evil as the temple. Recently a young girl was sold for eight hundred rupees, or nearly $400. There are places where the babies are brought up and trained for this immoral life. Thirty rupees a month is paid for a nurse for such a baby. Miss Carmichael has just lost another child, spirited away or kidnaped—a ten-day-old baby girl. I know of no greater moral contrast in India than to pass from the dark recesses of the Madura Hindu temple, with its life-sized obscene carvings in stone and its neighborhood of temple prostitution, to Miss Carmichael's radiant Christian institutions where one sees hundreds of beautiful little children who have been rescued from the very jaws of hell, now the very flowers of God. They were rescued when too young to know the infamy from which they were spared, the dark pit from which they were lifted.

Thirty of Miss Carmichael's lads are now in the Indian army, navy, and air force. Many of the girls have become earnest Christian workers. Hundreds of them are wives and mothers in good Christian homes. There is a fine medical work, under the charge of Dr. Webb Peploe and his colleagues, which reaches people from distant places. The hospital is thoroughly evangelistic and has yielded spiritual fruit. Direct evangelistic work is also carried on in the district, and many lantern lectures are given. But the work cannot be measured by statistics. Much of it lies in the unseen realm of the Kingdom of Heaven, which is "within," hidden in human hearts. At the radiating center of it all lies this Christlike saint, now an invalid unable to move from her bed of pain, but still joyous and indomitable after fifty years of service.

DR. IDA SCUDDER

The first Dr. John Scudder (1793-1855) was a stalwart medical missionary to India and Ceylon a decade and a half before Peter Parker went to China. He must have been, as reputed, a giant and an athlete, for every mother's son, grandson, and granddaughter of the Scudder family that I have known has been an athlete. The Scudders and their wives have given more than twelve hundred years of service in mission lands.

John Scudder entered Princeton in 1809, at the age of sixteen, and graduated in 1813. Because of his father's stern opposition to the ministry young Scudder turned to medicine, and this providential choice made him the first medical missionary to India and one of the first in the world. As a young man of twenty-six Dr. Scudder was practicing medicine in New York City. As he waited to enter the sickroom of a patient one day, he picked up a booklet with the title, *The Conversion of the World, or the Claims of Six Hundred Millions, and the Ability and Duty of the Churches Representing Them,* written by Hall, Gordon, Newell, and Samuel at Andover in 1818. He read and reread this until his heart was aflame with longing to go abroad as a medical missionary. When he spoke to his father of his proposal his father replied: "If you persist in this mad idea, I shall strike your name from my will." The stern, autocratic father was accustomed to obedience from his sons and from the Negro slaves on his large estate in New Jersey. He did not become reconciled to the choice his son had made until two decades later, when the son had his one and only furlough; but in the meantime he had set free his slaves—before Lincoln's proclamation.

The American Board was looking for its first physician to

send to India with its second installment of missionaries. When Scudder offered his services he was eagerly accepted, and he sailed with his young wife and child from Boston to India in 1819. He proceeded in 1820 to his first station in Jaffna, Ceylon, where he was ordained at the hands of Congregational, Baptist, and Methodist ministers. From the first, Dr. Scudder combined skilled surgery and medical aid with evangelistic preaching. When he was ordered to Madras for his health, it led the American Board to open a temporary mission in Madras; and it was there that Scudder later reopened medical missionary work in 1847. As a wide-ranging evangelist, Dr. Scudder preached and healed all over South India, though he was sometimes opposed and even stoned. After four years in Madras he was called to Madura by a severe cholera epidemic. An unbroken term of seventeen years of work in India resulted in failing health and drove Dr. John to America for a four-year furlough, where he toured the country speaking on missions. In 1846 he again sailed to India and joined the Madura Mission of the American Board.

During their first twenty-two years of service the Scudders had fourteen children. Seven sons and two daughters became missionaries and helped to form the Arcot Mission of the Reformed Church in 1853. Dr. Scudder ended his labors at the age of sixty-one, dying in South Africa, where he had gone for his health, after thirty-six years of fruitful service in the East. He was full of physical, mental, and spiritual vigor, deeply religious by nature, a fervent evangelist, and an irrepressible optimist amid all the trials and hardships of a hardy pioneer. Old Dr. John left his stamp upon his children and grandchildren to the third and fourth generations of one of the great missionary families of the nineteenth century. All his children became Christians; nine of the ten living children became foreign missionaries and returned to India, and the other died in preparation for the same great work. Five of the seven surviving brothers were doctors of medicine, as well as pastors. Twelve grandchildren became foreign missionaries, six of the fourth generation of Scudders went to India and two to Arabia, and ten great-grandchildren have entered the same high calling.

The youngest son of the original Dr. John was also named John Scudder; and he had five stalwart sons and one beautiful daughter, Ida, who became a medical missionary, almost in spite of herself. "Bonny Ida" was born December 9, 1870—a birthday that eventually became Founders' and College Day for several hundred graduates of her women's medical school. During her childhood, in 1878, a severe famine swept India like the Black Death, carrying away three million people. Dr. John Scudder, Ida's father, was fighting the famine in Vellore and North Arcot; and Ida, then a child of six, remembers feeding the starving children with her own hands, and seeing others lying dead by the roadside.

Dwight L. Moody, then at the height of his powers, admitted Ida to his school for girls in Northfield. Here she was full of fun and pranks, determined that she was going to enjoy life and never, never be a missionary. A cablegram telling of her mother's illness called her unexpectedly to India. One memorable night in 1894 Ida Scudder's whole life was changed by three desperate situations which seemed to constitute a threefold call for her to become a medical missionary in India. Listen to her story as told in her own abbreviated statement:

As I sat alone at my desk, I heard steps coming up to the verandah and looking up I saw a very tall and fine-looking Brahmin gentleman. He said his little wife, a mere child, was in labour, having a very difficult time, and the untrained barbers' wives had said that they could do nothing for her. He asked if I would go and help her. I told him that I knew absolutely nothing about midwifery cases but that my father was a doctor and would gladly help. The man drew himself up and said, "Your father come into my caste home and take care of my wife! She had better die than have anything like that happen." Later I took him over to my father's study and together we pleaded with him and I told him that I would do everything in my power to help his wife, with my father, if he would only let us come! I would be an assistant! Still he refused.

After a time I heard steps again on the verandah and I saw a Mohammedan who had come to see me, and I was horrified to hear the same plea from him. His wife was dying, a mere child, and would I come and help? I took him to my father, and we both reasoned with him and I said that I would go with my father who was a doctor. He utterly refused, saying that no man outside his family had ever looked upon the face of his wife. "She had better die than have a man come into the house," he said. I went back to my room with my heart burdened. I again heard footsteps, and, running to the door, I was more than horrified to have the same plea coming from a third man, a high-caste Hindu. He refused to have my father just as the others had done, and vanished in the darkness.

I could not sleep that night—it was too terrible. Within the very touch of my hand were three young girls dying because there was no woman to help them. I spent much of the night in anguish and prayer. I did not want to spend my life in India. My friends were begging me to return to the joyous opportunities of a young girl in America. I went to bed in the early morning after praying much for guidance. I think that was the first time I ever met God face to face, and all that time it seemed that He was calling me into this work. Early in the morning I heard the "tom-tom" beating in the village and it struck terror in my heart, for it was a death message. I sent our servant, and he came back saying that all of them had died during the night. Again I shut myself in my room and thought very seriously about the condition of the Indian women and after much thought and prayer, I went to my father and mother and told them that I must go home and study medicine, and come back to India to help such women.[7]

These three cases of child wives dying in childbirth served to make India's desperate physical need the more vocal. Into a space half the area of the United States three times our own population is crowded in deep poverty. Few of the fifty million annual cases of malaria receive any medical treatment; malaria accounts for a million deaths a year, disables two million, and saps the vitality of many more. The toll of plague, cholera, typhus fever, hookworm, tuberculosis, leprosy, and venereal dis-

[7] Mary Pauline Jeffery, *Dr. Ida: India* (New York: Fleming H. Revell Co., 1938), pp. 49-51.

ease takes millions annually. India's mortality rate is double that of England and three times that of Australia.

With a population increasing almost a million every two months, the majority are worse fed than they were fifty years ago. Eighty-five per cent of the population is illiterate and with no interest in sanitation or understanding of disease germs. Abbé Dubois found more than a century ago that if you "try to change a social institution you meet an unconquerable people." The British government has perhaps done the best it could, but after spending, as the Simon Commission found, $62\frac{1}{2}$ per cent of the central revenues on India's little army and its pensioned foreign officers there is an utterly inadequate sum left for the development of education, medicine, public health, modern industry, or agriculture. A fifteen-year government plan requires twenty times as many midwives, seventy times as many health visitors, and a hundred times as many trained nurses as there are now in India. The British have failed to develop a system of public health that distantly approaches the system in Russia. According to the director-general of the Indian medical service there are in India:

Doctors	42,000, or 1 to 10,000	population
Nurses	7,000, or 1 to 57,000	population
Health visitors	1,000, or 1 to 400,000	population
Midwives	5,000, or 1 to 80,000	population

In British India there are but 6,700 hospitals and dispensaries with 69,000 beds, or one to every 5,700 inhabitants. The total cost of all hospitals is $12,000,000 a year. There are but 800 maternity and infant welfare centers in all India. This is but a fraction of the medical aid so abundantly provided in the United States and in Soviet Russia. While 5,000 doctors graduate annually in the United States, India graduates less than 1,600 for a population three times that of the United States. Viscount Wavell states that health and communications are to be the first concern of the government after the war. Only one fifth of the children born alive live one year in India. Except for China, India has the worst factory conditions in the world. Only an insignificant fraction of the sick and diseased in India receive any medical aid whatever. All this explains why the great medical and surgical work of the Scudders was and is so desperately needed in British India.

The abysmal need of India, physical and spiritual, voiced by the deaths of the three child wives in a single night, enabled Ida Scudder to find her true self and her appointed task in a world that needed her. In 1895 she entered the Women's Medical College in Philadelphia. After that she studied at the Cornell Medical College in New York City. A request had come to the board for a hospital for women in Vellore, South India, and that Ida Scudder be allowed to raise the money. After hearing of Dr. Ida's work a Mr. Schell gave her ten thousand dollars toward a Mary Taber Schell hospital, in memory of his wife. On January 1, 1900, in her thirtieth year, Dr. Ida returned to India as a doctor in her own right. Five months after she landed, her father, Dr. John Scudder, died of cancer at Kodaikanal. I was present at the funeral and vividly remember every detail. In 1903 Dr. Ida fought the bubonic plague, which took a toll of a million deaths.

Beginning her work in India, Dr. Ida had to compete with superstition and destructive forces such as the belief in Kali Athal, the goddess of death, in the South. This goddess of destruction is also called "Mother of India," and she holds powerful sway in her fortress in Calcutta—reeking with the blood of goats sacrificed—and in hundreds of other temples. Great disease epidemics have been Kali's instruments for centuries. As one instance of the sway of such evils, a thirteen-year-old temple girl, Laksmi, "dedicated to the gods," was brought to Dr. Ida's hospital saturated with venereal infection. Not only was she cured, but the possibilities of her character so blossomed under Christian care that she became a center of attraction for nurses, patients, and doctors. Suddenly the old head temple woman, of sinister mien, made her appearance to take Laksmi back to her old life in the temple. Dr. Scudder strove to save the girl, but she obtained legal advice and offered money in vain; for nothing could tear a girl who was under age from the clutches of

133

temple prostitution. After Laksmi's return to the temple she attempted to escape, but was seized by the priest and dragged back into the abyss. The next day she was found dead in the well. She considered suicide preferable to temple prostitution.

All of us should be eager to welcome every value in a non-Christian religion and every beauty in its sacred books, yet we cannot be blind to its evils. To this day the stone carvings in the depths of the Madura and other temples, unbelievably obscene and pornographic, testify to Hinduism's inability or unwillingness to eliminate the worst evils; on the other hand, they testify to the need of Christian medical, educational, and evangelistic missions like those of the Arcot Mission. Anyone who had seen the dark side of life in India, who could then have seen in contrast the group of a hundred women medical students, nurses, and compounders seated on mats about Dr. Scudder, as she gave them spiritual instruction, would realize the difference between darkness and light in this desperately needy country.

In addition to her work in her hospital at Vellore, Dr. Ida started a roadside dispensary service that has been multiplied fourfold in the succeeding years. A donation of the first motor car to appear in the district greatly extended this work. Sometimes Dr. Scudder had to see three hundred patients a day in these roadside dispensaries, while members of her staff carried the ministry to other centers. When Dr. Ida saw three blind men being led across the fields for her aid, she found that one of them, before he became blind, had been suffering from a high fever and had gone to the priest for advice. The priest had prescribed ground glass, cayenne pepper, and gingelly oil to be placed in the eye to relieve the fever—and it had left the man totally blind. At that time there had been no roadside dispensary that might have saved the sight of these three blind men.

Dr. Scudder has shown not only compassion but also driving force and executive ability in opening successive branches of the work. The school of pharmacy in Vellore furnishes compounders and graduates for Dr. Ida's own establishment and for other hospitals in India. From 1913 to 1918 Dr. Scudder thought and talked and dreamed of a medical college for women in Vellore. The British surgeon general gave his consent to try the experiment, saying to Dr. Scudder that she would be fortunate if she got three applicants, but if she got six to start the school. The first year 151 applications came in, and the number was doubled the second year—from all of which she could select only eighteen for her first class, because of her limited accommodations.

In an old bungalow and a temporary shed erected for the dissecting room, Dr. Ida began to teach her first class in anatomy with one microscope, one or two books, and a few bones. She proved herself to be a born teacher. Fourteen out of the eighteen original students completed the course and sat for the presidency examinations. Of the four hundred men who took the examination, only 20 per cent, or one in five, passed. All of Dr. Scudder's fourteen women graduated. Some of the girls' beautiful drawings took prizes in the "presidency exhibit." Of the students from Vellore, four secured first class in the final year, one heading the whole presidency in obstetrics; and one carried off the medal in anatomy in the second year, "making us fear," said the surgeon general, "that the girls were setting a standard too high for the men."

It was not the original group of timid girls who had stood before Lord Pentland as he opened the medical school but a band of seasoned women that Dr. Ida addressed at graduation:

You will not only be curing diseases, but will also be battling with epidemics, plagues, and pestilences, and preventing them. You will be teaching mothers how to nurture their children so that they will make more efficient reliable citizens to take their rightful places in their nation. The practice of medicine affords scope for the exercise of the best faculties of mind and heart. . . . Last and greatest of all, may you follow always and closely in the footsteps of the Great Physician, Christ, who went about doing good, healing the sick, outpouring his wealth of love upon a sinning, sorrowing world, encouraging, uplifting, and carrying joy wherever he went.

In the future may we together help India to take her rightful stand among the great nations of the world.

Five years after the first beginning, in 1923, the Cole dispensary and medical ward were opened at Thotapalayam by Lady Willingdon, wife of the governor of Madras, who was later viceroy of India; and additional buildings containing 268 beds were opened by Viscount Goschen, governor of Madras. Four miles south of Vellore, Sir George Stanley and Lady Stanley opened the fine buildings of the Union Medical College for Women, with its laboratories, lecture rooms, a hostel, a chapel, and two bungalows; with added buildings for the use of radium and deep X-ray therapy. This college is one of seven interdenominational colleges in the Orient, three of which are in China, one in Japan, and three in India. For these colleges John D. Rockefeller, Jr., gave one million dollars when the joint committee raised the remaining two million for the needed three-million-dollar fund in 1920-23.

The record at Vellore has been a brilliant one. The college has graduated over 300 licensed medical practitioners entitled to write the letters L.M.P. after their names. Of these, nearly half were in mission service, 114 in government service, and 30 in private practice. Nine had died. With few exceptions those who entered mission hospitals have rendered excellent service. Many have refused posts with higher salaries. The Women's Medical School started in 1918 with three foreign doctors and an Indian assistant. Including Indian assistants, it has now fourteen Western doctors, eighteen Indian doctors, seven nursing sisters, fourteen Indian staff nurses, eleven post-graduate nurses, an English pharmacist and her Indian assistant, and a Western X-ray technician. The nursing school has sent out 122 trained nurses, on an average of twelve nurses a year; and 75 compounders and technicians have been trained in the hospital.

If we compare the work done in the first little hospital in 1902 with that of the present time, we note the following contrasts:

Date	In-patients	Out-patients	Major Operations	Minor Operations	Maternity Operations
1902	103	12,359	21	428	35
1939	3,474	36,062	466	5,631	1,396

During the year 1942, the total number of patients treated on the four roadside itineracies was 29,000. The past forty years of Vellore's history make a very thrilling story centered around the radiant personality of Ida Scudder, to whom the hospital and medical school buildings are a glorious living monument.

No less than eleven boards of missions in the United States, Canada, and Great Britain co-operate in the Union Missionary Medical College of Vellore. Members of the Vellore staff include American, British, Canadian, Australian, German, Danish, and Indian in this truly international union service. The fine-looking laboratory of the college was built and equipped in memory of Laura Spelman Rockefeller.

Dr. Scudder has won a reputation for a very difficult gynecological operation. She was awarded the D.Sc. degree by Rutgers in 1935, and an honorary F.A.C.S. The president of Rutgers College, when conferring upon her the degree of D.Sc., said:

Your direction of the Mary Taber Schell Hospital at the Arcot Mission of the Reformed Church in America at Vellore, India, was rightfully honored when you received the celebrated Kaisar-i-Hind medal from the government of India for distinguished public service. The famous Union Medical College for South India, which you served as first president, exists today as a direct tribute to your fruitful labors. I greet you today as the third member of your distinguished family to receive recognition at the commencement exercises of this institution, and so, at the direction of the trustees of Rutgers University, I confer upon you, *honoris causa,* the degree of doctor of science.

In 1939 Dr. Scudder received a gold bar for her Kaisar-i-Hind medal.

It is not easy to live a solitary life for forty years in India. But many times Dr. Scudder has refused the offer of a happy home life for herself in order to remain at her lonely post. She has escorted several thousand babies into the world and has opened a children's home for unwanted babies and orphans.

In support and sponsorship, the medical center at Vellore brings East and West together in one of this generation's most inspiring causes. Young women have gone out from the institution as licensed medical practitioners, to engage in a ministry of healing throughout India where, as one visitor said, "religion and science move forward together."

Vellore's Medical College for Women was in its twenty-fifth year when a new milestone was reached. No longer would graduates be prepared for the intermediate degree of L.M.P.—licensed medical practitioner. In July, 1942, classes opened at the college to prepare young women for the full university degrees of bachelor of medicine and bachelor of surgery, representing the Indian equivalent of the American M.D. To bring Vellore standards for training and practice to the university level is not only desirable but essential. India's problems in health are so vast that the official preference of the government for the more specialized and complete training is wise and progressive. To provide these advanced courses the college requires a much larger investment in buildings and equipment, additional facilities for hospital practice and research, a larger and more specialized staff, and an adequate endowment. The present annual budget of the college and its hospital is $123,000. Within five years the total will rise to $230,000 a year. Of this amount, $50,000 is to be provided in India and the balance in Great Britain and North America. The present endowment of the Women's College approximates half a million dollars, income from which must be used exclusively for women's work. The enlarged institution should have a greatly increased endowment to insure basic regular income. The Foreign Missions Conference of North America acts as depository for funds received.

Notable additions to the staff have already been made, including the appointment of Dr. Robert G. Cochrane, outstanding British physician and authority on leprosy, as principal of the institution. Now a complete medical center is projected, using the Missionary Medical College for Women as a foundation. A Men's College is included. The center has the unqualified endorsement of leading physicians and of the National Christian Council of India, for this becomes India's only institution offering Christian medical education of university grade. Thirty-four boards and societies in Great Britain, Canada, and the United States join Indian Christians in endorsing and contributing to the All-India Christian Medical College. Their advance gifts made the first steps possible, but only as large resources are obtained promptly is the future of this unique institution secure.

In 1945 at least one million dollars is needed for plant and equipment, plus additional sums to be sought from contributors in Great Britain. Generous gifts are also necessary for the rapidly expanding annual budget of the institution, with its hospitals, surgery, clinics, rural work, and comprehensive health program, all of which will utilize and train more students and serve more patients.

BISHOP AZARIAH OF DORNAKAL

Vethanayahan Samuel Azariah was the first Indian I met when I arrived in Calcutta in 1896, and for fifteen years he was my best friend, Indian or foreign. Since we were both entering Y.M.C.A. work together as young secretaries—I was twenty-five and he some two years younger—we had much in common. Both were adventuring into new experiences in new fields where we were beyond our depths and had to sink or swim. I remember an early conversation between us that was crucial. When I questioned Azariah about our friendship, he replied that he supposed we were as close friends as an Indian and a foreigner could ever be. This seemed to me to imply that he felt some subtle racial barrier between us and that I would be kept at arm's length in a sort of second-class friendship. When I showed that his attitude struck me like a blow, he was amazed that any foreigner would want a complete and equal friendship with an Indian.

Emerson said, "A friend is a person with whom I may be sincere." From that frank moment Azariah and I became close and equal friends, with all that such a friendship could imply. Any results I may have had in my work in India I owe first to the fact that I had such a friend as he among the people with whom I wished to identify myself. I found at once that I was, like every other foreigner, making all sorts of mistakes in my dealings with Indians in general, and especially with my servants and with my fellow workers; and these mistakes Azariah sympathetically but unsparingly corrected. When I first arrived in India, an old veteran missionary, who held the power of the purse over his poorly paid workers, advised me never to shake hands with a "native," for he thought that the foreigner must keep the Indian in his place. If such advice were followed, it would ruin the life and the meager influence of any young missionary, for he would never accomplish much as long as he remained a "foreigner."

Azariah was helping me far more than I could help him, though there were some things that the West could contribute that were of priceless value to him. As I shared with him the methods of historical criticism that I had learned from my professors, such as William Rainey Harper and President McGiffert, he started on a course of lifelong reading and study that enabled him later to train the workers in his great diocese as modern men who could cope with the modern world. Azariah avidly formed the habit of good reading, of utilizing every precious moment of time, even on trains and trams, and the efficient habits of Western organization which would enable him to organize and administer as a bishop the greatest mission field in India.

As a student worker I began traveling through the colleges of India speaking chiefly to Hindu and Mohammedan students in English, but I could learn of no one in India at the time who was successfully and consistently winning student converts from among high-caste Hindus or Moslems. Even when I concentrated for a time upon the most promising Christian college in all India, I found that I was breaking my head and my heart against a stone wall. As the Apostle Paul turned finally from the Jews, who had hardened their hearts, to the openhearted Gentiles, so I began to hear a clear call to turn to the Indian masses. But neither I nor any of the forty-six hundred Protestant missionaries in India at the time could reach singlehanded the nearly four hundred million people of India across the gulfs of race, language, religion, caste, custom, and prejudice, which separated us from them. However, if the million and a half Protestant Christians of India could be awakened and aroused to undertake a crusade for the evangelization and Christianization of their own country, nothing should be impossible. The awakening of the Indian Church and the arousing of Christian student leaders in the Indian colleges seemed the key to the whole situation, and that would require a fluent use of the vernacular. I finally decided, instead of working in English for a few high-caste students, to acquire the Tamil language, which would give access to the largest number of Indian Christians; and so I immersed myself in that vernacular. I lived in Indian homes and, after taking charge of a regular mission station and, temporarily, of a theological school, I toured the country preaching with Indian fellow workers, where I did not see a white man from one month's end to another.

Azariah now became my fellow worker, both in the vernacular and in English, among the churches and the colleges, in what we believed was nothing less than a crusade for the evangelization of the world. Our objective was both individual and social. Seeking to work with all Christian forces as one team, we hoped to raise up Indian leaders for the Christianization of their own land, and ultimately to change the whole social order, building a new India as part of a new world. If we were fellow workers with God, if the coming of the Kingdom of God was God's purpose, if infinite spiritual resources were available for the doing of his will, then no spiritual end was impossible.

As Azariah and I traveled together and visited the scenes of his boyhood I learned of his early life and background. Azariah's father was a pastor in the Tinnevelly field of the evangelical Anglican Church Missionary Society; and his mother, who had a profound influence on his life, was an earnest Christian of Spartan character. His Christian home and his Christian teachers were the chief forces in the molding of his character. He had been a pupil of Dr. William Miller, principal of the Madras Christian College, who had deeply influenced him and thousands of other students all over India. Azariah's family, belonging to the Nadar, or Shanar, caste, was so humble that his ancestors had been refused access to the temples. Sturdy and powerful tree climbers, his ancestors had eagerly seized upon the privilege of missionary or government education, and they became the most virile and rapidly rising caste in India. When the jealous Brahmans saw them capturing competitive examinations and government offices, and entering the Hindu temples, a test case was brought to the high court; and they were ruled to be outcastes who must be excluded from the right of Hindu temple worship. But they never belonged to the forty to sixty million untouchables.

I visited Azariah's home church, far from any railway. Here I found three hundred earnest Christians coming out every morning at five o'clock for a service of worship before going to their work in the fields. Four miles away, where Azariah attended high school in Megnanapuram—"The Town of True Wisdom"—I found the site of the ancient devil temple and the stone once reeking with the blood of beasts sacrificed to the demons, where his ancestors had worshiped. When the last man in that community became a Christian, the men of Megnanapuram with their own hands tore down this devil temple and erected a fine stone church seating three thousand Christians. The threshold of the church, over which the new Christian community entered to worship the God and Father of Jesus Christ, was the old altar stone of the former pagan shrine. As in the early apostolic centuries, Christianity appears in India and China today as a virile new religion challenging the paganism, pantheism, polytheism, and idolatry of the old order, which is now beginning to crumble.

When in 1732 the poor, persecuted Moravian community of six hundred souls at Herrnhut began their first missionary work, they little dreamed what it would mean for John Wesley, for the evangelical revival, and for world-wide missions. When the shoemaker at Hackleton hung out his sign, "Second-Hand Shoes Bought and Sold," he could little know of the significance of William Carey for India and for all future Protestant missions. Similarly the young men of India, especially Azariah and K. T. Paul, could not possibly know to what an extent they were making history in the founding of the first indigenous missionary movement in India. In 1899 the Jaffna Student's Foreign Missionary Society was organized, and a young teacher, J. K. Sinnatamby, was sent to India as the first "foreign" missionary from North Ceylon.

When Azariah and I, who were now fellow Tamil evangelists, were visiting Jaffna in 1902, Azariah was deeply impressed by the heroic missionary enterprise of little Jaffna. In Azariah's own mission in India there were fifty-four thousand relatively prosperous and educated Christians in the churches of Tinnevelly, who had been signally uplifted by the gospel in every way, but who were doing practically nothing for the evangelization of their country. One night after a meeting in Jaffna, Azariah went out under the palm trees along the seashore to pray; and he shed bitter tears to think of his own great churches unawakened. When he returned to India, he gathered together the young men of the churches and they organized the Indian Missionary Society of Tinnevelly on February 12, 1903, at Palamcottah. The object of this society was: "To develop by an indigenous organization the missionary spirit of the native Church in order to spread the Gospel in India and other lands." [8] In April, 1904, Samuel Pakkianadhan left the prosperous Tamil churches of Tinnevelly to work in the society's newly chosen field among the poorest outcastes in the Telugu country, at Dornakal, in the Hyderabad State.

[8] The whole history of the Indian indigenous missionary movement has been written with painstaking care by Donald F. Ebright under the title *The National Missionary Society of India, 1905-1942*, Ph.D. thesis, 1944; and I am indebted to this history in this portion of the narrative.

After intensive study of the government of India census of 1901, Azariah published his findings, showing that a hundred million people in India were utterly beyond the reach of any existing Christian agency. It was found by correspondence with the principal mission boards in Britain and America that they could not possibly open new missions to reach these unevangelized portions of India. Azariah and the young Indian leaders next corresponded with a hundred representative missionaries and Indian Christians to ask their opinion regarding the founding of an interdenominational national missionary society, with Indian men, Indian money, and Indian management, to undertake the evangelization of these unoccupied fields. The response was so enthusiastic that they decided to call together a score of young Indian leaders to meet at Serampore, where Carey began his work. "A Call to Indian Christians" was circulated throughout the Christian community, signed by Raja Sir Harnam Singh, Kali Charan Banerji, and Professor Samuel Satthianathan, the three outstanding leaders of the Christian community. None of these prominent leaders, however, but only the younger men, were present at the organization of the first two missionary societies.

Seventeen delegates, speaking eight languages and representing every part of India, Burma, and Ceylon, assembled at historic Serampore College. After an all-day discussion on Christmas Day, Professor Sirajuddin of Lahore moved the resolution to form the National Missionary Society, seconded by K. T. Paul of Madras, and supported by J. R.—later Bishop—Chitambar, of Lucknow. V. S. Azariah was chosen as general secretary; Raja Sir Harnam Singh, president; K. T. Paul, treasurer and organizing secretary for the South. English was necessarily chosen as the conference language, although at the close all delegates recited John 3:16 and sang the doxology in their own vernaculars.

The delegates finally agreed upon the following statement:

In Carey's historic library at Serampore on December 25, 1905, with delegates present from each province of India, Burma, and

144

Ceylon, there was organized the National Missionary Society of India. Uniting as it does the Christians of all churches and of all provinces into one society for the evangelization of India and adjacent lands, its organization marks a new era in the history of India. It is remarkable that just 200 years since Ziegenbalg came to India as the first Protestant missionary, exactly 100 years since Samuel J. Mills at Williamstown, Massachusetts, with his fellow students at the haystack prayer-meeting began the great missionary movement in America, and 100 years since the saintly Henry Martyn landed in India, the Christians of this land have now united in the first national, indigenous missionary movement of its kind ever organized in India. While the sessions of the conference were held in the great library where William Carey labored, the constitution of the new society was adopted in the old pagoda where Henry Martyn worked and prayed for the evangelization of this land. With Indian men, Indian money, and Indian management, the society is controlled by a central executive committee and a national council with representatives from each presidency. Founding no new denomination, but preserving the strongest loyalty to the churches, soliciting no funds outside of India, but laying the burden of India's evangelization upon her own sons, we believe the society is organized on a sound and safe basis. Only after months of careful planning and after securing the approval of hundreds of representative Indians and European missionaries in every part of the Empire was this important step taken.

Azariah was now the general secretary of both of the new indigenous missionary societies. In one sense, the whole missionary movement in India was an outgrowth of the Student Volunteer Movement of the West. Characteristically, it advocated the evangelization of unoccupied fields "in this generation." As the secretary of both movements, Azariah traveled across the country preaching this new missionary crusade, with all India for his pulpit, calling on the students to go as workers and the churches to give their offerings for their own country. Two men, Azariah and K. T. Paul, were to become the leaders of two very different movements—the National Missionary Society and the Indian Missionary Society of Tinnevelly. Azariah was the evangelist, the churchman, the future saintly bishop who was to lead and mold the most successful and spiritual Christian mass movement in India under the Tinnevelly mission in Dornakal, Hyderabad. K. T. Paul was the statesman, more gifted in practical wisdom than any man I ever knew in all Asia. He was later to lead the National Missionary Society in the Indianization and indigenization of Christianity, in a truly Oriental and nationalist Christian movement.

The National Missionary Society is a demonstration of cooperation and church unity in action which looks toward ultimate church union. Most of the leaders do not believe that any isolated Western denomination will be the basis of the future church of India. The leaders are increasingly Oriental, not quite so orthodox as many Western missionaries, but more modern. They are more tolerant, they have a deeper appreciation of the spiritual values in the indigenous religions, but some of them seem to have a less vivid realization of the undoubted evils in Hinduism, such as idolatry and caste, than had Bishop Azariah—or than the founders of the movement had four decades ago. The National Missionary Society and the Tinnevelly Missionary Society, with its most successful and spiritual mass movement, may represent two wings of the advancing Indian Church, both of which, however, are agreed upon the need of union among the churches.

Thus far, we have followed the development of the National Missionary Society, of which Azariah was the leading spirit and first general secretary. We must now return to the earlier Tinnevelly Missionary Society, which he organized in 1903, which sent out Reverend Samuel Pakkianadhan as its first missionary to the then unknown village of Dornakal, Hyderabad, in 1904. As Azariah preached this missionary crusade in the colleges and churches, challenging the students to give their lives, and Christians to give themselves and their sacrificial offerings, he described the depths of need of a hundred million of their Indian fellow countrymen, largely outcastes and primitive animists, sunk in idolatry, devil worship, carrion-eating, drunkenness, and robbery. He naturally became more and more possessed by the missionary spirit, until at last he felt called to go himself to the neediest field he knew. Many felt it would be disastrous to lose this most useful leader in all India, the general secretary of the two great indigenous missionary societies, who seemed to be irreplaceable. It would be like Mott and Speer both going to Africa if they were the only board secretaries in America and leaving their work in the American colleges and churches without adequate leadership. When I visited Dornakal, the outcastes of Hyderabad seemed to me so debased, so sunken almost in savagery, the men such drunkards and thieves and the women so stupid, that no great fruitage, no adequate results could be expected in our lifetime. I did all I could to dissuade Azariah; but I might as well have argued with William Carey, or Judson, or Morrison against going to the mission field, for nothing could now stop him.

In 1909, four years after launching the National Missionary Society, Azariah turned over the general secretaryship to K. T. Paul and went as a humble worker to the wilds of Dornakal in Hyderabad under the Tinnevelly Missionary Society. I felt that he was falling into the ground to die and that I would never see him again. The poverty of the people, who were the lowest outcastes, struggling to live on four or five cents a day, was abysmal. I watched Azariah begin his work in Dornakal, and one day saw him buying a few acres of land for an industrial school. The price of the land was fifty cents an acre, which by a strange coincidence was the price Booker Washington paid for the wasteland for his industrial school at Tuskegee. A few miles away from Azariah's field, in British India, land was costly, but the former Nizam government of the Indian state of Hyderabad was so sunk in corruption at the time that land was of little value. The people feared the grafting agents of the Nizam, who deprived them of much of their crop, more than they feared the local robbers.[9] To live and perhaps to die among these poorest of the poor in this mission in Hyderabad was a heroic sacrifice for Azariah to make, for the people were so

---

[9] The present Nizam of Hyderabad is more friendly to Christians than his father was. He writes a poem on Christ every year before Christmas, which is a very striking thing for the Moslem ruler of a prevailingly Hindu Indian state.

degraded that I did not expect to see any appreciable results in his lifetime. I said good-by to him fearing I would never see him again. When I did next see him, however, in 1912, he was being consecrated as the first Indian Anglican bishop by a group of English bishops. They were graduates of Oxford and Cambridge, with a thousand years of Christian civilization and culture behind them, while behind Azariah was the abyss of the past. As the Bishop of Dornakal he was long the strongest and most effective bishop in all India.

Years later, when I went back to visit Azariah in Dornakal, my weak faith was utterly rebuked. Here where I had expected to see but little fruit in our lifetime I found in Bishop Azariah's diocese a growing Christian community—which today numbers nearly two hundred fifty thousand souls, with several thousand more under instruction. There have been 9,000 baptisms during the past year. With Uganda this is now the largest mission field in the world. Yet forty short years ago it seemed the most discouraging and hopeless mission field I had ever seen. It is a matter of profound thankfulness to God that the leader of the most successful and deeply spiritual mass movement in all India was not an American or British foreign missionary but a humble and able Indian Christian, Bishop Azariah. Whole communities have been lifted above their former drunkenness, devil worship, carrion-eating, and ignorance. Their children are now in schools and they meet in intelligent worshiping congregations on Sundays. But, more remarkable, most of the new converts, with an attendance of some seventy thousand in their scattered churches, gather every night in the week for the study of the New Testament in order to conform their lives to the way of Christ. So great has been the moral transformation of these people that over ten thousand from the higher and middle castes, convinced of the moral superiority of the Christian way of life, have joined the church within the diocese. Before such a community, the Apostle Paul might well say, as he did to the Romans: "I am not ashamed of the gospel of Christ." It is able to transform each life and to uplift the whole of society.

I saw among the converts in Dornakal a former robber, Lakshikadu. He was not an outcaste but a Yerukala, proud of his caste. At the age of sixteen he was taken with a gang of robbers until he became a daring and noted dacoit. He described to me personally his whole former technique of robbery. He found the adventure exciting as a youth, but he spent the plunder upon drink and was caught and imprisoned for six months. His wife begged him to go to the holy men, as she called them, of Bishop Azariah's mission in Dornakal to find deliverance from his bondage. When he found that he would have to give up his life of robbery, he realized that he had no other trade or means of livelihood; but when he heard that Jesus, his Saviour, had worked as a carpenter, he eagerly learned that trade. He took the baptismal name of Thomas and his wife the name Prema, meaning "love." Even after three years, he would not take the communion with outcaste converts; but now Thomas has no caste prejudice or spirit of segregation left in his heart. He supports his family, working six days a week as a carpenter; and on the seventh day he goes out to tell the good news of the Kingdom of God to his former fellow robbers and to the outcastes, working without salary and giving his message without price. He has won two small congregations of new converts, and he shepherds these flocks on Sunday while his wife teaches the school—which Thomas is not able to do for lack of early education. At the other end of the social scale, two of the early Indian missionaries under Bishop Azariah were Brahman converts, who worked without salary and received only their food and clothing. Personal transformation of the converts and social change in the community seem equally evident in this work.

Azariah was neither a foreigner nor a bigot forcing his religion down the throats of an unwilling people. His own ancestors for a thousand years had themselves been devil worshipers excluded from Hindu temples. He knew in his own experience and in that of thousands of enlightened, educated, progressive Christians in South India, that this message of the Kingdom of God for these multitudes who were beneath the dregs of Hinduism was their only possible way of uplift—spiritual, intellectual, economic, or social. It meant for them a truly Christian civilization as against their recent condition bordering upon savagery, under the grossest forms of paganism.

When I asked Azariah the secret of the spiritual power in this community, which had overcome the most stubborn human and seemingly superhuman obstacles, he attributed their success to several things. He said that all the new converts and, as far as possible, all members of the church either personally observed a daily quiet time of Bible study and prayer or, if their educational level was not yet up to this, they met every evening in the churches to study the New Testament and pray that their lives might be not nominally but truly Christian. Nearly a hundred thousand meet each evening and some twenty thousand each morning for such services. Again, each Christian was taught that he was a living witness and a voluntary worker, and no man was paid as a professional evangelist to preach the gospel, which was as free as in apostolic times. And finally, Azariah felt that the weekly observance of the Communion of the Lord's Supper was a powerful means of grace. All were thus taught the central principle of sacrifice in Christianity, that each was to take up his cross and follow Christ, and each for himself was "to feed on him in his heart by faith with thanksgiving."

The whole movement in Dornakal was spiritual, yet it involved a complete social transformation of life. It was a continuation of the same spiritual struggle which Paul had with the gross paganisms of his day, and it was waged by the same spiritual weapons against more subtle enemies than flesh and blood. In 1897, even before the organization of the National Missionary Society, an annual day of prayer was called for all India; and this was widely observed by the most spiritual Indian Christians and missionaries. At least once each year Azariah and I, either together or more often alone, spent a whole night in prayer for India. There was no vain repetition and nothing artificial about this very real spiritual struggle, for ours was a crusade infinitely more difficult than a military crusade for the possession of an empty tomb. We lived by prayer, we believed in prayer, we were convinced that prayer had an answer (I John 5:14, 15), and we had constant evidence of its reality.

I had once bought a little land for Azariah's industrial school for fifty cents an acre, but for some years I had been sending him nothing for his work. Then one day I suddenly felt called on to scrape together all I could and to send him one thousand dollars. When I did this, I had quite forgotten that I had once financially helped in a very small way Azariah's neighboring American Methodist missionary in Hyderabad. Quite unknown to me this young missionary had come to the end of his rope. This relatively isolated foreigner could not seem to succeed in getting the same spiritual results as the great Indian bishop and his fellow workers next door. Moreover, here were two competing denominations in a field which could be more effectively served by one united church. Finally the Hyderabad Annual Conference decided to concentrate their efforts elsewhere. They offered to leave the whole field to the Anglicans under Indian leadership, turning over all their property—residence, churches, and schools—if the debt upon them could be paid. This involved a few thousand dollars, with the immediate need of one thousand dollars in cash. Azariah said to his wife, "We will pray about this tonight, and tomorrow I will write to Sherwood Eddy asking if he can secure the money for us. This opportunity of one united church for this whole region must not be missed." In the morning, before he could write, my letter arrived containing a draft for a thousand dollars, postmarked just a month before.

The work in Dornakal and Hyderabad was practical, involving men, money, and organization; but the central issue and core of it was always spiritual. The matter of the division of a hundred Protestant sects was one which growingly troubled many of us, and we were burdened with the prayer that we might all be one. Azariah was an Anglican and I was a Congregationalist who had been only too eager to bury the already attenuated denominationalism, of which I was never proud, in the larger unity of the United Church of South India, which included the Congregational, Presbyterian, Reformed, the Established and Free churches of Scotland, and the Basel Reformed churches in one. But why should these two great bodies, the Anglican and the newly formed United Church, and the third great Methodist Church, be separated? If there was indeed but one Lord, one faith, and one baptism, why could we not have one Lord's table and recognize our unity and final union in one body of Christ?

Both before and after the Edinburgh Conference of 1910 Azariah and I had begun to pray about this, and we were soon joined by the saintly Bishop of Madras, Henry Whitehead, brother of the philosopher A. N. Whitehead. We three were willing to do anything on God's earth to end our unhappy and costly divisions, which prevented us from praying and working as one and from presenting a united front to the almost insuperable obstacles which confronted us. A group of young Indian leaders, especially pastors and teachers from the three bodies mentioned above, similar to the group which had formed the National Missionary Society, met in Tranquebar to confer and pray regarding such a union. Soon the South India scheme for union was launched and brought before the churches concerned. It met with the approval of the Lambeth Conference of Anglican Bishops, and is still before the churches of the three bodies in India which are considering the union. Such a union requires time and must be a normal and healthy spiritual growth; but, whatever the delay, it begins to look as if the bridging of the gulfs that have separated the Episcopal and non-Episcopal churches since the Reformation might first of all be realized either in India, or in China, or in some other mission field. This would be a worthy product of the whole great missionary enterprise.

Bishop Azariah contrasted the growth of the work in his diocese in twenty-five years, from 1919, when the whole Anglican Church in the Telugu country was placed under the jurisdiction of the Dornakal diocese:

	1919	1943
Total Christian community	77,000	230,000
Number preparing for baptism	29,000	33,000
Baptized	57,000	192,000
Communicants	16,100	57,000
Clergy, European missionaries	72	177
Lay workers	710	1,736
People's contributions (in rupees—about 37c each)	40,000	104,000
Baptisms	.....	8,300

During the annual "week of witness" 34,400 men and women went out as voluntary evangelists, visiting over 3,000 villages and enrolling 7,250 inquirers. Of the Christians mentioned above, 9,000 are from the caste communities while nine tenths are drawn from the outcastes. The census commissioner admitted to Bishop Azariah that tribal Christians were included under the tribal groups but were not added to the Christian community. This would indicate that there are now many more in the Christian community than the 230,000 reported.

Bishop Azariah died January 2, 1945. He is significant not only as an individual and as the first Anglican Indian bishop but also as a symbol and a pathfinder. He first realized the full implications of the missionary crusade for the Indian Church and, with his successors in the National Missionary Society, kindled the missionary fire among the leaders of the Indian Church all over India. He led in the movement for church union of the divided sects in India; and at the time of his death he thought that this union would probably be realized within three years, though two of the councils in the London Mission area of South India might for a time hold aloof. He was probably the most successful and deeply spiritual leader of the mass movement in India, a movement which has not only gathered in hundreds of thousands of the outcastes but is now beginning to gather in tens of thousands of the middle castes in India. This account of Bishop Azariah's work may fittingly be closed by a brief account of the transformation of one of the lowest outcastes, the Reverend V. Santiago, who was Azariah's close friend, working with him for church union and for indigenous missionary evangelism.

A generation ago V. Santiago was a little outcaste Pariah boy playing in the streets. The dogs might enter the Brahman street but not he; the sacred cow was welcome in the Hindu temple, but there was no room for the polluted outcaste, dwelling apart in filth and ignorance and superstition. There were 2,378 principal castes in India at the time—1901. In the Hindu *Laws of Manu:*

The Brahman is by right the lord of this whole creation. . . . Whatever exists in the world is the property of the Brahman. . . . The dwellings [of outcastes] shall be outside the village . . . and their wealth shall be dogs and donkeys. Their dress shall be the garments of the dead, they shall eat their food from broken dishes. . . . A man who fulfills a religious duty, shall not seek intercourse with them.

But an elderly American made it possible for this outcaste boy to go to school. Twenty dollars a year sent him to the mission high school, and a somewhat larger sum helped him to work his way through college. After serving as a teacher in the theological school, he became pastor at Batlagundu, South India, with the care of some twenty schools and over a thousand Christians.

When the non-Christians could not find an honest man to be the mayor, or chief official, of the town, the Hindus and Mohammedans sent a written petition to the government that pastor Santiago should be made mayor. He was the first low-caste man ever permitted to walk down the Brahman street, or invited to sit in the Brahman homes as a beloved and honored guest. When the Madura Mission of the American Board placed its work under the charge of a district conference, composed of ten missionaries and fifteen representative Indians, he was elected as a member, and finally became the chairman. When all the Presbyterian, Congregational, and Reformed Christians from the missions of America, England, and Scotland joined in the United Church of South India, with one hundred and fifty

thousand members, Santiago was chosen its able moderator.
I watched this man go through stirring scenes and win
through to great spiritual victories. He was a glorious character,
sunny, attractive, lovable; an earnest evangelist; a spiritual
pastor; and a wise leader of the Indian Church. When I met the
man in America who paid his school fees of twelve dollars a
year, and the veteran missionary who educated him, I almost
envied their investment in the leadership that was to build
up the new India. Just as one could not tell the story of the
Apostle Paul and omit Timothy, or Titus, or the Roman
Church of Paul's day, so we cannot tell the story of Azariah and
omit Santiago, or Thomas, the converted robber, or K. T. Paul,
Azariah's successor, or the indigenous missionary movement, or
the mass movements of the Indian Church. For Azariah was
both a pathfinder and a crusader.

BISHOP ABRAHAM OF TRAVANCORE

Bishop Abraham was born at Kalloopara, Tiruvalla, November 2, 1881, into a Syrian Jacobite family. He was educated in
the Church Missionary Society College at Kottayam, in Trichinopoly, and the Madras Christian College. He experienced
his first spiritual awakening in a meeting conducted by the
Reverend Thomas Walker in 1894, and he was challenged regarding his life work to devote himself to his ancient Syrian
Church and to India while a student in Trichinopoly in 1905.

Abraham was just a boy when first I saw him in that meeting
in the High-Church Anglican college in Trichinopoly, South
India. He is now a white-haired bishop of the ancient Syrian
Church in Travancore. In that meeting on a hot night in 1905
I saw before me a score of boys from the Syrian Church who
seemed to me to be professing a Christianity they were not practicing. I fear I was blunt and tactless when I spoke to those
Syrian lads from Travancore, as I said: "Boys, you claim that
your church was founded here in India by the Apostle Thomas
nineteen centuries ago. Whether it was or not, in any case your
church has been spiritually asleep for a thousand years. The
impoverished masses in your country are sunk in idolatry, su-

perstition, and ignorance. Many of you are cramming to get your degrees, to rush out into life and make money while you leave your church and country in bitter need. Will none of you dare to take up the cross of Christ and follow him for the awakening of the Syrian Church and the evangelization of your own country?"

The meeting ended apparently in failure. But Abraham told me afterward that out under the stars he paced up and down and could not sleep. As he wrestled with himself, he said: "It is true. Our church is asleep, our country is in desperate need, and I am going out to make money and live for my own selfish ambition." He told me that for days, for weeks, he fought his battle, until finally he yielded his life for the service of his own people—though I heard nothing of him for a decade.

Abraham took his theological education in Wycliffe College, Toronto, beginning in 1912, and there took his M.A. and B.D. degrees. During this period, he one night crossed the Canadian border and came to Buffalo to attend a conference with a group of Canadian students. The Canadians registered at an American hotel, but as soon as Abraham's darker face appeared the clerk said the hotel was "full." In protest, the Canadian students left in a body and went to another hotel, where an Indian could be received. But Abraham could not sleep. He was humiliated and lacerated in spirit by the indignity. Then he remembered the outcastes of India who had long been excluded by his proud, prosperous, and respectable Syrian Church. He had never supposed they cared about this exclusion, but if they were men of like passions with himself they suffered from indignities just as he did. Instead of becoming embittered against Americans for their race prejudice, he resolved to return to India and to give his life for the awakening of the people of his ancient church, that they might receive the outcastes, end the practice of segregation, and throw themselves into a missionary crusade for the evangelization of India.

When I next saw Abraham, he had become bishop of the Mar Thoma Syrian Church, consecrated in 1918. He asked me to come down and speak to his people, as Thomas Walker, E.

Stanley Jones, and other missionaries had been doing. Annually the Syrian Christians had gathered in a convention like the Feast of Tabernacles among the Hebrews. Erecting a simple palm-leaf pavilion to shut out the sun, and sitting in the clean white sand of a river bed which is empty during the dry season, some thirty thousand of them gathered in a convention each year. A large flat sounding board over the head of the speaker enabled all to hear, in what was perhaps the largest Christian audience in the world. With deep emotion I saw them receive the outcastes publicly into membership, and heard the reports of these Indian workers who had been sent as missionaries to the lowest and neediest of their own countrymen.

It meant much for Bishop Abraham to attend the World Missionary Conference at Jerusalem in 1927, to tour the Holy Land with deep devotion, and to meet the patriarchs of the ancient Coptic and Greek churches. From 1917 to 1942 Bishop Abraham was almost continuously on tour in his diocese, especially taking charge of the "forward movement," of the evangelistic work of the church, and of its missionary outreach. He was always aided by the Reverend C. P. Phillipose, who was also an outstanding spiritual force in the life of the Syrian community. Abraham's silver jubilee was celebrated at the end of 1942. On the death of the late Metran, Abraham was made metropolitan and enthroned on July 17, 1944.

Tracing briefly the history of the ancient Syrian Church as far as the records permit, we find that it claims a first-century origin, when seven churches were supposed to have been established on the Malabar coast by the Apostle Thomas. According to their tradition, in A.D. 345 there landed here a bishop from Edessa accompanied by presbyters, deacons, and Christians from Jerusalem, Bagdad, and Nineveh. During a severe persecution of Christians in the Persian Empire a large emigration from Syria and Mesopotamia seems to have taken place. This would explain the ecclesiastical dependence of the Syrian Church upon the Patriarchate of Antioch, the Syrian ecclesiastical language and literature, and the Syro-Nestorian type of theology and life during the Middle Ages.

The church came successively under the influence of the Nestorians, the Roman Catholics, and the Jacobite Christians of Antioch, as well as of the Hindu community round about, from whom many abuses and corruptions had permeated the community. At the beginning of the nineteenth century the Syrian Church presented a sorry spectacle. The Bible was not read, nor had it even been translated into the vernacular. Heathen customs and practices had crept in, such as guidance by omens, seeking horoscopes, gifts to Hindu temples, and the accounting of the approach of outcastes as pollution. But a hundred years ago the arrival of English missionaries of the Church Missionary Society led to the translation of the Bible into the vernacular, the education of their youth, and the exposure of the ancient Syrian Church to the currents of modern life. Their leader, Father Abraham, nearly a century ago became the Wycliffe of Malabar and led a movement for reformation. This awakening of the church was followed by a high tide of spiritual revival. Now, a century after their indigenous reformation, these Mar Thoma Syrian Christians are a purified remnant with a community of some two hundred thousand Christians divided into 250 parishes.

As the result of the litigation launched by the reactionary section of the church from 1837 to 1847 against the reforms of the saintly Abraham Malpan, a serious division took place between the reformers and the orthodox. This culminated in a lawsuit that was finally decided in favor of the orthodox party in 1889. The reformed Mar Thoma Church was deprived of most of its property, just as the Free Church of Scotland had been. In 1900, largely through the influence of the Reverend Thomas Walker and other evangelicals of the Church Missionary Society, the Mar Thoma Evangelistic Association was organized, with its remarkable annual convention at Maramannu. The church has experienced a great spiritual awakening that has resulted in new ventures in evangelism, in missionary extension, and in the social uplift of the depressed classes. English and Malayalam schools were started, the prayer book was revised, and Sunday school work was reorganized. Since 1915 Bishop

Abraham has been the inspirer and leader of all these movements. He has been their "apostle to the Gentiles" in leading the Syrians to recover their mission to the outcastes and to men of all classes. He gathered about him a band of gifted, able college graduates who gave up all for the sake of the church and the Kingdom of God, and threw themselves wholeheartedly into the work under his leadership.

The Mar Thoma Church, and to some extent the Jacobite Church, is now providing leaders in education, medicine, and other Christian work all over India. Many headmasters and others in positions of leadership in mission and church institutions throughout the country are Syrian Christians, and these are also found in leading government positions. Because of the deep spiritual life of its workers, the Mar Thoma Church is exercising an influence throughout India out of all proportion to its size. It entirely supports a mission field in South Kanara in connection with the National Missionary Society, and its evangelistic association has over two hundred workers laboring in five fields and has won several thousand converts. God was moving as truly in the lives of Bishop Azariah and Bishop Abraham as in that of St. Augustine in his little bishopric in Hippo in North Africa in the fifth century, when the Roman Empire was being Christianized as India is today.

The Reverend H. A. Popley of Erode, South India, furnishes the latest statistics for the Mar Thoma Syrian Church, as follows:

Total Christian community	200,000
Number of churches	280
Number of bishops	3
Number of clergymen	133
Total number of converts up to 1943	10,000
Number of converts in the year 1943	360
Congregations of new converts	90
Sunday school scholars	50,000
Voluntary teachers	4,500
Dispensaries maintained by the church	3
Theological seminaries and training schools	5

In a recent letter containing a report of the work of the awakening of this ancient church, Bishop Abraham writes:

The ashrams, or missionary fellowship homes, have been a new feature for the development of the work. Realizing that the rank and file of church members have not fully awakened to the need of missionary work, a few devoted servants have gone to different centers in India to start ashrams as centers of evangelistic activity for the districts around. Five such have come into existence in recent times. The Christu-Mitra—"Friends of Christ"—Ashram at Ankola in North Canara, south of Bombay, where the Reverends P. J. Thomas, B.A., B.D., Philip Oommen, B.A., and Mr. P. John Thomas, B.A., with three women from the women's branch of the ashram, has later come into existence. All these ashrams have been started on "faith lines." It is wonderful how a Roman Catholic gentleman, a retired government doctor, alive to the good work these friends were doing, made a handsome present of two plots of land with two bungalows on them and a few thousand rupees for the uplift, education, and spiritual help of the Agyars, an illiterate caste which had for generations been among the suppressed classes in India.

Quite recently a few of our graduates from the Serampore University got a vision of service, and they have already gone and settled at Sigora in Central India. At first the people of the place were very hostile and would not allow them even to rent any of their country sheds for habitation. In spite of the natives' hostility, these men, after learning the new language, began to teach their children and help their sick. They are now slowly winning their way into the hearts of the people and giving them the gospel message. Their immediate need is a plot of land on which they can build a small fellowship house, a school, a small dispensary, and a chapel. And there is the Perambavoor Ashram, in Travancore itself. It is a wonder how in an area backward in point of education, a band of young graduates, without any money in hand, were led to open a high school outstanding in efficiency and character training. As a result young men flock to it even from distant places. The teachers, receiving just enough for their daily bread, live with the students night and day, teaching, guiding, and helping them in every possible way. The women's ashram under the Sevika Sangam at Tiruvalla has four or five sisters who work among the non-Christians and help the Christian women in their missionary activities.

All of these have come into existence as a challenge to the Mar Thoma Church and perhaps to other Christian denominations in the state as well, commanding the appreciation of the public, who, though slowly, are beginning to realize the great possibilities before them if only they will unloose their purse strings and offer their hearty prayers to God for the evangelization of their countrymen. We are praying earnestly for a similar fellowship home to be started in South Travancore, where about 2,500 have already come into the church during the last four years.

Side by side with these fellowship groups are our "volunteer workers"—men and women—about a hundred, who, leaving their own families at home to look after themselves, have gone to different parts of the Malayalam country in order steadily to carry on evangelistic work by means of house visits, personal interviews, night schools, magic lantern lectures, and the like. It is as a result of such steady, unselfish labors that hundreds are coming in, month after month. The committee of the Evangelistic Association, which met last week, decided to take over charge of another congregation of over a hundred people in South Travancore. In Kottarakara district I myself have baptized, on two occasions, over a hundred and fifty. I am anxious that the large number of non-Christians should be approached regularly and won over to Christ.

On the seacoast field the work is progressing equally well. There have been some converts from the middle class, Ezhavas and Arayas. These baptisms raised a protest, and a persecution was launched against the converts. Beyond human calculation, the Spirit of God is working, awakening the ancient Mar Thoma Church to its missionary vocation and blessing it with many souls won for the Lord. I am sure you will join with us in thanking God for his mercy in awakening us to the great missionary call.

K. T. PAUL, INDIAN STATESMAN

Kanakarayan Tiruselvam Paul (1876-1930) was the first Christian statesman that India produced. He lived during the creative period of India's emancipation and took a leading part in that movement. The year of his birth, 1876, was marked by the organization of the Indian Association, the first indigenous political movement, which in 1883 became the National Congress. This voiced the growing demand of the educated classes for representative government, and their increasing resentment at what they regarded as the arrogance and domineering of the foreign bureaucracy. With the fervid approval of K. T. Paul and the students, the Indian National Congress by 1904 was demanding *swaraj,* or self-government; and by the time Paul became a man the common people were part of the revolution. K. T. Paul saw that India had surged forward, not only under the sympathetic reforms of a great viceroy like Lord Ripon, but even faster under the arrogant contempt of the last great autocratic viceroy, Lord Curzon. Paul early became a follower of the great nationalist Gokhale, and also a friend of Gandhi on his return from South Africa. While Paul favored dominion status within the Empire in his able book *The British Connection with India,* he regarded foreign rule by a self-proclaimed superior race as a curse.

I used to visit K. T. Paul in his home in Salem, where he was born; and his home life was one of the most beautiful I have ever known in any land. His father had been an able government servant of high character, but had died early, leaving the family in charge of Paul's remarkable Spartan grandmother. She, more than any other, molded his character until he became of age and could assume the oversight of the family estate. In Salem College, Paul took courses in English literature with distinction, winning a government scholarship for graduate study in the Madras Christian College. In Salem he gathered about him a group of men who met in his home, including C. Rajagopalachari, who became prime minister of the Madras government, and on whose cabinet Paul might have served had he lived. In Madras he drew his inspiration from the great principal William Miller, whom he regarded with reverence and affection all his life, indeed as his guru, or venerable teacher, and from a noble group of Scottish professors. Here he joined the college church, then attached to the Presbyterian body. His chief interests at this time were politics, social reform, and Tamil literature, although his religion was the central motivation of each. He next studied law and took a position in the government secretariat. Then he took a course in the teachers' college, passing his examination with the highest rank in the whole presidency. For a time he served as headmaster in the Arcot Mission High School at Punganur, and in 1903 he became history tutor in the Madras Christian College under Principal Miller.

In 1905 K. T. Paul was one of seventeen delegates who assembled at Serampore to found the National Missionary Society of India. Here Azariah, who was a little older, became the general secretary and K. T. Paul was wisely chosen treasurer of the new society. He now began to visit the churches, first of South India and then of the North, to kindle the missionary spirit and increase the sacrificial giving of Indian Christians. In 1906 he became the organizing secretary of the society, traveling all over India founding branches. In 1907 he forfeited the security of a permanent place on the faculty of the Madras Christian College to become joint secretary of the National Missionary Society with Azariah. As traveling organizer he published monthly his *Diary of an Organizing Secretary.* In this job he knew all the hardships of traveling third class, on the bare boards of uncushioned seats. But he carried a song in his heart as Indian Christians gave even their jewelry and prized personal possessions to the new crusade.

On one New Year's Eve, in the stillness of the night, Paul heard his simple boatman in Travancore fervently praying for India's salvation, informing the Almighty of the moving statistics Paul had given of India's need. As simply as a child Paul received this New Year's gift, saying, "The joy that then entered my heart is indescribable." During these early years Paul would sometimes approach the foreign missionary's bungalow with some fear and trembling, uncertain of his reception as a "native." Relationships between foreign missionaries and their Indian workers were then frequently strained, and Azariah delivered at the Edinburgh Convention his loving but much-needed challenge to missionaries to treat their Indian colleagues as equals. In 1909 Azariah had gone as a missionary to Dornakal, and K. T. Paul became the general secretary of the National Missionary Society and editor of its magazine, the *Intelligencer*. In the years that followed, Paul came to know India as a whole, in all phases of its life, as probably no other Indian knew it. From the first he was the moving spirit in the Indianization of the church, which was seeking to develop its own indigenous liturgy and a suitable lyrical order of service. With his organizing genius, Paul visited the National Missionary Society Mission in the Punjab, established the base of its financial support in the churches, and opened up its missions in South and Central India, wherever practicable advocating "ashrama."

Azariah and Paul inaugurated a monthly English journal for the National Missionary Society, *The National Missionary Intelligencer*, which has appeared monthly for forty years, as well as five vernacular missionary journals. Together they began, as board secretaries, to educate the Indian churches on missions. They opened their first mission in the Montgomery district of the Punjab with James Williams as the first missionary. With Azariah, Williams was one of the eleven Indian delegates to the Tokyo conference of the World's Student Christian Federation in 1907, and it was in Tokyo that he offered his services to the new National Missionary Society. A true nationalist patriot, Williams' methods were refreshingly Oriental. With his old school friend and fellow worker Basil Singh and a qualified physician, Dr. Dina Nath, he opened a school and a dispensary. These first Indian missionaries had surrendered more secure and better paid positions under foreigners to give their lives sacrificially for their beloved country. Dr. Dina Nath was so successful in treating ten thousand patients during the year that the government voted a generous grant for the support of the medical work.

The Indian ladies of South Travancore also contributed to the support of a school for outcastes. They began with no Christian community, no house, and no building; but soon they built "Dina Nath's Cathedral" and made it "big enough for

God"—without walls or roof, under the blue arch of heaven. Later they erected their own church buildings. The workers were invited to preach to the crowds at the Islamic melas, or fairs, and developed their own Christian mela, on the Moslem pattern, with its music and drama, its sermons, fellowship, and inspiration. The Christian mela became a "holy week," visited by Christian sadhus reportedly belonging to a Secret Society of Jesus, as India was turning from Occidental to Oriental forms. James Williams was ordained under the bishop of Lahore, and the work was carried on by three missionaries, four helpers, three schools, one dispensary, and one church. Prem Chander, of good family, then joined the staff. He took the vow of poverty, to work without salary as a Christian sadhu. The devoted band got the permission of the society to experiment with the system of voluntary self-extension. They borrowed a principle from Islam and advocated that every Christian should consider himself a missionary. A volunteer youth band of "cross bearers" devoted themselves to evangelistic work. When their formerly barren district, irrigated by a newly built system of canals, blossomed with well-watered green fields, it rapidly increased the population. The National Missionary Society then founded the Christian village of Bethlehem and later other Christian communities, which became known all over India as models of the Christian life. They sought to root Christianity in the soil of the Punjab by creating communities of Christians based upon sound spiritual, economic, and cultural foundations. They formed training schools for village head men, and tried to build their villages on the ancient and rich culture of India, not on a Western pattern. They challenged the social evils of the district to emancipate their people from the slavery of debt, and developed cottage industries and agricultural aids for the poor peasants.

In 1931 the brilliant and gifted Miss Komolini Sircar, B.A., resigned her well-paid and secure post as vice-principal of Kinnaird College to become a humble missionary in Bethlehem, and within a few years it became a transformed village. The Bishop of Lahore wrote: "People in English parishes wonder whether Christian Indians are doing anything to spread the Christian faith. Come with me to Bethlehem, then I will convince you that they are. . . . Here lies what must be eventually the line of development of the future church in India. . . . The National Missionary Society are making their new village worthy of the name it bears."

In 1934 the 850 Bethlehem Christians added a large park and built a beautiful church costing four thousand rupees. Then Miss Sircar and her associates decided to launch forth upon a faith basis and accept no more salary from the National Missionary Society. The money came, however, from unexpected sources, so that they lacked nothing; and Miss Sircar was invited to speak all over India in colleges, churches, ashrams, and conferences, about her work and the National Missionary Society. Bethlehem, founded as a Christian colony with fifty families, soon grew to a community of over a thousand. There are now over three thousand Christians scattered in over ninety-five villages in the district. When the head of the mission organized the Masihi Ashram, he was joined by Sadhu Banerjee; and the May harvest thanksgiving service was conducted by Bishop Banerjee. Five paid Indian workers and thirty volunteers now constitute the mission staff, and the whole work is both Indian and Christian.

The Mar Thoma Syrian Christians of Travancore decided to join the National Missionary Society and open up a "foreign" field in another language area of India. In 1933 Bishop Abraham had become the president of the National Missionary Society. In 1909 the Syrians chose the district of North Kanara in the Bombay Presidency, and four of their most brilliant young men were sent as missionaries, including P. O. Philip, who later became general secretary of the National Missionary Society and then in 1924 was called to the National Indian Christian Council. P. O. Philip has been a frequent contributor to *The Christian Century,* in America, and other journals. The Syrian missionaries had to master three new and difficult languages to reach the people. They journeyed from far Travancore to Western India by "faith" and depended solely on voluntary gifts to supply all their needs. The unpaid religious pattern, common to non-Christian religions in India, has characterized these ancient Syrians. Even their bishops receive no fixed salary. When the Syrian missionaries organized the Christa Mitra Ashram, a Roman Catholic doctor presented his property, with two buildings and seven and a half acres of land, for an outcaste Agyar colony; and an endowment of 16,154 rupees—about $7,000—for educational work. About the same time a Moslem gentleman offered fifty thousand rupees if the National Missionary Society would take over St. Andrews College, Garakpur, in the United Provinces, North India, when the Church Missionary Society was compelled to close it. The National Missionary Society accepted the offer and sent the Reverend E. C. Dewick as principal of their first college.

After Azariah and K. T. Paul had presented the cause of the National Missionary Society to the Lutheran Christians of South India, three different Lutheran bodies requested that an indigenous mission field be opened for them. Finally an all-India Lutheran body to administer the work was organized, and a field in Central India was selected, including the Indian state of Rewah, which was deeply hostile to foreigners. The Reverend S. Gnanabaranam was the twenty-sixth volunteer for the service of the National Missionary Society, going from ancient Tranquebar, where Ziegenbalg had begun work in 1706. He was assisted by a medical worker, Dr. Goswami, a Brahman convert, and by a second medical worker, Dr. Nallathambi, who was willing to serve in an honorary capacity and who made a great name for himself. The missionaries were assisted by a score of workers, with a Christian community numbering eighteen hundred. They also ably occupied fields vacated by German missionaries who had been expatriated during the first World War. For three decades the relations have been most cordial between the National Missionary Society and all the Lutherans, who have been drawn into closer co-operation with each other through its uniting agency.

The National Missionary Society has two ashrams affiliated with it. The Indian doctor S. Jesudasen, while in England for graduate study, won the friendship of a fellow medical student, Dr. E. Forrester Paton, a Scotsman of some wealth. Being dissatisfied with service in a more formal foreign hospital at Poona, the two offered their services to the National Missionary Society, and opened the Christu-Kula—"Family-of-Christ"—Ashram at Tirupattur, North Arcot, in South India, in 1921. Their beautiful buildings at first sight resemble a Hindu temple, but their whole symbolism is Christian. The ashram embodies the idea of the reconciliation of peoples of all groups, castes, and races in one brotherhood. They have made a portion of the Indian desert to blossom as the rose, and the story of their humble Christlike service reads like the record of Jesus in Galilee. The ashram not only serves as a source of power and inspiration for an immeasurable body of earnest Christians in South India but also ministers to hundreds of Hindu patients in its hospital. No menial work is beneath the dignity of any of the members, and the necessity of a paid staff has been eliminated. They report about as many statistics of conversions and of healings as Jesus did—which means none at all—and the truly Oriental National Missionary Society never demands these.

The second most influential Christian ashram of India is also affiliated with the National Missionary Society. The Christa Prema Seva Sangha is situated at Poona, Western India. The acharya (head of the ashram) of the Poona brotherhood is the Reverend John Copley Winslow. The brotherhood adopted the beautiful High-Church eucharistic liturgy of the Syrian Christians of Travancore. Eight gifted young Englishmen followed Winslow to Poona, where they were joined by young Indians. They seek the spirit of the primitive Franciscans combined with that of the Asiatic Indian sadhu. Bishop Azariah was the visiting bishop; the ashram is ecclesiastically Anglican and High-Church. The Indian and non-Indian members are all members of an equal brotherhood.

The National Missionary Society has become a leading factor in the Indianizing of Christianity. It has felt the full pulse of social unrest, especially after the shooting in the Amritsar tragedy of April 13, 1919, in which 379 Indians were killed and

1,200 wounded, in General Dyer's attempt to create "a moral effect from a military point of view," or, in plainer language, to terrorize the Punjab. According to H. A. Popley's very fine *K. T. Paul, Christian Leader*, Calcutta, 1938, from which the facts in this sketch are chiefly taken:

The National Missionary Society successfully holds all-India conferences every three years, as the Student Volunteer Movement has held its quadrennial meetings of spiritual power in America. When the Silver Jubilee of the Society was celebrated in Allahabad in 1930, the Lord Bishop of Lucknow led the procession of more than a score of the missionaries of the National Missionary Society, and J. R. Chitambar, Principal of Lucknow Christian College and the first Indian bishop of the Methodist Episcopal Church in Southern Asia, gave the address.

At the triennial conference of the society in 1935, the National Missionary Society president, Bishop Abraham, led a spiritual retreat. The society now owned its own headquarters building in Royapettah, Madras, after twenty-nine years in rented buildings. Following Azariah and K. T. Paul, two able men had held the post of general secretary, P. O. Philip (1916-24) and Rai Bahadur A. C. Mukerji (1924-36), and they were succeeded by the present secretary, S. J. Duraisamy, N. M. S. Building, Royapettah, Madras. There were four full-time traveling secretaries. There was a growing volume of business of the National Missionary Society Press, and the proposal was considered of sending a National Missionary Society worker to Uganda, East Africa. An able ladies' auxiliary raised a budget of 10,000 rupees of the total National Missionary Society budget of 90,000—from $30,000 to $45,000 according to the rate of exchange. The amounts were small compared to amounts raised in the opulent West, and the Indian Christian community was poor; but a much greater volume of work was done when there were no costly foreign missionaries to support in a tropical country, and when so much of the work of the National Missionary Society was conducted on a voluntary basis. The whole National Missionary Society has been an experiment in the naturalization of Christianity in India by the adoption of indigenous, Oriental methods of work. The society felt it had much to learn from India's ancient religions, which emphasized renunciation and self-sacrifice and which stressed the spiritual character of religion in contrast to the activist and more materialistic West. They wished to combine this Oriental element with the efficiency and scientific spirit of the Occident.

The National Missionary Society has been working in ten major areas in India, always looking toward indigenization and the building of a genuine Indian Christian culture. The society at present operates in some fifty places in eight provinces. Its manifold work has included ashrams, brotherhoods, hospitals, schools, and a college. Its nationalistic Christian leaders are critically examining church architecture, methods of worship, music, discipline, theology, and organization, regarding their society as a laboratory for experimentation. They seek to root Christianity in the life of the East. They believe that the future Church of Christ in India will be the result of a spontaneous Indian movement and will not be imposed from without by Western missionaries, or Western sects. In this indigenous service, they have an enormous advantage over highly organized, highly financed, and sometimes hidebound Western foreign organizations.

In 1912 E. C. Carter invited K. T. Paul to become associate national secretary of the Y.M.C.A. in India with a view of Paul's becoming his successor. The department for which Paul first became responsible was that of Christian rural reconstruction. Paul utilized the studies of the co-operative societies of Denmark and the co-operative credit societies of Germany and applied their methods for the relief of the village people in their bondage of poverty and debt. He used these principles in the social, physical, and religious rural work which he supervised. By 1920 he had 30 rural secretaries of the Y.M.C.A. and 160 rural co-operative or credit societies in South India alone. Under specialists, these were developing poultry breeding, carpet weaving, and co-operative stores, and organizing village sports, educational lectures, Bible classes, and Christian Endeavor societies throughout the villages, to lift them to a higher economic and spiritual level. To reduce the unsupportable burden of debt for the depressed classes, Paul organized the Christian Central Co-operative Bank at Madras to finance depressed class societies, with an able Swiss businessman as the first honorary secretary. By 1931 the paid-up share capital of the bank had reached $57,000, with deposits of over $300,000 and an annual turnover of over $1,000,000. Paul served as president of the board of directors, a position in which he demonstrated his financial and administrative genius.

In 1912, when Dr. Mott visited India to carry out the purpose of Edinburgh to establish representative Christian councils in each province, K. T. Paul was wisely selected as the one Indian to accompany him throughout his tour, for Paul was the organizer, the Mott of India. During the first World War, K. T. Paul's burdens were increased; he served as acting national general secretary of the Y.M.C.A. for India, Burma, and Ceylon. He was the first Indian Christian to become all-India minded. Twenty-five army centers with seventy-two secretaries were opened in India; and seventy-seven secretaries were sent with the Indian armies to France, Egypt, Mesopotamia, and Africa. Paul presided at the all-India secretaries' conference in 1917, with 250 secretaries on his team—Indians, British, Americans, and Swiss.

Paul was always chief; he held his place intellectually, spiritually, and administratively as *primus inter pares*. There were brilliant men on his team like L. P. Larsen and the great scholar J. N. Farquhar, who organized other scholars, Indian and foreign, for a hitherto unheard-of production of literature. But no man among them was Paul's equal as an administrator. He was long editor of the *Young Men of India*, and he hoped to write the life of his beloved Dr. Miller. He organized the School of Physical Education in Madras, with large government grants, for training physical directors for all India. At the same time he supervised a large building program for new Y.M.C.A. buildings.

In 1919 Paul made his first journey to the West, looking

after the war work in Iraq, visiting the battlefields of Flanders and France, and completing his first odyssey to Britain and America. He visited the general assemblies of the Church of Scotland and the United Free Church of Scotland. In making an address at the latter, he was introduced as "the most eminent layman of the Indian Church, and a staunch Presbyterian." He spent a memorable day with his greatly beloved college principal, Dr. William Miller, at the Bridge of Allan; and on a later journey, in 1922, he was with him just before he died. After speaking before a great audience in the assembly hall at Edinburgh he wrote to his friends in India: "I was privileged to pay a humble but most deeply felt tribute to my master, William Miller of Madras. . . . The response of the vast audience was enthusiastic throughout. To me there was but one vision, the solemn and sacramental farewell I had taken that very noon at the bedside of him, the greatness of whose soul I was struggling to analyse."

It was not easy for Paul to speak to Scottish businessmen in Glasgow on India's case for self-government, with Sir Robert Bruce in the chair. In speaking at Oxford, Cambridge, and Edinburgh universities, in answer to the question, "Is there any more a real career for a Britisher in India?" Paul's kindly but frank reply was No, unless men went out with a sense of mission as friends, for the mutual benefit of both countries. India was no longer a field to be imperialistically exploited. Paul spoke in many of the principal cities of England and Scotland. He visited Bristol to pay his tribute at the grave of Raja Ram Mohun Roy, the first great Hindu reformer, founder of the Brahmo Samaj, and loyal friend of Alexander Duff. Paul raised funds for opening a hostel in London for Indian students, at a cost of over a hundred thousand dollars. He reveled in his visits to Italy, Egypt, and Palestine; for he was interested in their history, art, literature, and religion. He drank in the beauty of the pictures of Italy, for his father had brought him up to appreciate Italian art.

Paul visited America for six weeks and placed before the International Committee a chart showing the probable development of the Y.M.C.A. work in India from 1920 to 1924. He was infected by the optimism of the time in America and asked for 324 men on the staff of the Indian National Council and for new buildings to the value of over a million dollars. In New York he joined the Commission on Village Education in India, headed by Principal A. G. Fraser, and made a study of "Education for Life" in the famous Hampton and Tuskegee institutes. In 1924 Paul made a third visit to England and Europe and a second visit to the United States. Important conferences were held with the International Committee, Dr. Mott, former President Taft, and many others.

Paul served as national secretary of the Y.M.C.A. for India almost continuously from 1916 to 1931, when he retired. He, more than any other, was able to consolidate the position of the association as a progressive force in national life and made it an influence second to none in the rebuilding of the young manhood of India. He flew by airplane as a delegate to the Helsingfors conference of the Y.M.C.A., where he was one of the "big five" who chiefly guided the conference. In 1919, when the movement toward union between the Anglicans and the South India United Church was started by the Tranquebar conference of Indian leaders, he became, and was until his death, an influential member of the Committee on Union. In 1925 he was elected for two years as the first layman president of the South India United Church, and to the church he gave the most devoted service of his life.

Paul's manifold activities mentioned above have not included his splendid work in political citizenship—local, provincial, and national. His friend C. Rajagopalachari, prime minister of the Madras Presidency and leader of the non-co-operation movement in South India, who is often called the Tamil Gandhi, said of Paul: "For the first time in the history of Christianity in India, he grafted Indian national aspirations and Indian self-respect on to Christianity." Paul always protested against missionary education which left youth ignorant of the great heritage of India, severing them from their roots. His closing years were spent amid bitter political turmoil, but not even the darkest days could dim his conviction, expressed in his book *The British Connection with India,* that India's place in the Empire was due to the providence of God. He was deeply grieved over Gandhi's first term of six years' imprisonment, and at each of the subsequent confinements of Gandhi, as well as that of Nehru, and those of tens of thousands of Indian patriots. Paul's effort to bring Lord Irwin—now Lord Halifax—and Gandhi together for reconciliation was not successful until after his death, when it resulted in the famous "peace pact."

After seven years of service for the National Missionary Society and eighteen years with the Y.M.C.A., Paul resigned from leadership in both of these organizations that he might devote himself to public service, feeling that he must now "speak out" on behalf of Indian nationalism and self-government. With S. K. Datta, Paul strenuously opposed the dividing of India into helpless fragments by a competitive communalism, under the ancient "divide and rule" strategy of the conqueror. He favored the reservation of certain seats for Christians in the provincial councils in a *general* electorate, not forcing each jealous community to vote only for itself. As one of the last acts of his life he served, by invitation of the viceroy, as a member of the first Round Table Conference in London, in 1930. Here he was a force for reconciliation between Hindus and Moslems, whose conflict was one of the chief factors in keeping India in bondage to Britain. He made a strong presentation of the Indian Christian position before the full conference, as a representative of the Christian religion which had been in India for seventeen hundred years. His health was undermined at the Round Table Conference, and he wrote home: "When forty thousand or more are in prison, can I endure this much for India?" During his last days before his death at his home in Salem he spent much time looking at a picture of Jesus, and he often asked his children to sing the Tamil lyric "I Know That My Redeemer Liveth." He said to his wife: "I have done my duty to my God and my country. I die in peace."

After Paul's death, telegrams came from Geneva, Canada, New York, London, Cairo, Australia, China, and Japan, as well as from the governor of Madras on behalf of the prime minister and secretary of state. The viceroy, Lord Wellingdon, who had known him well for many years, wrote a personal letter to Paul's wife. The word of Gandhi was: "The nearer I came to him the more I respected him. His Christianity appeared to me to be broad and tolerant. It not only did not interfere with his being a thorough nationalist; on the contrary, in his case it seemed to have deepened his nationalism." After two hours with him, Romain Rolland said of Paul: "A great and impartial mind, filled with the thought alike of the East and West, who unites the historical precision of Europe and its science of facts with the science of the soul, a peculiarly Indian science."

Personally, I had the great privilege of being a guest in the homes of Gandhi, Nehru, and Paul. I considered Gandhi the saint, Nehru the patriot, and Paul the wisest man I ever knew in all Asia. He was always the reconciler between factions and conflicting opinions—between British and Indian, Hindu and Moslem, at Jerusalem between the Continentals and Anglo-Saxons, and above all between East and West, rulers and ruled. Utterly different as they were, Azariah was the churchman and Paul the statesman. They supplemented each other. In the infinitely varied interests of the Kingdom of God, no two men mentioned in this book were alike. The mold was broken after each was produced. Each was a triumph of the handiwork of God.

4

PATHFINDERS IN CHINA

CHINA, like India, is a vast subcontinent with a population of some 450 million. China has never had a scientific census, though for many centuries estimates have been made that vary from 270 to 700 million. The Chinese are one of the great root races of the world. The bones of the Peking man are the oldest remains of their kind known upon the planet and are probably half a million years old. Before 3000 B.C. China was the center of neolithic culture. No other ancient people developed such a massive, homogeneous, and continuous civilization. The whole of Western civilization owes a debt to China for her early discoveries, inventions, and arts. Silk culture and weaving, the making of paper and printing, the mariner's compass, the finest porcelain "china" ware, wall paper, lacquer, tea, all the citrus fruits, together with literature, painting, and all the arts, were known in China long before they were discovered or introduced in the more backward countries of Asia and Europe.

Christian missions entered China under the Nestorians and existed there from 635 to about 900. A missionary, A-lo-pen, probably from Syria, introduced Christianity in the year 635, in the reign of the greatest Tang emperor, the tolerant T'ai Tsung. A-lo-pen was received with honor by the emperor, who studied the Nestorian religion and its sacred books and gave orders for its dissemination. Other missionaries arrived, monasteries and churches were built in various cities, and bishops were appointed. The edict of the emperor in 639 declared:

The monk A-lo-pen has come from afar with the Scriptures and the doctrine in order to present them to our capital. On examining the spirit of this doctrine we find it excellent, separate from the world, and acknowledge that it is quickening for mankind and indispensable. This religion succors human beings, is beneficial to the human race, and is worthy to be spread over the Celestial Empire. We decree a monastery to be built by the appropriate Board and twenty-one priests to be appointed there.

The Nestorian tablet gives a summary of the tenets of the faith, which include the creation of the world, the story of original sin, the mystery of the Holy Trinity, the incarnation, and the redemption. Christianity was alternately encouraged and persecuted by various Chinese monarchs. The infamous empress dowager Wu instituted in 698 a persecution that was a prototype of what the yet greater empress dowager was to attempt in the Boxer uprising of 1900, twelve centuries later. Nestorianism, however, was primarily the faith of a foreign community—of missionaries, merchants, and soldiers. It never became indigenous nor trusted itself to Chinese leadership.

The Franciscan Roman Catholic missionary John of Montecorvino arrived at the Mongol capital of China in 1294 and did a noble work for a third of a century. He was followed by various Dominicans and Franciscans. After an interval of nearly two centuries, during an awakening period of world exploration and missionary zeal, the great Francis Xavier, after his period of fervid evangelism in India and Japan, sought to enter China in 1552. Before Xavier could enter China, however, this great "Apostle of the Indies" died on an island off the coast. The longing in his heart was voiced by his follower, the Jesuit leader Valignani, as he also gazed toward China ere he died a half century later in Macao, in 1606, with the cry: "O rock, rock, rock, when wilt thou open to my Lord?"

The brilliant Italian Jesuit, Matteo Ricci, who became the real founder of Christianity in China, reached Peking in 1601. There his knowledge of the Chinese classics and of Western astronomy and mathematics, his scientific instruments, and his maps of the world made a deep impression on the scholar class, whom he sought to reach. He tried always to conciliate and to adapt Christianity as far as possible to Chinese customs. He dressed in Chinese robes, adopted Chinese customs, and held in high respect China's ancient civilization. He also, however, taught Western sciences, disproving the Chinese belief that the sky is round and the earth square. He cured diseases and established a hospital. At length he was allowed to come before the emperor and plead for the recognition of his religion. He was permitted to build churches in Peking and to give public lectures on Christian doctrines. Ricci was followed by the famous German astronomer, Johann Adam Schall von Bell, who held offices and enjoyed the favor of the emperor until there were many Catholic converts.

The Jesuits adapted their methods to Chinese prejudices and counted the ceremonies in honor of Confucius and of ancestor worship as permissible to Christians. After decades of controversy over this issue between the Jesuits, Dominicans, and other orders, each seeking to gain a favorable decision from the pope and the Inquisition, the Chinese emperor became disgusted at outside interference in the internal affairs of China and imprisoned the papal envoy in Macao until his death. Some of the later Catholic priests adopted a superior attitude of authority toward the Chinese, often intervening in lawsuits and, in the judgment of the Chinese, interfering in political affairs. Intermittent periods of persecution of Roman Catholic Christianity followed.

We have already seen that Robert Morrison as the first Protestant missionary entered China in 1807. When a leader in the new Republic of China was asked when the Chinese revolution began, he replied: "On the day that Robert Morrison, the missionary, landed in Canton." In less than a century after Morrison, in 1925, there were twenty-four Protestant colleges and universities in China, enrolling 2,811 students, a number that was to be doubled within a few years. There were also some three hundred thousand students in teachers' training, high and middle schools, industrial institutions, and Protestant primary schools. There were 7,663 Protestant foreign missionaries, with 27,133 Chinese fellow workers, serving 5,424 organized churches and a Protestant Christian community of nearly a million.

The Catholic community was four or five times as large as

the Protestant body, for the Catholics had been in China nearly three times as long and had counted some two hundred thousand on their rolls when Morrison landed. The Protestant community, however, was growing faster than the Catholic. It engaged more in public evangelism, and it believed more in the widespread dissemination of general educational and Christian literature. It also believed in delegating authority wherever possible to Chinese nationals and in training a great lay leadership for China's economic, political, and religious life. It was consciously seeking to influence the whole of China's national life by the building of an indigenous Christian civilization at the heart of it.

If space permitted, I should like to tell of the life and work of S. Wells Williams, James Legge, W. A. P. Martin, Calvin W. Mateer, John L. Nevius, Arthur H. Smith, Young J. Allen, Laura Haygood, and many able veterans of the first century of missions in China. Instead I shall confine myself to a very few modern workers of various types. I shall recall the work of the great pathfinder Timothy Richard; the veteran educators Bishop Schereschewsky and Francis Hawks Pott; the founder of the China Inland Mission, Hudson Taylor; the student leader, Fletcher Brockman; and the Buddhist worker, Karl Reichelt. I shall then consider typical Chinese leaders like Chang Poling; the principal of the woman's college, Dr. Wu Yi-fang; and James Y. C. Yen.[1]

TIMOTHY RICHARD

Timothy Richard [2] was a Chinese scholar who was equally the trusted counselor of the national leaders and the recognized

---

[1] As I have referred to several of these men in previous writings, I here include some paragraphs which have been rewritten from two books now out of print, *The New Era in Asia*, 1913, and *I Have Seen God Do It*, Harpers, 1940.

[2] For the facts in the life of this great missionary see W. E. Soothill, *Timothy Richard of China*, Seeley, Service & Co., London, 1924; also Timothy Richard, *Forty-five Years in China*, Unwin & Co., London, 1916, and Richard's autobiography in one chapter of his *Conversion by the Million*, Christian Literature Society of China, 1907. In this account of Timothy Richard I have used several paragraphs which are rewritten from my book *I Have Seen God Work in China*, Association Press, New York, 1944.

friend of the masses, whose Chinese name, Ti-mo-tai, was more widely known than that of any other foreigner in the land. I admired Richard as a veteran pathfinder and trail blazer and as a younger worker I took counsel with him eagerly, for he was always ready to share his rich experience. Timothy Richard was born in 1845, in a little village in South Wales, Ffaldy-brennin—"The King's Fold." At twelve years of age Richard was baptized in the river under the open sky, as Jesus had been by John the Baptist, and he became a member of the local Salem Baptist Church. He contracted no bad habits in his wholesome youth that could dog his steps in later life, but built up a strong body, a keen mind, and an earnest spiritual life that enabled him to devote fifty years of sacrificial service to China. At fifteen he had finished the village school; and he began to work with his father on the farm, acquiring a knowledge of practical things that would be useful all his life in dealing with the peasants of China. He taught school in the winter and earned enough to complete his education in the normal college and at Haverfordwest College, where he prepared for the ministry, enjoying educational privileges that his fellow Baptist, Carey, had never enjoyed.

In 1870 Richard arrived, among the first pioneers, in Shantung, the province of Confucius, when the doors to most of China were closed to the foreigner. Working with the great Americans, John L. Nevius and Hunter Corbett, in Chefoo for seven years, Richard tried out the traditional methods of mission work. He found that preaching in a street chapel yielded few converts and that the distribution of Bible portions did not bring magic results. He began to think that the immediate message of the Bible was for the Jews, and that its living principles, especially as embodied in the life and teaching of Jesus, should be applied to the world of today in messages suitable to the environment and daily life of each people. He studied the Epistles especially, to find the clue to winning converts. In 1877 he read a sermon by Edward Irving that suggested following the original apostles in the injunction in Matthew 10:11: "Into whatsoever city or town ye shall enter, inquire who in it is worthy; and there abide till ye go thence." That meant to Richard that he was to seek first the devout leaders, the guileless Nathanaels, the prepared souls, those who had been striving to walk in the "real light, which enlightens every man." What if God, who never left himself without a witness in any age, had been unable to send Isaiah and Jeremiah—known only to the prepared Jews—but had sent instead their contemporaries Confucius, Lao-tzu, and Gautama Buddha as "the light of Asia" to prepare the Orient for "the Light of the World"? Richard never did anything by half. This hopeful thought of going first to the worthy, contained in the enlightening sermon by Edward Irving, so impressed him that he had the sermon published and sent a copy to each leading missionary in China, India, and Africa.

Richard now heeded the injunction of his Master to seek first the worthy among Chinese Confucian and Buddhist scholars, who would probably prove good ground on which to sow his seed. Having great ability, he mastered the Chinese language, much of its voluminous literature, and its three religions—especially all that was best in them—in order that he might fit himself to meet the gentry and officials on equal terms. When on tour, he healed as well as preached. Timothy Richard was not a physician, but he carried medicines for epidemics like cholera and malaria. This was at least better than the Chinese doctors, who were poking needles a foot long through the intestines to "let the demons out" that were supposed to be causing disease—a belief prevalent in modern China as it had been in medieval Europe. Throughout his life Richard sought both to make new men and to build a new social order.

Richard visited the leaders of the Chinese secret societies, who were the cream of the religious community, the chosen or advanced seekers after truth, and studied their religious books to understand their thoughts, their ideals, their vocabulary, and their mental climate. He then translated Christian principles into their own terminology and prepared booklets and tracts that would appeal to the Chinese, including a catechism and a hymn book of understandable hymns. He abandoned the old apologetic of attacking the people's religion to prove that his religion was better than theirs. He made his appeal directly to the heart and mind and, in China especially, to the conscience. He found in actual experience exactly what I discovered in India, long before I met Timothy Richard, that there are four courses open to one in dealing with non-Christians: wholesale condemnation, wholesale commendation, comparison or contrast of the two religions, and "completion" in the sense that perhaps Jesus meant when he declared, "I am not come to destroy, but to fulfill." I found, as Richard did, that to condemn the other man's religion is to repel him, just as it would if you condemned a man's wife or child; to commend it with unstinted praise leaves him self-satisfied; to contrast the two religions, endeavoring to prove that we have a better religion than his, throws him on the defensive, which is the worst possible attitude if you want results. If, instead of any of these approaches, the man can be made to realize first his own need and sin, and then the reality of the Saviour who is able fully to meet that need and bear and overcome that sin, the results may be as effective as in apostolic days.

I consulted Timothy Richard and other experienced missionaries and Chinese leaders before beginning our meetings in China, and on three successive nights spoke on three topics in this order: Sin, God, Christ. We could not baldly announce these bare subjects to materialistic students who frankly neither knew nor cared whether or not they were sinners, whether or not there was a God or a spiritual universe, and who cared least of all about Christ. They did care supremely about just one thing: what could save China? Instead of technical theological subjects, we would announce such topics as "The Crisis in China," "The Need of China," "The Hope of China." Before the meetings were over, many of the students realized that the desperate crisis in China was at bottom a moral crisis, centered in sin; that if China was rich in precepts but lacking in moral dynamic, perhaps the deepest need of China was the discovery of God; and that the hope of China was in a fundamental and unique way related to Jesus Christ—in a way that it was not related to Confucius or Lao-tzu or Buddha, to materialism, to nontheistic humanism, or to any other system or person. Paul used the same method when he said in Second Corinthians 4:2 (Moffatt) : "I state the truth openly and so commend myself to every man's conscience before God."

First and last, we always appealed to the conscience which God had been preparing for more than two thousand years— long before the time of Confucius. Richard did not believe that the mere reiteration of proof texts as shibboleths, or the repetition of phrases such as "nothing but the blood," had any magical effect upon non-Christians. He believed in Paul's "foolishness of preaching," but not in the preaching of foolishness. He repudiated the horrible doctrine that he was called to preach the gospel as a testimony *against* these poor people, who were as sheep without a shepherd, and the belief that once he had proclaimed some incomprehensible shibboleth, or "transaction," at Calvary, the "heathen" were without excuse and that their blood was now on their own heads. He was not like my old theological professor who would calmly consign ninety-nine per cent of humanity to an endless burning hell and then go home to toast his feet by the fire and then enjoy an untroubled sleep.

After studying Chinese history and civilization, Richard drew two startling conclusions: (1) that there was a providential order among the Chinese as well as among the Jews and the Christians—he believed that God as Creator and Saviour had not left them in ignorance and that his first missionaries to the Chinese had been their own sages who had taught righteousness, benevolence, truth, and faithfulness; and (2) that the new Buddhism from India, teaching faith in a merciful God and the salvation of one's fellow men, had prepared many "worthy" men in China as conscious sinners who needed salvation.

Instead of using the strange names "Jesus" or "Christ," Richard spoke of the Saviour and presented the gospel in Chinese terms. He would put up his tracts and posters on the walls of a Chinese town or village and then go to eat in the inn. Sometimes while he was eating men would come and kneel to ask him to tell them his good news. When Richard visited the leader of a Chinese Mohammedan mosque, the Moslem received him kindly, served him with tea, and asked to be allowed to tell him of Mohammed in order to make him a good Moslem. When asked by the Moslem to state his own case, he said he would gladly do so later. Richard carefully prepared, so that when the Moslem leader and his students paid him a return call he was ready to tell his story and interpret his religion in a way that would appeal to the Chinese mind. He made no claims of miracles or of an infallible Koran, such as the chief, Ahung, had done, but appealed always to the conscience and reason, to the mind and heart of his hearers, as sinners, like himself, who needed a Saviour just as he did. He took the approach: "What shall it profit a man, if he shall gain the whole world, and lose his own soul?" and "I came not to judge the world, but to save the world." Richard rediscovered the all-important message of the Kingdom of God—the message of the prophets, of John the Baptist, of Jesus and the apostles. After a fair trial of this method, instead of winning four or five men a year as formerly, within two years he had won a thousand converts and inquirers.

When in 1876 there broke out an appalling famine, in which nearly twenty millions perished, Richard organized what was perhaps the first widespread famine relief, raising a fund of some three hundred thousand dollars. This brought him in helpful contact alike with officials and with the common people, and incarnated the spirit of the religion he was trying both to live and to teach. He thus became an expert on relief, ready to meet each succeeding famine. Richard sent his appeals for the starving in the famine to Chefoo, to Shanghai, and to London. Relief committees were organized, tons of rice and wheat were delivered to the famine areas, and Richard was sent to Shansi to distribute food to the starving. Here he won the gratitude and affection of the people in the capital of Taiyüan-fu, whom he was later to rescue from the vengeance of the foreign powers after the Boxer massacre. The British consul reported to Lord Salisbury, the British prime minister: "Richard is known far and wide among all classes as the chief of the distributors. By his great tact and power of organization, he has been a powerful agent in bringing the relief through to a successful termination." Richard preached to the masses of sin and salvation as hundreds lay with their faces to the earth, weeping, confessing their sins, and seeking mercy from the Lord.

After the famine, instead of meeting the missionaries with their former hatred and scorn, as "foreign devils," all classes were now ready to give a favorable hearing to the Christian message. Richard became the most widely known and deeply loved Englishman in China. He now settled in Taiyüanfu, the capital of Shansi, where he won acceptance with the literati, the mandarins, and the common people. Seeing the vast resources and raw materials of China undeveloped, Richard lived on rice while he scraped together five thousand dollars to buy books and scientific apparatus in order to lecture to the Chinese and to write on the applied sciences. By lectures and the printed page, he showed the need for building roads and railways, for opening mines, for the development of manufactures and industries, for flood control, famine prevention, reforestation, and scientific agriculture. Where scholars and officials were unawakened or too rapacious to care to meet China's need, he showed the necessity of spiritual motivation and religious self-sacrifice, and still sought those who were worthy. He paid no professional agent, but inspired laymen to live and tell the good news of the gospel and opened schools for the poor. He guided his missionary friend Whitewright to open a museum to illustrate the principal inventions and techniques of applied science of the West and to lecture several times each day to crowded audiences of officials, scholars, and students on needed reforms and the modernization of China.

When forced to return on furlough for a needed rest, from 1884 to 1886, Richard pursued advanced studies in science and education in London, Paris, and Berlin. He was ambitious to establish a new sytem of education in China, with one Christian college or university in the capital of every province, as a center for the evangelistic work in each district. He was also intent on the more thorough preparation of missionaries, before they were sent to the field, in the science of missions and comparative religions, just as medical missionaries were professionally trained. But Timothy Richard was in advance of his time, just as William Carey had been; and his missionary society sent him back without funds or liberty to try his new methods of work. Instead, he was subject to a local committee of six inexperienced and ultraconservative juniors. In consequence, he was forced to leave Shantung for the wide, open spaces of the western province Shansi.

Richard now entered Taiyüanfu, capital of the province of Shansi, and tried to enlist the support of the leading statesmen of China for the opening of modern universities, hoping that they might save China from her impending doom. He was invited by the great viceroy Li Hung-chang to become the editor of a Chinese daily—the *Shih Pao,* or *Times.* He soon developed a widely circulated weekly, and became editor of a widely known magazine, *The Review of the Times.*

In 1891 Richard became the secretary of the Society for the Diffusion of Christian and General Knowledge, which later became the Christian Literature Society. He continued in this position for twenty-three years, until 1914, when he retired as secretary emeritus. By a steady stream of magazines, newspapers, books, and pamphlets, Richard deliberately sought "the conversion of the Chinese mind." He instructed the leaders and officials regarding the governments, industries, and civilization of the West, looking toward the reform and development of China. He tackled the vast problems of illiteracy, of opium, of mass poverty, and of official corruption. When he found that the government "blue books" were inciting to riot and the persecution of Christianity by wild tales of missionaries gouging out the eyes of children to make medicine or electricity, he challenged the leaders in Peiping to do away with this menace by insisting upon a more tolerant attitude on the part of officials. More than any other missionary, Timothy Richard became the friend and adviser of the reformers, especially of the modern sage of China, K'ang Yu-wei. His most brilliant disciple,

Liang Ch'i-chao, acted as Richard's temporary secretary while he was in Peiping. He was asked to be president of Peiping government university, but he declined this and all other government appointments.

At this time Richard was editing three magazines, with the aid of the American Southern Methodist, Young J. Allen. Together they were publishing books, booklets, and pamphlets in ten provinces, especially in the capital cities, where over a hundred thousand students from all over China met triennially to take their second-degree examinations. The object of the Christian Literature Society was "the publication and circulation of literature throughout China based on Christian principles." Richard believed that the power of the printed word was more potent among the Chinese than among any other people. Under his leadership the Christian Literature Society published 250 booklets in eighteen years, and they were circulated by the thousands, and finally by the millions, all over the Chinese Empire and later the Republic.

In 1898 the youthful emperor appointed K'ang Yu-wei secretary of the Foreign Office—Tsung-li Yamen—and issued a bold series of edicts in rapid succession during the "hundred days of reform." These edicts proposed: (1) to abolish the essay system of examination, which had been in vogue for at least five hundred years, (2) to establish a university for the study of Western science in Peiping, (3) to convert temples into schools for Western education, (4) to establish a translation board, to publish books on Western learning, (5) to establish a patent office, to further new industrial developments, (6) to protect Christianity, (7) to make the reform paper *Chinese Progress* the official organ of the government, (8) to abolish useless offices and waste in government, both in Peiping and in the provinces, and (9) to send young Manchus abroad to study foreign languages.

The young emperor, who had been reading Richard's books and papers for some time, asked Richard to become his adviser; but before the latter could do so, the dowager empress seized and imprisoned the emperor for life. After the Boxer uprising, when the Allies had atrociously avenged the Paoting and other massacres, it was feared that they would seek similar vengeance in Shansi. The viceroy, Li Hung-chang, and Prince Ch'un asked Richard to endeavor to save the province and to aid in a plan of restitution for the massacre of some two hundred missionaries including their families. He believed that their blood was too sacred to be requited with financial indemnities. If the cause of the Boxer uprising had been ignorance, would not these martyrs themselves have desired not vengeance but an indemnity that would establish a university that might in time dispel the ignorance of a province so stained with innocent blood? The Catholics were demanding large indemnities, which would have embittered the whole province against them. Since some punishment seemed necessary to prevent future massacres, Richard proposed a fine of $500,000, spread over ten years, to be used exclusively for the education of the province, centering in a university in the capital city of Taiyüanfu, where the worst massacres had taken place. And Richard was asked to be chancellor of the university for a stipulated period of ten years, and he chose several associates to help in founding the institution.

After Timothy Richard had opened the University College in Taiyüanfu, with eight foreign and twelve Chinese professors, teachers, and translators, imperial edicts were issued that similar colleges were to be opened in every province of the Empire, at a cost to the government of $500,000, which by a strange coincidence was the very sum Richard had suggested fifteen years before to the missionary societies of Great Britain for a chain of Christian colleges in China. The throne also issued an edict commanding the Chinese foreign office to consult Timothy Richard and the Roman Catholic Bishop Favier on how to promote a better understanding between the Chinese government and Protestant and Catholic missions. The red button of the first grade of officials was conferred upon both men. Several regulations were drawn up by Richard and Bishop Favier, which were approved by the Archbishop of Westminster in London, who agreed to send them to Rome with his favorable recommendation; but Bishop Favier died before negotiations could be completed.

Having proposed plans to the officials for a modern university as the keystone for an educational system in each province in China, Richard returned to complete his work of producing Christian literature in Shanghai. He had become an authority on Mahayana Buddhism; he had made friends with the leaders of all religions in China—with Catholic, Buddhist, and Taoist priests; with Confucian scholars; with peasants, workers, and coolies; in short, with all who were "worthy." This Welsh farmer boy had become a Chinese scholar and gentleman to his fingertips. He had fulfilled Confucius' ideal of the princely or superior man. For fifty years he had been granted the priceless privilege of pouring out his life, with all his rich gifts, to build new men and a new social order in China, and to widen the horizon and deepen the sympathy of many of the younger men, Chinese and foreign, who would seek to carry to completion his unfinished work. He sought to impose no irrational doctrine upon prejudiced men, but to transform individuals and society for the building of a new China as part of a new world.

On April 20, 1919, a cable from London announced the death of this elder Christian statesman, Timothy Richard. He was a many-sided man, a bold dreamer who expected great things from God and attempted great things for God, like his fellow Baptist, William Carey. He had long been a prophet in his own country, and after fifty years of service for his beloved China many of his early dreams had already come true. Worthy Chinese leaders and younger foreigners were now ready to take up the work that Timothy Richard had laid down and carry it on to full fruition and completion.

BISHOP SCHERESCHEWSKY AND
FRANCIS HAWKS POTT

St. Johns University in Shanghai was the creation of two men, Bishop Schereschewsky (pronounced Sher-e-sheff-skie) and Dr. Francis Hawks Pott. Both were remarkable men. The Bishop, a Russian Jew, was born in 1831. At the age of fifteen he entered a rabbinical school and there first saw a New Testament, which finally convinced him that Jesus was indeed the Messiah. He left the Jewish school at the age of nineteen and with his pack on his back walked some five hundred miles to Germany, where he studied for four years. At the age of twenty-three he emigrated to America, and at a Passover Supper celebration of a group of Christian Jews in Brooklyn, he decided to make a public profession of his Christian faith. He studied in the Presbyterian Western Theological Seminary at Allegheny and graduated from the Episcopal General Theological Seminary in New York City. When, in 1858, Bishop William J. Boone of Shanghai called for volunteers to enter the newly opened treaty ports of China, the young crusader Schereschewsky offered himself. As a brilliant linguist he became one of the foremost Orientalists of his time, proficient in Mandarin, Wenli, Mongolian, and the Shanghai dialect. While working in Peking, he translated the New Testament into Mandarin and then the Old Testament from the Hebrew two years later. These were priceless and monumental gifts to China.

After fourteen years in China, Schereschewsky took his first furlough to America, and the House of Bishops elected him Bishop of Shanghai. He declined because of his linguistic duties, but was re-elected in spite of his refusal. He accepted on the one condition that the bishops would assist him to raise money for a Christian college in China. This condition was realized, and Bishop Schereschewsky founded the school that later was to be St. Johns University, of which in 1879 he became the first president. This departure in higher education gave a new turn to the Episcopal and other churches in China. Bishop Lawrence of Massachusetts pronounced Schereschewsky "the liveliest man with the liveliest manner and brain of any person I had met."

In 1881 the Bishop suffered a sunstroke while working in the heat of Wuchang, six hundred miles inland, and was almost completely paralyzed for the rest of his life. When the mission board would not send him, as a crippled invalid, back to China, he courageously continued his work of translation, although the paralysis had left only one finger that he could use in type-writing his manuscript. Inevitably, after nine hours of work a day, this middle finger on his right hand failed from exhaustion; but the Bishop, still undefeated, continued to typewrite with a stick. In one of the most amazing literary undertakings of all time, he completed the revision of the Mandarin Old Testament in a year; and in the next six years he revised 2,500 pages of the entire Bible in Easy Wenli. After this feat the board sent him back to China in 1895, and he saw his Chinese Bible through the press in Japan. At his death, in 1906—after having sat in one hard chair, paralyzed, for over twenty years— he had completed the further revision of the Mandarin, the Easy Wenli, and the Chinese Reference Bible in both tongues. Bishop McKim of Tokyo said: "Bishop Schereschewsky is one of the most remarkable men I have ever met. His courage and energy are indomitable. Paralyzed in hands and feet, unable to move without assistance, his mind is as vigorous as it ever was." The Bishop was a true crusader and pathfinder, both in Bible translation and in the field of higher education for China.

Francis Lister Hawks Pott was born in New York City, February 22, 1864. After graduating from Columbia in 1883, young Francis Pott studied in the General Theological Seminary, New York; and it was here that he became deeply interested in China through teaching a class of Chinese laundrymen and others to read and speak English. As Pott considered his future field of work, it seemed to him that the greatest need in the world and the greatest spiritual opportunity that he knew were in China. In 1886, at the age of twenty-two he went to China; and, after studying the language, he began evangelistic work in Shanghai. When it seemed to him that a greater opportunity in educational work was offered him, he became headmaster of the school that later developed into St. Johns University.

In 1879 Bishop Schereschewsky, who was in charge of the China Mission of the Protestant Episcopal Church, planned to start a missionary college and theological school at a time— more than two decades before the Boxer uprising—when the Chinese did not appreciate the importance of Western learning. A fine site was acquired, and the cornerstone of the new institution was laid on Easter Monday, 1879, though the first educational work of the mission was begun as early as 1847. For fifty-three years Dr. Pott was headmaster of the college and president of St. Johns University, from 1888 to 1941, when he became president emeritus. He organized the college proper in 1892 with but four students, but the growing demand for an education in English rapidly enlarged the institution. Dr. Pott finally decided to limit the student body to eight hundred, five hundred of whom were in the college proper. The beautiful and impressive campus of St. Johns, covering forty-six acres, contains thirteen university buildings and thirty-two residences, with a strong school of arts and sciences, a school of medicine, a school of theology, and a school of civil engineering.

Because of its wealthy families, St. Johns sent a large proportion of its students to study abroad—some forty a year went away for a long time. A considerable number of these students after their return entered government service and occupied prominent positions, so that St. Johns has held a unique place in the development of leadership in shaping the destiny of China.

The father of the statesman W. W. Yen—who was prime minister and foreign minister in Peiping—was in charge of St. Johns until Dr. Pott relieved him. T. V. Soong, China's great financier and the senior male member of the "Soong dynasty," is a graduate and an active and earnest member of the board of directors in China. Wellington Koo, Alfred Tzu, and a hundred more are among the graduates who entered government service. As Dr. Pott was one of the earliest educators who sought spiritual results in his work, from very early years there were Christian converts in the college. Among St. Johns graduates who were great Christian leaders were David Yui, T. Z. Koo— one of the most brilliant spokesmen for China and the cause of Christ in America, in Britain, or in the world—Bishop Y. Y. Tsu, and many others. St. Johns was always frankly a religious institution, and about a fourth of the students were Christians. Among its thousands of graduates during the last sixty years, many have led the way in various reform movements, such as the emancipation of women. Because of the high quality of its able staff and of its curriculum, St. Johns early became a model for government colleges; and it has helped in the molding of government education, especially during the last three decades.

Through all of St. Johns' development Francis Hawks Pott was the guiding spirit. A perfect gentleman, a scholar, a great teacher, and a devout Christian, he was one of the builders of the new China. He was elected a bishop in 1910, but declined the office in order to complete his great life work. He was decorated with the Chinese Order of Chiaho. Beyond all earthly honors and offices, Dr. Pott remains a great Christian path-finder, still continuing, at the ripe age of eighty, his Christian service in America on behalf of China.

Less than a century after Morrison—in 1925—there were twenty-four Protestant colleges and universities in China, enrolling 2,811 students, a number that was to be doubled within a few years. There were also some three hundred thousand students in teachers' training, high and middle schools, industrial institutions, and Protestant primary schools. There were 7,663 Protestant foreign missionaries, with 27,133 Chinese fellow workers, serving 5,424 organized churches and a Protestant Christian community of nearly a million. During the last three decades I have had the privilege of meeting a considerable proportion of the Protestant missionary leaders and a larger number of Chinese Christians. It has seemed to me that they were doing perhaps the greatest piece of work for human uplift and betterment—spiritual, intellectual, and material—of any body of men in the world.

Dr. Pott agrees that even World War II has proved to be a great opportunity as a demonstration of the power of Christianity in ministering to China's desperate need—in service to the army, the wounded, and the often homeless and starving population. Christian leaders have been able to minister to colleges despoiled of their plant and equipment, and some of them have trekked more than a thousand miles to places of refuge, where they have had to start all over again. These men have gratefully welcomed every aid in supplying textbooks, buildings, equipment and even food. The Generalissimo and Madame Chiang have both testified publicly and enthusiastically to this practical ministry and to the heroism of Christian service and sacrifice in the war. This has gone far beyond any possible measurement by statistics. Out of a population of over four hundred millions, little more than four millions in China are professing Christians. While only about one in a hundred are members of churches, an analysis of China's *Who's Who* shows that of these educated men who have in some way distinguished themselves one in six is a Christian; and of those listed in *Who's Who* one half received their education in Christian schools and colleges. If we turn to the score or more of outstanding leaders who have most helped to mold every part of China's life, about half are Christians.

HUDSON TAYLOR AND THE CHINA INLAND MISSION

I heard Hudson Taylor first at the Detroit convention of the Student Volunteer Movement in 1894, and I was able then to feel his deeply spiritual influence. He was one of the purest, humblest, most sensitive souls I ever knew, fervent in prayer, mighty in faith, his whole life dedicated to the single object of doing the will of God. I felt myself in the presence of a man who had received a Kingdom which could not be shaken, without or within. He told us students of his deepest spiritual experience, which had come to him in the heart of China twenty years before in connection with the passage in John 4:14: "Whosoever drinketh . . . shall never thirst." The thirsty years for him had ended forever twenty years before when he had learned continuously to drink of the living water.

Even before his birth, his godly parents in Yorkshire had prayed for a son who might become a missionary in China. Born in 1872, Hudson Taylor experienced conversion at the age of fifteen. He tells us in his *Retrospect* that at an early age he had become skeptical. In his father's library one day he found a tract; and to while away the time he began to read it, hoping to find an interesting story at the beginning and to omit the dismal moral at the end. Arrested by the expression "the finished work of Christ," he thought: "If the whole work was finished and the whole debt paid, what is there left for me to do?" There flashed upon him the conviction that to be saved there was nothing left for him but simply to fall down on his knees and, "accepting this Saviour and his salvation, to praise him forevermore." At that very moment his devout mother, who on a distant journey was wrestling in prayer for him, knew with sudden assurance and thanked God that her prayers were answered. Few men have ever turned so completely to God and have sought with single eye so wholeheartedly to do his will all their lives as did Hudson Taylor. At that moment joy and peace and power seemed to enter his life forever.

When Taylor was seeking his field of work, he came across Medhurst's book on China, which emphasized the appalling need in that land and the value of medical missions. Accordingly, to prepare himself, he studied medicine and surgery in Hull and later in London. In the expectation of meeting great hardships in China, he began to live the simple life, subsisting mainly on oatmeal, rice, and bread. He practiced living by faith, that all his needs might be thus met. When he went to minister and pray for a dying woman and her starving family in the slums of London, he had but a half crown, or sixty-two cents, in his pocket. Could he have divided the one coin he possessed, he would gladly have given fifty cents to the poor family; but he was afraid to part with his last sixpence for his next meal. He felt that he could trust God plus sixpence, but not God alone, without any money in his pocket. In agony of mind, feeling himself a hypocrite, he gave his last coin, all that he had, to the poor family. The woman's life was saved—and his own faith. The next morning a half sovereign, or $2.50, came in the mail without any signature or explanation. He felt he had a 400 per cent return upon his venture of trust. He literally lived by trust in God in all that he did while in England and during the opening years in China, until he became convinced that God answers believing prayer. He finally felt that he could absolutely rely upon the promise "My God shall supply all your need," whether for himself as an individual or for a whole mission with hundreds of workers and no human guarantee for their support.

In 1853, at the age of twenty-one, having finished his preparation, he sailed for China, under the Chinese Evangelization Society, on a salary of $400 a year. On the long five-months' voyage he and his shipmates barely escaped shipwreck among the cannibals of New Guinea. He believed that, in answer to prayer, they were saved for future service. After studying the language in Shanghai, Taylor began evangelistic tours with some fellow workers and soon adopted the Chinese dress, queue, and manner of life. For seven months he toured China with the great William Burns, beloved over all Scotland. The name of William Burns was a household word, for thousands remembered him from the great revival of 1839, when as a young evangelist he had toured Scotland with pentecostal results. Burns was cultured, genial, a delightful companion overflowing with mother wit—a great human, while Hudson Taylor was a great saint. Burns had escaped with his life from violent mobs in Ireland, and now in China he had left his flock in Amoy to tour Chekiang Province with Hudson Taylor. When they felt called to separate, Burns went north to labor in Peking and then to carry the gospel beyond the Great Wall as a pioneer in Manchuria; while Hudson Taylor, after a time in Ningpo, set his face toward the unoccupied, fast-closed interior.

In 1860 Taylor returned on furlough to England as an invalid, but he continued to work for China. He was especially burdened in prayer for the inland provinces. Finally, on Sunday, June 25, 1865, being unable to bear the sight of a congregation of comfortable Christian people at Brighton who were rejoicing in their own security, he, in his own words,

wandered out on the sands alone, in great spiritual agony; and there the Lord conquered my unbelief and I surrendered myself to God for this service. I told him that all the responsibility as to the issues and consequences must rest with him, that as his servant it was mine to obey and to follow him—his, to direct, to care for, and to guide me and those who might labor with me. Need I say that peace at once flowed into my burdened heart. There and then I asked him for twenty-four workers, two for each of eleven inland provinces which were without a missionary, and two for Mongolia.

He wrote on the margin of his Bible: "Prayed for 24 willing, skillful laborers, at Brighton, June 25, 1865." For Hudson Taylor and for China, that prayer made history.

As he could not continue under the Chinese Evangelization Society, which was continually going into debt, he was led to organize the China Inland Mission. He resolved that in the new society there should be no collections taken and no appeals sent out, so that the work could go on only so long as it had God's approval. With frugal living, the average worker under the China Inland Mission needed $300 a year. The workers must be men and women of faith, with "a restful trust in God for the supply of all needs, apart from human guarantees," and they must be soul winners before going abroad. They held "the fundamental doctrines of the Scripture: that Jesus is the Son of God; that the saved are saved through faith in Him; that the lost *are* lost because they sin against the light they have; that the Bible is the inspired, authoritative Word of God." The China Inland Mission appeals strongly to fundamentalist and to the most orthodox believers. After a Chinese asked Hudson Taylor why his father and the people of China had not been told the gospel, he wrote in his *Retrospect* of two hundred million who had been swept into eternity, into "Christless graves," without an offer of salvation.

In answer to unceasing prayer, the twenty-four workers offered their services and were accepted; and $10,000 was given to send them to China. In 1865 the Lammermuir party of twenty-two sailed for China. In 1888 and again in 1893 Hudson Taylor visited America and spoke for Mr. Moody at Northfield, and in many places in the United States and Canada. In 1885 the celebrated "Cambridge seven" sailed for Shansi. They included Stanley Smith, stroke oar of the Cambridge eight; C. T. Studd, captain of the university cricket eleven, perhaps the greatest gentleman bowler in England; and also an officer of the select Royal Artillery; and another from the aristocratic Dragoon Guards. All of them had renounced careers of promise in order, like a grain of wheat, to fall into the ground and die in Inland China. I well remember the blessing that came to my own life through this band of consecrated men. I studied their record as I went abroad in the summer of 1892, and decided that I too must prepare to be a missionary. By 1900 there were 780 missionaries, including wives and associates, who had reached the field under the China Inland Mission, and there was an annual income of approximately a million dollars. There were, however, only 774 Chinese fellow workers, which was less than the number of foreign missionaries. There had been 10,500 converts baptized, of whom 7,000 remained in Christian fellowship in 200 stations.

At the present time the head office of the mission is in Chungking, where Bishop Frank Houghton is the general director. It is, of course, now impossible to get complete statistics in occupied China; but I give here a few of those available. The present number of missionaries is 1,176, of whom 740 are in war-torn China, and 436 are on furlough or on the home staffs. This includes 402 associate workers, chiefly missionaries from continental Europe, who hold the principles of the C.I.M. but whose financial administration is distinct from that of the home countries, Great Britain, North America, and Australia. The home directors are Mr. F. Mitchell, China Inland Mission, Newington Street, London; the Reverend H. M. Griffin, 235 West School Lane, Philadelphia 44, Pennsylvania; and the Reverend W. J. Embery, 64 Elizabeth Street, Melbourne, Victoria, Australia. In 1940 there were 1,499 paid Chinese workers for the mission, and 2,911 voluntary workers. The number of communicants in association with the mission in that year was 110, 573, and today Bishop Houghton reports a total of some 125,000 Christians in the churches founded through the mission. Five years ago living was relatively cheap in China, but with inflation China has become one of the most expensive countries in the world for foreigners; but, as Bishop Houghton writes, the need has been met by "an astonishing increase in contributions from every one of the home countries. . . . God gives us what we need, and what God does not give we do not need." The total income of the China Inland Mission in 1943 was $870,740–$389,956 of which was received from Great Britain and $348,116 from the United States; and $47,368 of which was raised in China.

The pioneers of the China Inland Mission have led the way as pathfinders in entering all the unoccupied inland provinces of China. No body of men and women has excelled them in faith, in courage, in sacrificial devotion, in loyalty to the truth as they understand it. No group has furnished more fervid crusaders. But in certain respects they have not led the van of the great missionary advance. It is to be feared that they have not sufficiently developed their educational work to raise up an adequate body of Chinese fellow workers, nor trusted them with full responsibility. Consequently the China Inland Mission cannot show as large a proportion of students in schools, of Chinese fellow workers, and of converts, as most of the regular denominational missions. They have placed first emphasis upon the speedy evangelization of China rather than upon the long-distance Christianization of that land. They have not trusted all their missionaries with democratic self-government on the field to the same extent as the regular denominational mission boards. They have insisted upon a literal and orthodox interpretation of Scripture. We shall see in a later section, however, that the great Christian James Y. C. Yen, when a boy of twelve in a boarding school in the far western province of Szechwan, was won to Christ by W. B. Aldis, who was recently at the head office of the C.I.M. in London. If the mission could show only this one result, it would be great; but actually it can show many more. The mission has sought souls and has won them.

We are many members of one body. All are not evangelists, all are not educators. We need a right and a left wing in our missionary crusade. We need men and missions to supplement each other. There is a place for broad and tolerant orthodox conservatives, and for devout modernists: both for men like

Hudson Taylor and for men like Timothy Richard. Therefore, we thank God for Hudson Taylor, for "Jimmie" Yen, and for the whole China Inland Mission.

FLETCHER BROCKMAN AND THE STUDENTS OF CHINA

As an example of our pathfinders I shall take a country boy from a cotton plantation in Georgia—Fletcher Brockman. He was hindered in his early education by the impoverishment and devastation left by the War Between the States. Even after graduating from Vanderbilt University Brockman was not adequately prepared by his classical education in Latin and Greek to deal with the proud literati or to master the Chinese classics and literature, which are more voluminous and far more difficult than the whole of English literature combined. If one had seen Fletcher Brockman as a country boy on a plantation in Georgia, he would never have guessed that he was to be called to do a unique work among the literati, the officials, and the students of China. As a matter of fact, however, Fletcher Brockman was not a mere country boy from Georgia. By birth he was descended from the gentry of Virginia; and, as we study his life, some of us may come to believe that he was called of God to work for the gentry and the students of China.

Fletcher Brockman was born in Amherst County, Virginia, where the Brockman family had been friends and intimates of the families of George Washington, Thomas Jefferson, and James Madison. In England, the Brockmans were one of the oldest families in Kent, prominent there from the thirteenth century. While Brockman's ancestors did not go back for more than seventy generations to Confucius, as did those of some of his later friends in China, like H. H. Kung, he was a Christian gentleman who embodied the finest inheritance of the Anglo-Saxon West. He remembers as a boy driving with his father, who seemed to him the perfect gentleman. When the humblest laborer, black or white, greeted them with lifted hat, his father, always lifting his own hat in return, would say to his son: "I can let no man excel me in courtesy." The one ambition of Brockman's mother was that all her sons might enter Christian work. Of the three who grew to manhood, all became missionaries— two went to China and one to Korea.

Part of Brockman's unconscious preparation for China had been in the development of a fine attitude of appreciation toward men of all other races and geographical areas, including those whom his friends called "the damned Yankees," the Negroes, and the Oriental students in Vanderbilt University where he studied. His intimate friend in college was Baron Yun Tchi Ho, the son of a Korean nobleman, who became a national leader in the religious work in Korea and later helped Brockman to gain immediate entrance to the hearts of Korean leaders. Another of his lifelong friends was "Charlie" Soong, a universally popular and earnest Christian Chinese student in Vanderbilt. Little could Brockman—or the Chinese youth himself—have dreamed that this beloved, unassuming friend was to be the father of the great Soong family, which was to furnish so many of the able leaders of China under the new republic. During the seven years that intervened between Brockman's graduation in 1891 and his sailing for China he was national secretary of the student Young Men's Christian Association, assigned to work in the colleges of the South. Here he was one of the first apostles of racial brotherhood in the Southern states. His father had been a loyal Baptist who could never take the communion of the Lord's Supper with his Methodist wife. Brockman himself, however, learned in his seven broadening years of traveling student work in America to co-operate with all.

In America Brockman had been preparing to go out and work for the conversion of what he then called the "heathen" in the Orient. It was only after he had reached China and had humbly sat at the feet of Confucius, in his language study, that he learned that "all within the four seas are brothers." In America he dreamed as little that he had anything to learn from Confucius as the proud Confucian scholars then did that the Christian "foreign devil" had anything to teach the "superior man" of the Middle Kingdom. But Brockman was the bearer of a gospel that was more catholic than his limited comprehension, and that was destined in time to break down all middle walls of partition and segregation. He wrote in *I Discover the Orient:* "The next ten years were largely taken up with discovering and untangling the true from the false without destroying my sense of mission."

Brockman did not go as a missionary to China primarily as a Methodist, a Southerner, or an American, but as a humble Christian inspired by the vision of Christ and captivated by his teaching. He had come gradually to believe, not only with Confucius that all men were brothers, but with his Master and the great Apostle to the Gentiles that all may be one spiritually, so that there is neither Jew nor Greek, bond nor free, male nor female; neither white nor black, yellow nor brown, in racial, class, or religious divisions. In a word, Brockman was all unconsciously providentially prepared to reach the students of China by the broad, tolerant, sympathetic, and highly efficient statesmanship of modern missions.

When Brockman was preparing to go to China, he first offered his services to his own church missionary board. It was his beloved Bishop Lambuth who saw that, during his seven years of work in the colleges of the South, there had been placed in his hands a unique instrument for work among students on behalf of all the missions in China. Bishop Lambuth realized that the Y.M.C.A., as an interdenominational, international organization, might become the agent of all the churches, to do for young men what no single church or denomination could possibly hope to do in the way of furnishing costly equipment and attractive buildings in the great cities teeming with temptation to young men. If this instrumentality could lose itself and be loyal to the churches, it could utilize its many points of contact and activities to reach and to win men and to train leaders for the churches, the community, and the nation. The most farsighted Christian statesmen saw that here was an adaptable unique instrument, long prepared, that could unite the leaders of all the Christian forces with the non-Christian young patriots of the newly awakened Chinese Republic, and satisfy at once their nationalistic and their spiritual aspirations. The veteran missionaries themselves had called the Y.M.C.A. to enter China. Just when access to this long-impregnable Rock of Gibraltar was about to be given, just as the ancient walls of China, like the walls of Jericho, were falling, these veterans, holding up Brockman's hands, urged him to unite all the co-operative Christian forces and to go up with faith to this mighty and exclusive citadel.

When Brockman landed in China, in 1898, he could hardly have realized the gravity of the national and international crisis. During "the hundred days of reform," the young emperor had issued a series of liberal edicts looking toward the emancipation of China and the modernization of the entire life of the nation, so far as that was possible within the framework of the old order. But the reactionary and murderous old empress dowager, jealous of the emperor's growing power among the people, had dethroned him and made him a prisoner. As Brockman sailed into Shanghai harbor he saw proud battleships flying the flags of all the nations—except China. The division and break-up of China among the European nations and Japan was then taken for granted.

With his frail but courageous wife and their baby, Brockman was landed upon a muddy flat on the river bank at midnight, only to find the great iron gates of the city of Nanking barred against him until daylight. In a mud hut, shivering over a charcoal brazier, he had never in his life faced such a black night. Those barred city gates were symbolic of the exclusion of the proud Middle Kingdom, then under the Manchu empress dowager, whose venomous Boxer massacre was to menace the lives of all foreigners and missionaries, including Brockman's wife and child, in a mad endeavor to exterminate every "foreign devil" in the land—for that was the name by which foreigners were called by the children of every Chinese city. Those fast-barred gates meant that China did not want a single element of Western civilization—neither its railways, newspapers, modern science, education, nor, least of all, its religion. Brockman was now at the end of his long journey, the goal of twelve years of waiting, hoping, and striving; but he wrote: "The city wall rose sixty feet above us in the darkness. It seemed to me that the giant doors of the city gate, locked and barred, were a symbol of the hearts of the people within the walls." The next morning, however, he entered the city, began language study, and started with his work in Nanking.

The year 1900 was tragically marked by the Boxer uprising, which flaunted its banners: "Protect the Empire; Exterminate the Foreigner." This was the last spasm of China's isolationist, antiforeign reaction. On August 14, 1900, the news was flashed around the world that the allied forces had reached Peking, the legations had been relieved, and the foreigners and Chinese Christians had been rescued. When Brockman later made a tour from Peking through North China, he found that the death toll of the Boxer massacre exceeded thirty thousand. And he wrote with heavy heart: "The atrocities committed by the armies of occupation far surpassed in barbarism the deeds of the Boxers." Every village on the line of march from Tientsin had been looted; a whole year was spent in the looting of Peiping. George Morrison, distinguished correspondent of the *London Times,* testified that one foreign army alone had been guilty of more atrocities than the Boxers had committed throughout all China, Manchuria, and Mongolia. As a result, the Chinese were yet more convinced of the moral inferiority of foreigners to themselves.

In 1900 Brockman was deeply moved at the sight of the examination halls in Nanking, where nearly thirty thousand Chinese scholars were about to gather to compete for the second degree in the great state examinations under a system that had been in operation for many centuries. Chinese tradition held that the great Emperor Shun (2200 B.C.), with the ideal of "employ the able and promote the worthy," examined his officials every third year. In 1115 B.C. the government was examining candidates, as well as officials, in the "six arts." When Brockman arrived in China, the examinations were held in three grades. Some two thousand competitors, from fifteen to seventy years of age, in each county, or hsien, each entered his narrow

cell to compete for the first degree of "Flower of Talent."
Sometimes only one in a hundred succeeded. Once in three
years these first-degree men came up to the provincial capital—
nearly thirty thousand at Nanking—each seeking to become
the one in a hundred who would win, as an Olympic victory,
the second degree of "Promoted Scholar." The following year
the second-degree men from the whole Empire went up to
Peking to compete for the third degree, "Fit for Office." These
first-, second-, and especially third-degree men became mandarins, or officials; and they might rise to become viceroys or
members of the imperial cabinet, or join the Hanlin Imperial
Institute as poets, historians, chancellors, or state examiners.
The three degrees were far more difficult to obtain than are the
American B.A., M.A., and Ph.D. The two or three millions of
the scholar class who secured these degrees ruled the Empire.
Brockman had the prophetic vision to see the strategy of reaching the members of this proud and conservative scholar class,
who not only were furnishing most of the rulers of China but
who constituted the one dominant group whose opinion could
call to account officials—even viceroys—and who, in extreme
cases might advise or, with the aid of some military leader, even
depose an emperor or overthrow a dynasty.

Brockman's reports of 1900 show that he not only had a
vision of the dynamic potentialities of both the ancient scholar
and modern student classes, but that, in a strange way, a burden
seemed to be laid upon him for reaching them. He began to
move heaven and earth to secure, first, a great scientist, or at
least a popular lecturer, who had the gift of visualizing and
explaining the principles of science to educated audiences, and
then a group of technically trained men, both Chinese and
foreign, who could reach these strategic classes. Awakening Chinese scholars were now asking eager questions. Few of them had
ever seen a railway locomotive; they wanted to know how fast
one could go, if it was true that a wire could carry the human
voice over long distances, and what were the possibilities of this
new mystery of electricity. Brockman wrote to his friend John
R. Mott and implored him to secure the best man in America

with scientific training to meet China's need. The letter reached Mott in Chicago, and in the elevator that was taking him to the street he saw the man who seemed to be ideally fitted to meet this challenging opportunity. It was his friend C. H. Robertson, professor of mechanical engineering in Purdue University, affectionately known by the students as "Big Robbie," former captain of the football, baseball, and track teams, and leader of the Christian work in the college. In a flash Mott thought, "There's the man!" He handed him Brockman's letter, and in a few months Robertson and his family were on their way to Nanking.

Within a few years Brockman's dream was realized in a remarkable way. The popular young educational genius Brockman had secured from America was addressing the largest audiences of officials, gentry, ancient scholars, and modern students that had ever listened to any man, Chinese or foreign, in all the history of China. In Peiping and a score of provincial capitals and port cities the numbers in attendance at Robertson's lectures rose from ten to more than fifteen thousand a week. Indeed, they included practically all the leaders of awakening China during this critical and formative period; and their interest and attendance continued for some three decades.

When Brockman sought to reach the official and student classes of this most ancient educated nation on earth, he was grieved to see the all but universal humiliation of the Chinese by most foreigners of the West, who subjected the Chinese to a lower social status, to subordinate positions, and sometimes to brutal treatment. This policy of subordination and exclusion was observed in business, in industry, in social clubs, in hotels, and in almost all secular and, unfortunately, in some religious institutions. As an illustration, Brockman was startled to find that his dearest Chinese friend, Charles Soong, who had long prepared for the Christian ministry, was not permitted to enter Christian work in China as an equal of non-Chinese graduates of American and English colleges. This meant that few of the best Chinese cared to enter Christian work.

To right this wrong of treating the Chinese as inferiors,

Brockman threw himself with unshakable conviction into a campaign not only to bring the members of the races of East and West together on a basis of complete social equality but to develop Chinese leadership throughout the country in all institutions and in all walks of life where the two races worked together. Brockman's view was that the Chinese and the foreigner were to be equal fellow workers from the start, but that the foreign workers were to decrease in responsibility and the Chinese steadily to increase. At the earliest possible moment the Chinese were eager to assume the major responsibility, assisted by the foreigners as advisers and fellow workers. The result of this policy of developing Chinese leadership led ultimately to its being extended to the presidency and professorships of colleges, to the organization and conduct of church bodies, and to other secular and religious organizations. Brockman and the most farsighted missionaries were determined that the Chinese should be advanced to the leadership of their own work, for there was always a danger of the lurking influence of foreign imperialism and the feeling of superiority of Western nations.

Early in his career Brockman placed himself under the direction of Chinese leaders. His emphasis upon Chinese leadership was prophetic, and his example in this respect kindling and contagious. He inspired his fellow missionaries to feel that they were humble learners and enthusiastic discoverers of the priceless treasures of China's classic culture in the past and of its yet greater possibilities in the future. The title of his book *I Discover the Orient* was thoroughly characteristic. He wrote: "I am rich. I have come into a great inheritance. My wealth has been gathered for thousands of years. Confucius, Mencius, Mo Ti, Buddha, Abraham, Moses, Isaiah, Paul, Jesus—I have entered into their inheritance. I am heir of the ages. I am sent not to dig up roots but to gather in the harvest."

Many missionaries testified that they had been inspired and helped by Brockman's faith and influence: Bishop Bashford, Bishop Birney, Bishop Roots, Leighton Stuart, Dr. A. J. Bowen, Dr. R. J. McMullen, and scores of others. The Chinese leaders whom Brockman helped to inspire and mold form a considerable portion of China's *Who's Who*. Brockman led in organizing the Edinburgh Continuation Conferences of 1912-13 in China, and helped to form the National Christian Council of China, to seek ultimately to unite all mission work under Chinese rather than foreign leadership.

When Brockman addressed the first board of directors of the Hong Kong Y.M.C.A., they were facing what seemed to them a huge budget with an empty treasury and almost no visible resources. When he spoke on faith, the chairman, Tong Kai-son, interrupted to say: "You tell us to have faith; you deal in faith. But we are businessmen; we have to pay our debts in dollars. If you could turn your faith into dollars, it would be all right." Brockman at once replied: "You are quite right, Mr. Tong. If I cannot turn my faith into money, it is of no use. I promise you that I will not leave Hong Kong until we have the necessary funds to carry us through the rest of the year."

When Brockman found that every Christian in the city was poor, he called upon the most influential Confucian Chinese in the city and placed the entire budget before him. This Confucianist said: "Do you mean to do all of that work with so little money? Leave this budget with me. I will take care of the expenses." A second Confucianist, without hearing what this man had done, also offered to meet the entire budget. When the board was called together, Brockman was able to report that each dollar of faith had been turned into two dollars of Hong Kong currency. From that time these men began to grow in faith, and then other national and local boards began learning the same lesson. They saw that faith was not trying to believe something in spite of evidence but daring to do something in scorn of consequences.

Early in his career in China, Brockman had gone to the great Welsh missionary, Timothy Richard, to ask how he could most successfully serve and win the Chinese scholar and student classes. Richard said to Brockman: "Follow the scriptural injunction: When you enter into a city, seek out the most worthy." He showed that the worthy included not only Christians but also Confucianists, Buddhists, Taoists, and Moham-

medans as well—"every man that worketh good," who seeks for
the moral, the spiritual, and the eternal, instead of the immoral,
carnal, and temporal. He assured Brockman that these moral
and tolerant Chinese gentlemen would give not only their service but their financial support to make the work for China's
young men a success, even in an avowedly Christian organization. At this point Confucianism was the most tolerant, the
most undogmatic, and the most moral of the non-Christian
religions; next to Judaism, it was best fitted to provide a kind
of "old testament" to Christianity in China.

Members of the chamber of commerce in the proud classical
city of Soochow, in the Yangtze valley, had complained to Brockman that when the modern railway and all the allurements of
Western material civilization came to their city, just at the
hour when their old family life was disintegrating, their sons
began going to modern hotels and scandalous resorts, with their
popular lure of dances, drink, and imported women. They
asked what they could do to save their youth, who were being
so rapidly demoralized. Brockman suggested the counter-attrac-
tion of a modern Y.M.C.A. building, with its auditorium, gymnasium, baths, roof garden, dining hall, educational classes,
sports and athletics, coupled with its moral restraints, religious
motivation, and character-building activities.

These Confucianists were so impressed that they asked Brockman to address the whole chamber of commerce the next day,
and then and there formally adopted a resolution to raise sub-
scriptions and erect such a building for their young men. A
year later the new building was erected at a cost of more than
twice the amount that Brockman had suggested. The bulk of
the money was given by Confucian businessmen and members
of the great Chinese guilds. They knew that the board of directors had to be composed exclusively of Christian men, representing all the churches. But many of these non-Christian spon-
sors preferred the Christian character of the work when they
came to see that it had the moral dynamic to reach and hold
their young men, which their own ancient religions, classic
ceremonies, and traditional family life could no longer do.

When one of these Confucian businessmen was frankly told by Brockman that the control of this Christian association must be in the hands of Christians, he replied: "Yes, of course, but cannot a non-Christian contribute to a Christian organization?" This man and other great Confucianists were thereby honoring the broad tolerance of Confucius himself and teaching a much-needed lesson to the Christian foreigners in this virtue. The same principle of going to the most worthy, of enlisting the earnest service and generous giving of Confucian businessmen, later proved valid in every city in China. This tended to vindicate the policy of establishing self-governing, self-supporting, and self-propagating churches as rapidly as possible throughout China.

Brockman and his fellow workers organized courses of lectures on modern science, social welfare, and many other practical and helpful subjects for young men, so that they could be trained in mind, body, and spirit, and organized for unselfish service to their own people on behalf of underpaid impoverished labor, in work for ricksha coolies, and in the teeming factories, industrial centers, and city slums. Such sacrificial service had never been conceived by China's old religions. Scores and often hundreds of Chinese young men in a single city were also early enrolled in Bible classes to develop a Christian conscience for individual character and social service. For centuries foreign missions had been handicapped by Chinese prejudice against Christianity. The classical scholar would not deign to lose face by listening to the preaching of "the foreign devil," either in a chapel or on the street. His prejudices were aroused by the foreigners' dogmatic and exclusive theology, which seemed so to conflict with Confucian tolerance and broad humanism. The missionary found it extremely difficult to discover a natural or social point of contact with self-satisfied Confucianists, for the Chinese and foreigner were living in two worlds, poles apart, and it seemed that never the twain could meet. But awakening China, long self-satisfied, at last realized that she needed everything, and needed it all at once; for she was helplessly medieval, centuries behind the modern world.

When Brockman, with joy, saw C. T. Wang succeed him as national secretary of the Y.M.C.A., and saw him in turn followed by David Yui and later by the present national leader, S. C. Leung, he felt that his quarter of a century in the Orient was complete and that he could accept a call to return to America, leaving his work to a Chinese leadership that was even better than his own. In this respect, he was one of the most advanced and far-seeing missionary statesmen of his generation. It was a true word spoken by one of the mission board secretaries: "Brockman thinks in continents." When he left the Orient, where he had been secretary for the Far East, he had been working in intimate relations with all the principal religious and political leaders of China, with such men as Prince Ito and Count Okuma in Japan, and with all the leading men of Korea. They saw in him a blood brother as well as a great organizer and religious leader.

Brockman was eager to learn from others. He was never glad when others went wrong, but "always gladdened by goodness, always slow to expose, always eager to believe the best, always hopeful, always patient." Yet he could flame in moral indignation at the sight of money-changers in the temple—when men would sell out their country for private gain. He had his limitations; but his gift for spending himself and losing himself in his cause, his ability to give his entire attention to the person with whom he was speaking, his rare sense of humor, especially when the joke was on himself, his quick sympathy, his instinctive tact, and his fearless integrity—all these made him winsome and very human. In a rare degree Brockman combined the Oriental courtesy of Confucius' "superior man" with Christian humility.

Brockman's intimate associates will remember his deep "cello voice" and his unique ability as a platform speaker; for, when he was at the top of his form, Brockman was in the best sense a real orator. An outstanding contemporary churchman and board secretary who has observed his work throughout the Orient writes: "He was the best beloved missionary in China in his day. His personal touch was felt all over the country. He

211

had the rare gift of prophetic insight. He was really a great Christian statesman, and his life qualifies him to be counted amongst the great missionaries of his generation."

Brockman had said, during his apprenticeship in Nanking, that he would gladly give forty years of his life if he could win even twelve of the literati or their successors, the student leaders of China. For long years he could not win even one of them, and he began the painful process of apparently "falling into the ground to die." If he had to fail, however, he was resolved to try to raise up a great Chinese leadership to take his place. But he lived to see great throngs of Chinese students attending his evangelistic meetings. He saw several thousand Confucian students join Christian Bible classes and hundreds of them join the churches. As I write these words news comes of his last illness in a Columbia, South Carolina, hospital. Spiritual seer and statesman, he saw the vision of the new China. He was both a pathfinder and a crusader. As a fellow worker with God, as a master builder who kept himself out of sight, "he was waiting for the City with its fixed foundations, whose builder and maker is God."

KARL REICHELT

As I am seeking in this volume to describe the lives and work of varying types of missionaries, I include Karl Reichelt, the Norwegian Lutheran missionary, who has seen more than forty years of service on behalf of the Buddhists of China.[3] All of the four hundred and fifty millions of China have been affected by the three religions of Confucianism, Taoism, and Buddhism, even those who, like the Communists, have tried to repudiate all religion as superstition. If we estimate the number of real Buddhists in the world as approximately a hundred and fifty million,[4] the importance of Karl Reichelt's work in concentrat-

[3] In this account of Professor Reichelt I am indebted to Henry P. Van Dusen's *For the Healing of the Nations*, Scribner, 1940, pp. 66-67; and to Phillip J. McLean's article "To Christ by the Buddhist Path" in *The Christian Century* of September 23, 1926.

[4] For statistics of the various religions of the world, and of the denominations of Christendom, see the Appendix. Though all in China were tinged or affected

ing upon these most religious people in China is obvious. Timothy Richard made the first sympathetic study of Chinese Mahayana Buddhism, but no one has been able to build up all the techniques of an institution uniquely designed to influence and to win Buddhists, except Professor Reichelt. Without any missionary society behind him, having secured some support from individuals and groups, Reichelt with his wife and a Norwegian colleague, Thelle, secured a small house in Nanking and in 1922 started the mission which was maintained there until he moved to Hong Kong as a safer refuge.

From the first the work attracted Buddhist and Taoist monks. Funds were so lacking, however, that Reichelt was forced to sell his summer home to maintain the work into which he had put his whole heart. The success of this unique mission was so marked that the Lutheran Church in China gave its support, and the Norwegian Lutheran Missionary Society has assumed responsibility for the salaries of the workers. The enterprise is known as the Christian Mission to Buddhists. Reichelt describes it as "strictly Christocentric, but consequently very broad-minded." The aim is to give Buddhists an understanding of Christianity in an environment that makes them feel at home, so as to lead them, if possible, to a living faith in Christ. The study of Chinese Buddhism has shown that its higher forms approach Christian conceptions in many ways and, under sympathetic guidance, the final step to Christianity is not too difficult.

The noble soul of Gautama Buddha (563-483 B.C.) was in revolt against the evils of Hinduism and its distorted views of God. He believed that the final revelation came to him of "the four noble truths": that all existence involves suffering; all suffering is caused by indulging our insatiable desires; therefore all suffering will cease when all desires are suppressed; and this may be achieved by the noble "eightfold path" of right belief, aspiration, speech, action, livelihood, endeavor, thought, and concentration. This austere religion of Gautama virtually died out in India, the land of its birth; but it was the first religion

by the three religions, we cannot say that there are 450 million Buddhists, Confucianists, and Taoists in China.

in the world to become international. As it spread eastward toward China and Japan, where it won its largest triumphs, it gave birth to a pantheon of deities like Kuan Yin, the goddess of mercy and the hope of salvation through faith in Buddha. It was at best, however, a dim "light of Asia," with no God and Father of Jesus Christ shining as the sun of righteousness for the whole world.

Buddhist and Taoist pilgrimages are very popular in China; and all over the country holy mountains and famous temples, decrepit but beautiful, are visited by pilgrims. The pilgrims stop for a night or for several days at each temple, in whose "pilgrim hall" travelers are cared for during their stay. The Reichelts have wisely set apart a pilgrims' hall similar to those of the Buddhist monasteries and temples. There is the customary long platform for the bedding of the pilgrim, with a shelf above for his possessions. In the Reichelts' mission, opposite the platform, there is a table with an incense burner and, above it, a picture of Christ. Around the walls are suitable scripture quotations, such as: "God so loved the world, that he gave his only begotten Son," and "Come unto me, all ye that labor and are heavy laden, and I will give you rest." Visiting monks are made to feel at home in this room and invited to remain for a day or two to hear of Christ and to join in the periods of worship, meditation, and explanation.

A new literature is also being produced to meet their special need. A deep-toned Chinese bell, similar to those used in the temples, is sounded to call the worshipers together into the hall, fitted up in Chinese Buddhist style. There is a red lacquer altar with symbols in gold. These include the lotus lily, a symbol used by the Buddhists to illustrate the state of man in the world. As a lotus rises out of the slime and filth to beauty and purity, so the soul may blossom in beauty above the sin of the world. There is also the monogram of Christ in Greek; the symbol of the sun of righteousness; the ancient Chinese crosslike symbol of cosmic union and perfect peace; and the special emblem of this mission, the cross rising out of an open lotus lily. Over the altar is hung a copy of Hofmann's painting of Christ in Gethsemane, and above this, in black and gold, are four characters which mean, "In the beginning was the Word." Candlesticks are used on the altar, and incense is burned between them during the service of worship. Everything in the place fosters the spirit of worship in order to make these seekers, who may think they are orphans, feel at home in their Father's house. All of the symbols, and the whole setting and environment, seek to make contact with the worshiper's past experience and lead him upward and onward toward the Christian life.

At the services selections from Buddhist scriptures, in harmony with the Christian message, may be read along with passages from the Bible. The aim is to gain points of contact through truths recognized by all, from "the light that lighteth every man," and then give a positive and constructive Christian message. A monk from a neighboring Buddhist monastery near Nanking once bought a Bible and entered an old-fashioned street chapel, where he heard Buddhism so bitterly and unfairly attacked by a man who had no accurate or sympathetic understanding of it that he went away saddened. Reichelt believes that he has come not to destroy one value of truth or beauty realized in the past but to fill to the full the heart hunger, aspiration, and need of every seeker. The broad tolerance and sympathy of the mission spring from the conviction that all that is true, noble, and good comes from God, the Father of lights and the author of every good and perfect gift, and that Christ has other sheep not yet gathered into any denominational Christian fold.

At the heart of Reichelt's experiment is a brotherhood. This was begun in 1923 with six adults, one of whom had been a Buddhist monk who had taken an ascetic vow never to bathe or shave, and had locked himself in his tiny cell as a prison. Today he is the Christian Chinese secretary of the mission. The testimony of such a man naturally carries weight with other Buddhists. All members of the brotherhood bind themselves to follow Christ in all things and to seek to interpret Christianity to Buddhists. The members have all things in common, like the first disciples in Jerusalem, and eat simple vegetarian food, as Buddhists do. The order is not celibate, though most of the members have not married. Hundreds of monks from all over China have visited this Buddhist home and Christian shrine. During a normal year between eight hundred and a thousand stop here, and many gain a new conception of Christianity. Some hear of it in the far interior of China and come great distances to seek the truth, just as many of them formerly went on Buddhist pilgrimages. A number of orphans were handed over by the various temples for instruction, and a Christian school was opened.

When China was first threatened by Japanese invasion, Reichelt sought a safer retreat on a promontory high above the green hillsides near Hong Kong, with magnificent panoramic views between the steep hills toward the open sea. This Christian Buddhist center is one of the most remarkable communities in China or in all Asia. In English it bears the name "The Buddhist Christian Institute," but the more picturesque Chinese title, "Tao Fongshan," represents the three words "Truth-Spirit-Hill." It is indeed the Hill of the Spirit of Truth, or the Hill of the Word of God. The Hong Kong institution is a retreat or study center where Buddhists, especially Buddhist priests, who wish to know more about Christianity may come to live, to study, and to meditate. After their period of retreat they may return to their Buddhist work or, if they desire, they may decide to follow Christ, to be baptized, and even prepare for the Christian ministry.

Henry Van Dusen after his world trip through mission fields considered Reichelt's institution the most notable meeting place of two great religions in the world. He counted his day there one of the most memorable of his life. There Buddhism and Christianity are brought into sympathetic relation with each other, and the bridge from the pre-Christian to the Christian religion may be readily crossed. The Hong Kong buildings are all in graceful Chinese style, many of them being adaptations of what one finds in the beautiful Buddhist monasteries. One dormitory is for preliminary inquirers; another for those in definite Christian training. The lecture hall has sides wide open toward the hills, the sky, and the sea. At the center is the chapel, which is a circular building, with a simple altar. Beneath the dome hangs the star of Bethlehem, and beneath that another star of symbolic meaning. Various symbols are interspersed with the insignia of the fellowship of the order—an open lotus lily, which is the Buddhist symbol of unfolding truth, supporting a cross. In the light of this symbolism Buddhism would seem to Reichelt to be the basis, the background, the pre-Christian "old testament" which prepares the way for the Christian gospel.

It is a picturesque sight to see a score of young Chinese emerge from the various buildings when the deep-toned bell reverberates across the valley. They make their way silently to the chapel, some in black robes, some in white, some with shaven heads after the fashion of the Buddhist priests, and some unshaven. Reichelt and his associate enter to conduct the vesper chapel service. There are hymns and psalms, scripture reading and prayers. The stillness of the spot, in the heart of the beauties of nature, the simple yet beautiful Oriental buildings, and the quiet voice of the elderly Norwegian saint whose life speaks through his words, all leave a profound impression, not only upon the worshipers, but even upon the foreign visitor.

It is a great occasion when a Buddhist monk is ready to take the final step of becoming a Christian. But many are ready to take at least the next step in an advance toward the truth of Christ. Many who visit this Christian mission to Buddhists spread the news of it and arouse interest in it in monasteries all over China. Apparently the leading Chinese Buddhist, Tai Hsu, wrote an article attacking Christianity in general and this mission in particular. Later he met Professor Reichelt, and his attitude was so altered that in 1923 he invited Reichelt to speak with perfect liberty as a Christian to a World Conference of Buddhists. After Reichelt had spoken on the prologue of John's Gospel, Tai Hsu, as chairman, explained the Buddhist use of the Tao or "the Word," and added: "Jesus Christ is the incarnate Word or Tao; this I now understand. But for us the chief thing is that the Tao can also be incarnated in us."

Only the divine mind that knows the secrets of the heart could tell the story of all the pilgrims who visit this Christian shrine, or monastery. Li Tao-si may be an example of many others. For years he had traveled to all the holy places of China he could visit, from the far south to Mongolia, and from the sea to Tibet, seeking peace for his heart and satisfaction for his soul. Some years ago, when passing through Nanking on his way to the sacred island of Pu-to, he stopped at a small Buddhist temple for the night. The local priest, who had often attended the services at the neighboring mission and who was in sympathy with the work, told Li of the pilgrim hall of the mission and advised him to visit it. As this was the first time Li had heard of the Christians doing anything special for Buddhists, he decided to visit the place. He came to the mission; and in the quiet, sympathetic Christian atmosphere of the spot he found Jesus Christ and the fullness of life that he came to give, which Li had been vainly seeking in Buddhism for years.

If Timothy Richard could know of all the Buddhists who have found blessing here, it would give him great joy. How it would gladden William Carey, whose heart was reaching out to the whole Orient, or the Apostle Paul, who carried the good news throughout the Roman Empire in Europe and Asia, but who had probably scarcely heard of China, or of Buddhism, or Confucianism! Surely Karl Reichelt is another scribe in the Kingdom of God who is bringing forth from his treasures things new as well as old. He is a worthy pathfinder in the world missionary crusade, that must include all the followers of Gautama Buddha.

CHANG PO-LING

On each visit to China I saw and worked with that great soul Chang Po-ling. I agreed with the judgment of President Eliot of Harvard that Chang was in many respects China's greatest educator. Chang Po-ling was a graduate of the old Imperial Naval College and an officer in the Chinese navy, from which he resigned because he felt that China's greatest need was education. Under the Manchus he was invited by the gifted

Yen Hsui to aid him in his educational program as vice-president and acting head of the imperial board of education for the whole Empire. Under his patronage, and with the generous contributions on the part of the gentry and officials of thousands of dollars, a model educational institution called Nan Kai was started in Tientsin. Chang was made principal, or president. So famous did this college become that it enrolled students from all the eighteen provinces of China; and Chang, as Arnold did at Rugby, left his stamp on many a student.

Professor Robertson came in contact with Chang Po-ling and helped him by lecturing in his college. Chang's mother had been an earnest Buddhist, his father a strict Confucianist; but through the materialistic writings of Spencer and Huxley, Chang himself had become a Confucian atheist. Oppressed by the problems of evil and human suffering, he became a confirmed pessimist and was deeply discouraged over the condition of China, which seemed to be drifting from bad to worse. When he unburdened his heart to Robertson, he said: "I notice that you Christians seem to have some hidden source of joy and peace and power. What is the secret of this power?" Robertson invited Chang to join him in studying the Bible, and together they began with the problems of the book of Job, and then the life of Christ. Months passed and their friendship grew.

Chang told me personally, as we talked till nearly midnight one evening, the thrilling story of his conversion. When he was appointed representative of his province on an educational commission that was to visit America and Europe, Robertson invited him to his home on the night before his departure. Robertson spoke to him again of Christ and asked him if he would join him in prayer. Chang said that as he knelt to pray it seemed as if a great light filled his soul and flooded his whole being. His conversion seemed almost as clear, as instantaneous and revolutionary, as the blinding vision of the Apostle Paul himself; and his came, as did Paul's, as the climax of a long struggle. He knelt an agnostic, he rose a Christian; he knelt a pessimist, he rose an optimist. The face of all the world seemed changed, and he could not sleep the whole night for joy. In the morning he said: "I have been drifting for ten years like a ship at sea without chart or compass; now I know where I am going." He hastened to Tientsin and spent the first day with his family, telling them of his decision. The next day he went to his college, calling together teachers and students, and finally the board of directors. With glowing face he told them all why he had become a Christian. Finally he resigned his college position, for he could no longer bow to the tablet of Confucius.

On the following day Chang journeyed to Peiping and spent the day with the officials, boldly telling them the reasons for his decision. A whole week was spent with these men, who finally said: "Well, be a Christian if you must, but be a Christian in secret. Simply bow to the tablet of Confucius; it is only an empty, outward form, and you can believe what you like in your heart." But Chang stood firm and said: "A few days ago, One came to dwell within my heart. He has changed all life for me forever. I dare not bow to any other, lest he depart." When urged by some of his Christian friends to be more cautious, he said boldly: "I want everybody to know that Chang Po-ling has become a Christian."

After spending six months in America and Europe visiting the leading institutions, he returned to give his report in China. He was then called to be the president of his old college, as a recognized Christian leader. Night after night he presided at the evangelistic meetings in Tientsin and swayed the two thousand non-Christian government students as he gave his ringing testimony for Christ, with such winsome reasonableness and joyous fervor that repeatedly the great audience broke into applause. A growing company of men is going out from his college with the stamp of Chang's life and character upon them. He still occupies the position of president today, although the college has been driven on the great trek for more than fifteen hundred miles into Western China.

WU YI-FANG

I might have told here the story of Miss Laura Haygood of the Southern Methodist Church, once principal of the Girls' High

School in Atlanta, who felt called to found her great school for the daughters of the leading scholar and official families in Shanghai. I might have told of her unconsciously influencing her former Sunday school pupil in America, Fletcher Brockman, to become a missionary, and of her winning some of China's most distinguished women for Christ. But instead, I shall do what Laura Haygood would have wished—and what unfortunately Dr. Wu would emphatically have protested against—tell briefly the story of one of her greatest pupils, Dr. Wu. I say *one* of her greatest pupils, for others included the wife of Charles Soong, and later her three famous daughters, Madame Chiang Kai-shek; Madame Sun, the wife of Sun Yat-sen, the father of China's republic; and Madame H. H. Kung—with many others of the leading women of the new China who studied in Laura Haygood's great institution and felt her enduring influence, which will reach to the third and fourth generations.

Wu Yi-fang, the first Chinese woman college president, was born in 1893 in Wuchang, Hupeh Province, China. Her father was a scholar-official who held office in Wuchang and northern Hupeh. Her progressive Confucian uncle opened one of the first schools for girls in China. Her older sister had great ambition for Yi-fang and herself and for women in general, and Yi-fang at an early age was reading new books and pamphlets urging reform. At this time in Peiping the young emperor was listening to K'ang Yu-wei and Liang Ch'i-chao and trying to introduce new ideas into the government. The edict favoring schools for girls was issued in 1907, and that same year Yi-fang started with her sister on a journey of eleven days by sedan chair, houseboat, and steamer to enter one of the new schools in Hangchow. Later they attended mission schools in Shanghai, Soochow, and Hangchow, where they received more of the "new learning," and training in the English language, the key to Western science.

When Yi-fang was eighteen years of age, her father, mother, elder sister, and brother died within a year; and she was left to care for her grandmother and a younger sister. She taught English in a girls' normal school for one year and then entered Ginling College in February 1916, becoming a member of the first class which graduated in 1919. Although interested especially in science, she ranked high in all subjects. Upon her graduation as a bachelor of arts she was invited to return to Ginling as an assistant; but she accepted instead a position in the Peiping Higher Normal School, where she was head of the English department from 1919 to 1922, the period in Peiping of the literary renaissance, the beginning of Russian influence, and the rise of anti-Christian propaganda.

In 1922 Miss Wu went to Ann Arbor as a Barbour scholar in the University of Michigan. She completed her master's work in biology in 1924 and received her Ph.D. degree in 1928. On June 18, 1928, from the commencement platform, President Clarence Cook Little of the University of Michigan looked out upon the twenty-one hundred candidates for undergraduate and graduate degrees. Wu Yi-fang was not among them, but was already on her way back to Nanking to sit in conference with the directors of Ginling College. With her diploma in his hand, referring to her brilliant work and her task of building the new China, President Little said:

I have the honor to make an announcement unique in the history of education. Today the University of Michigan confers upon Miss Wu Yi-fang the degree of doctor of philosophy in biology. . . . In her six years at Ann Arbor she endeared herself to those who knew her, and inspired in them a confidence that she can graciously fill this unusual post and render through it a high service to the great country from which she comes. The University of Michigan is proud to have had a share in the preparation of Dr. Wu for her new task.

Dr. Wu, this deeply humble but truly great woman, is even more impressive to see than her college, whether at Chengtu or in beautiful Nanking, where it will some day return. With her cultivated speech, her perfect command of English, her vigorous, poised, and experienced manner, she is obviously an administrator. The union of womanly gentleness, sensitiveness, dignity, and quiet strength shown in her clear eyes and firm mouth reveal a character of unusual quality. She is a scientist of distinction, a gifted educator, a prominent leader in national affairs—

> A perfect woman, nobly planned,
> To warn, to comfort, and command.

To see her is to be reminded of such pathfinders as Mary Lyon, Alice Freeman Palmer, Laura Haygood, and Mary Woolley, in America.

Not easily nor at a bound did Dr. Wu gain her place of distinction. As a proud and materialistic Confucian student she once opposed Christianity. For all her fine mind, she could for a long time see no meaning in life, and had no interest in it. When she looked into her own heart, or upon her family and her nation, all seemed dark. But at long last, as an agnostic student, she fought her doubts and gathered strength. Almost enviously she watched her earnest Christian roommate kneel to pray. When she went home with her on vacation and saw her roommate's radiant Christian mother and the hitherto undreamed-of beauty of a Chinese Christian home, she saw that religion was not mere superstition but a great reality, a comfort, and a moral dynamic. She saw that these Christians had something that she and her superior Confucian ancestors had never known. Finally, with tears of sympathy, her roommate's Christian mother said to this heart-hungry agnostic, this spiritual orphan: "My dear, whatever your doubts, we need you, the cause of Christ in China needs you." And finally, Wu Yi-fang, without much theological faith, replied out of her deep moral consciousness, "I believe—in part—God help my unbelief. Even though with faltering steps, I must be a Christian and follow Jesus' way of life." She joined the Baptist Church, but the wise Chinese pastor asked her no theological catch questions. She had simply heard Christ's call, "Come and follow me," and this she had begun to do.

At first Dr. Wu found it difficult to believe the good news of a God who was both the Father of Jesus Christ and her Father also. But Jesus' call to sacrifice and suffering, to take up her cross and follow him, deeply appealed to her. She was greatly helped by Fosdick's *Manhood of the Master, Meaning of Faith,* and *Meaning of Service,* as well as by her personal interview with Dr. Fosdick when she was in America.

In her college Dr. Wu's life speaks louder than her words, and she is loved and followed eagerly by her adoring students. No man can tell the story; but her character and life are written in the more than five hundred alumnae of the college. Dr. Wu says: "If a Chinese woman is well trained and qualified, she may compete equally with men for any position from the highest government office down. Only as women become educated can we expect them to step into their places as leaders."

China is giving greater opportunity to its new and educated womanhood than is Japan, or India, or any other country in Asia. Madame Chiang Kai-shek, who takes the deepest interest in Ginling College and who counts Dr. Wu as a trusted friend, remembering what she owes to her own education, said on one occasion: "Ginling is fine in everything save one point only—instead of a hundred and fifty undergraduates you should be training fifteen hundred here today." And doubtless some day they will be. Like the Union Medical College in India, the China colleges, where students have come from eighteen provinces and represent all classes of society, still need our help.

Ginling College was founded by a small group of American Christian women in the Yangtze valley, who realized the need for educated women leaders in the new social and economic world brought into being by the Chinese revolution of 1911. Mrs. J. Lawrence Thurston, of Mount Holyoke College, was president from 1915 to 1928. When the Chinese Ministry of Education wisely demanded Chinese leadership in its educational institutions, Dr. Wu Yi-fang became the first Chinese woman president of the only separate Christian college for women in all China, supported interdenominationally. During the following nine years, until the Japanese invasion in 1937, the college grew steadily, doubling its student body, enlarging and modifying its curriculum to China's requirements, building new buildings, adding to its campus. President Wu's policies as president and her activities beyond the college proper put her in the forefront of China's educational, political, and religious advance.

I had the rare privilege of speaking in beautiful Ginling—which is the literary name of Nanking, meaning "Golden Heights"—with its forty-acre campus facing Purple Mountain. It lay within the city wall of Nanking, the greatest city wall in the world, rising to a great height and twenty-two miles in circumference. There were fourteen buildings of inimitable Chinese architecture. The college was opened with a mighty faith in China's future, with nine students and six faculty members—resembling the first women's college in India. The original members of the class of five, including Dr. Wu, were among the first women to receive the A.B. degree in China. In 1937 there were 259 students with 63 members of the faculty, consisting of Chinese, American, and British teachers. In Dr. Wu herself I could see the type of womanhood she and her associates are developing in these future leaders.

Since 1937 the Japanese invasion has multiplied the difficulties of college administration a hundredfold. Forced, with other college executives, to decide where work could be continued best, Dr. Wu has taken Ginling College to the campus of West China Union University in Chengtu in the province of Szechwan, sixteen hundred miles west of Nanking. On a clear day it is now within sight of the snows of Tibet. Here four other colleges are also established in refugee quarters. As in other centers in China, a co-operative arrangement has been worked out between the institutions, each school maintaining its individuality and readjusting its specialized fields for more practical service to the country. These brief words cannot tell the story of that heroic trek to Chengtu. The students were not transported by airplane or Pullman sleeper. Dr. Wu herself led one of the groups on that arduous journey of over sixteen hundred miles—by boat, by bus, by truck, and on foot—to build a brave new China. Dr. Wu has ever been a pioneer, and I include her proudly among our great pathfinders.

Two thirds of the forty faculty members of Ginling College are Chinese, and the remaining third British and American. The high standards, even in wartime, have satisfied the regents in New York and the Ministry of Education in China. A degree on graduation is equivalent to a degree from a Grade *A* American college. Ginling was recognized by the Association of American Colleges in 1926. Literature, the sciences, social studies, philosophy, and music form the core of the curriculum. Extra-curricular activities include music, dramatics, athletics, student government, Y.W.C.A., and social service.

The board of founders has its headquarters at 150 Fifth Avenue, New York. The supporting units of Ginling include: The Woman's American Baptist Foreign Missionary Society; Woman's Division of Christian Service, Board of Missions and Church Extension of The Methodist Church; Domestic and Foreign Missionary Society, Protestant Episcopal Church; Board of Foreign Missions, Presbyterian Church, U.S.A.; Board of Foreign Missions, Reformed Church in the United States; United Christian Missionary Society; faculty, alumnae and undergraduates of Smith College. The total annual budget, amounting to $43,508 in United States currency, is raised by contributions from co-operating units, by gifts from individuals, by a share in the funds of the Associated Boards of Christian Colleges in China, by interest on investments, by fees paid directly to the college, and by grants from the Ministry of Education in China, as well as by gifts from alumnae. It also receives part of the offerings made on the World Day of Prayer. In 1940, the twenty-fifth anniversary of Ginling, a birthday gift of $30,000 was raised under the leadership of Mrs. Dwight W. Morrow; $15,478 of this came from Smith alumnae, who have been most loyal supporters of Ginling, in which they take great pride.

In 1938 Dr. Wu was head of China's delegation of distinguished men and women to the International Missionary Congress held at Madras, the first woman ever to head a national delegation to a world convocation. The Chinese delegation was generally recognized as the strongest sent by any one of the seventy nations represented among its five hundred delegates. Dr. Wu served as chairman of the section on the church and education, comprising distinguished educators from every quarter of the world. Among her other honors and titles only a few may be mentioned: She holds the degree of Sc.D. from St. Johns University, Shanghai; she is a member of Sigma Xi, U.S.A., of the National People's Political Council, and of the executive committee of the National Women's Association for War Relief; she is chairman of the national committee of the Y.W.C.A. and vice-chairman of the Chinese-American Cultural Relations Association, Chungking.

Dr. Wu has been closely associated with the development of the "new life" movement and the national organization of Chinese women for war relief. She is one of the fifteen women members of the People's Political Council, and the only woman among the seven chairmen of the council. She impresses all thinking Americans who meet her as a great woman, one who passes with dignity and grace through every door open to her, one whose greatness is rooted in character, in her inheritance from a long line of fine-minded men and women.

JAMES Y. C. YEN

I shall close this section on China with a brief sketch of James Y. C. Yen, known to a host of his friends in China and America as the beloved "Jimmie" Yen. His life is representative in a remarkable degree, because no other man, Chinese or foreign, has so studied and revealed the four chief weaknesses of his country; and probably no other man has done so much, practically and concretely, to remedy them. His life is of the greatest importance just at this time, for if the fourfold reforms he advocates are adopted wholeheartedly by the Chinese government, China can be saved. If these reforms are approved on paper by the Kuomintang, but actually defeated by the reactionaries, the landlords, the profiteers, and the grafters, who are trying now to control this war-torn land, probably nothing will be left for China but a Communist revolution. And such a revolution might be far more cruel and bloodthirsty than were the purges of Soviet Russia, if we may judge by the Taiping rebellion.

I first knew Jimmie Yen as a student in Hong Kong University and later at Yale, where he became the natural leader of the several thousand Chinese students then studying in America. Even before the time of Confucius, more than seventy-six generations ago, his celebrated ancestor, Yen Ping Chung, was honored by Confucius as a scholar and official "who knows the art of friendship." Jimmie Yen himself was born in a Confucian home of the old school and had memorized some of the Chinese classics before he was ten years of age. When the old examination system was abolished, his father sent him to acquire Western education. Before he was eleven he was sent to a school for boys in his far western province of Szechwan. The saintly and able principal of the school was W. H. Aldis, recently head of the China Inland Mission in London. Jimmie cried himself to sleep the first night in homesickness, but he implored the principal the next day not to send him home as too young to study in a boarding school. The second night he wept, but stifled his sobs in his pillow. Aldis' knowledge of Chinese was painfully limited, but he became a father to the lonely little Chinese boy; and in his character, life, and love, Jimmie saw the life of Jesus reproduced, and from this godly missionary's fatherly care he came to know God as a Father. Here in this school of the China Inland Mission he avidly studied the New Testament and became a Christian at the age of twelve.

But where did this Chinese boy get the adopted name of "James"? In a little churchyard in faraway Foochow there are the graves of eleven missionaries who were murdered by the mob just before the Boxer uprising. Among those graves are those of four members of the Stuart family—the father, mother, and two children. The eldest daughter helped to rescue her four surviving brothers and sisters, and these five orphaned children were sent back to England. After completing their education, they faced the question of their life work. England was home to them now; and China was the land that had murdered their father, mother, brother, and sister. Yet back to China all five went, constrained by the love of Christ to give their lives in missionary service to the people for whom their parents had died! Here was a motive beyond the dreams of Confucius. Here was the spirit of the early Christian martyrs.

The eldest son, James Stuart, went to the far western province of Szechwan and there came in touch with young Yen. James Stuart was the warden and Yen the assistant warden in a Chinese hostel and school. Here they worked together as brothers, and Yen taught Chinese to James Stuart. During the first World War, Stuart went to serve as a chaplain in France; and when he was killed on January 2, 1916, Yen told me that he knew by psychic telepathy that something had befallen his friend at that moment. Afterward, in sheer affection, Yen adopted the name of his friend James as his own. He now began to know something of the sacrificial spirit of that godly missionary of the China Inland Mission and of the martyred Stuarts.

Shortly afterward James Yen accompanied the two hundred thousand Chinese coolies who went to France to dig trenches for World War I. Here he was swamped by thousands of requests to write letters home to the families of the coolies, who were often in superstitious terror. Although it had never been known in Chinese history that coolies could be taught to read, and reading and writing had for several thousand years been confined to relatively few scholars, Yen suggested to the coolies that he teach them to read and write for themselves. And within six months the first fourteen laborers had learned a thousand of the most familiar characters; and as they stood reading the bulletins of the war, they were looked upon with amazement by the other coolies, as though they were miracles of learning, like Confucius himself. Then there was a rush, for all wanted to learn to read at once. Jimmie Yen then devised the "thousand character method," whereby within a few months illiterate Chinese could be taught to read and write a thousand essential characters.

Yen found that 85 per cent of these hitherto illiterate men were hardy farmers; and in his daily intimacy with them he began to see the significance of the Chinese word for coolie, *koo lee,* which means "bitter strength," or "bitter labor." In association with these Chinese laborers he discovered not only the hardness of their lot but the undreamed potentialities of these splendid men. He learned that China's chief wealth was not in her raw materials but in her undeveloped human resources. Even when, with a new wonder, these men could read, their chief problems were not thereby solved. They were afterward in dire poverty in China, often without work and the few pence a day it would bring. Then he saw that, partly as a result of their ignorance and poverty, a host of these men of "bitter strength" were suffering from serious diseases. He saw that China would need several million modern doctors and an adequate public health department. Moreover, he saw that, however much he and his fellow workers were able to do for China's impoverished masses, the three evils of ignorance, poverty, and disease still persisted because of gross misgovernment by rapacious officials. As he could not himself reform the hardened officials at the top, he decided to begin at the bottom.

Dr. Yen now took a whole Chinese county, Ting Hsien, south of Peiping, with some four hundred thousand inhabitants, in which to study the concrete needs of its people, to see if he and his fellow workers could find a solution for their problems. He began a training school for Chinese students returned from America, where as humble learners they might discover China's problems and practical means of meeting them. In time, in order to build up a model county, James Yen founded a people's school, to train Chinese peasants as successful farmers and citizens and to equip a new body of honest young officials who could go out to other counties and districts to help solve the four basic problems of China.

In the Ting Hsien experiment Yen and his fellow workers learned in bitter experience what all their study in America for their doctorates in philosophy had not taught them—what the four deep needs, or the four chief evils, of China were. And his own study was confirmed by that of China's great scholar, the father of her renaissance, Hu Shih. The latter, in his

"Which Road Are We Going?" in *China's Own Critics,* speaks of the great national enemies of poverty, disease, ignorance, corruption, and disorder. As disorder seems to be a result rather than a cause, and as two decades of lawless chaos under rival war lords, with their roving bands of soldiers and bandits, have fortunately ended, I shall confine myself to a discussion of the other four evils. That these are indeed China's chief problems is confirmed by the wholly independent experimental study for practical reform conducted by James Yen, which study showed the importance of these evils to fall in this order: ignorance, poverty, disease, and misgovernment.

Yen's mass education movement makes its first drive for the hundred million illiterate youths who are responsible and eager to learn. A four months' course of an hour each weekday night, or a total of ninety-six hours, at a cost of one dollar for the term, gives the bare rudiments of learning, the first start in education, for these eager students. Where facilities permit, the second period of the movement includes intensive training in citizenship. Book work is followed by instruction in sanitation and modern farming. The whole campaign is community wide, voluntary, and locally self-supporting. The millions of simple books that have been printed and sold are used by multiplied millions of people. Graduates proudly receive the diploma of "Literate Citizen." Dr. Yen believes that, with adequate official and voluntary planning and with government backing and enthusiastic popular support, once peace is restored, China's age-long problem of illiteracy can conceivably be solved within a generation, as it has been in Japan and, more recently, in Soviet Russia.

In the light of this hopeful new method of reform we may pause for a moment to examine these four needs, or problems, of China. When Dr. Yen began his work, he estimated that at least 85 per cent of the people of China had been left in illiteracy several thousand years after China's scholars had led the world in writing. While Japan, after a generation of amazing progress, claimed that 99 per cent of her children were in school and that an equal proportion of her people were literate, and while Soviet Russia had almost abolished illiteracy in two decades, the scholar-officials of China had complacently left their masses in ignorance. Fewer than a fourth of the men in China are able to read and write, and fewer than 2 per cent of the women.

Poverty is the most fundamental and basic material problem of China. Yen found that the average Chinese farm is less than 4 acres, compared to 14 in the Netherlands, 21 in Germany, 40 in Denmark, and 157 in the United States. Approximately half the land is farmed by tenants and part tenants. Rent takes from 45 to 60 per cent of farm production. Taxes, legal and especially illegal, for the current year or collected far in advance, fall heavily upon the Chinese peasant. When transportation by human labor is necessary, the cost is forty times as great as by rail. No wonder Sun Yat-sen dreamed of railways and roads, of scientific agriculture and industrialization for the people's livelihood. Floods destroy annually vast quantities of food and bring starvation and disease. The flood of 1931 affected some twenty-five million people. With all his medieval handicaps, the Chinese peasant on the average is only 7 per cent as productive as the American farmer. Instead of 1.2 man days to cultivate an acre of wheat, the Chinese peasant requires twenty-six days, so that wheat production per man in America is fourteen times what it is in China.

The experiment of James Yen at Ting Hsien showed that the whole standard of life in a given area might eventually be raised if, under able and honest officials, the farmers are given citizenship training, proper seed, help in modern methods of farming and animal husbandry, and aid through the hundreds of co-operative societies that are already functioning even under the tragic conditions of wartime. China has in her people, in her mineral wealth, and in her raw materials, vast undeveloped resources, which industrialization and modern transportation can help to utilize.

Disease is a further source of weakness in China. As Hu Shih says:

The slaughter from plague, phthisis, and syphilis is visible to all of us. There are, however, other diseases which do not so plainly kill men, but whose strength is enough to wipe out whole villages and weaken whole races, such as that dangerous and world-wide disease of malaria.

Regarding the fourth evil, misgovernment, Hu Shih said in 1931:

In corruption, China certainly leads the world. Not only is there an open and organized sale of offices in the state, not only has there been for twenty-five years no system of examination for government posts, but there is also the universal habit of bribery in every branch of Chinese society. It is exactly what Professor Huntington of Yale says: "In Chinese life there is one particularly hateful thing, and that is the practice of bribery." . . . There are districts where the taxes have been collected for a period of eighty years in advance. And these conditions, in spite of some general improvement, are still widespread.

Landlords and officials squeeze the peasant in his lack of capital by an average interest rate over wide areas in China of 32 per cent. Most of China's pawnshops in rural areas are owned by landlords and merchants. Their rate of interest in some districts is as high as 8 per cent a month. There is the closest connection between the rapacity of landlords, gentry, and officials, and the poverty of the peasants. Robbed to the point of starvation, the latter are driven into banditry or Communism. Misgovernment and corruption are not necessary traits of Chinese character, for in their business dealings the old Chinese guild merchants won a deserved reputation for honesty throughout the East; their word was as good as their bond.

Dr. Yen found that to meet China's four principal evils of poverty, ignorance, disease, and misgovernment, his country imperatively needs four things: (1) To meet the evil of poverty, China needs the fulfillment of Dr. Sun's "principle of the people's livelihood" by a program of land distribution and scientific agriculture, coupled with industrialization and the further extension of industrial co-operatives, to provide work for the landless poor and the great mass of the unemployed. (2) To meet the need of ignorance, she needs a vast program of education. (3) To meet the problem of disease, she needs a wide extension of her present excellent but limited medical training, coupled with an adequate program of public health. (4) And most of all, to meet the problems of misgovernment, of rapacious landlords and corrupt officials, China needs, not more moral precepts, but a new moral dynamic and effective religious motivation to meet her deepest and most long-standing evil.

Under the leadership of men like Dr. Yen, China could become a literate nation in a few decades, *if* such men were wholeheartedly supported by a liberal, united, intelligent, modern government. When Dr. Yen conducted his great experiment in Ting Hsien to study and abolish the ignorance, poverty, disease, and misgovernment in one county, he was confronted by seventy-five lawsuits that sought to kill his work, conducted by the gentry and the old officials who wished to continue to prey upon the peasantry and maintain their special privileges at all costs. They would have been quite content to keep China backward for the next four thousand years if they could have continued to batten upon the helpless poor. Opposition to his reforms, at Ting Hsien and in other places where they have been tried, has come from the local bad gentry, political bosses, unscrupulous landlords, and money lenders who are protecting their vested interests.

His fourfold program is evolutionary and nonviolent. If given right of way it could in time do away with the old semi-feudal power of the landlords and not only educate but emancipate the common people according to Dr. Sun's plan. China's standard of living, her literacy, and her efficiency will all remain low until these imperative, interrelated reforms are *introduced all together*. China can have neither scientific agriculture without industrialization nor industrialization without scientific agriculture, and both will be impossible without transportation. These reforms cannot be realized against the centuries-old inertia of the peasants, and the special interests and profiteering of the possessing classes, without adequate moral and spiritual dynamic and motivation. China does not need more moral precepts, for she has had more than any land on earth; she needs a spiritual revolution even more than economic and political reform.

Despite the close censorship in Chungking, it is constantly becoming more widely known in America that there are re-actionary forces in the Kuomintang, or Nationalist Party, that control the educational system of China, the propaganda in the army, the appointment of officials by a system of patronage, and that have their own secret police. To repeat, things have reached such a state in China that, if these reactionary forces, together with rapacious landlords, speculators, and grafting officials, have their way, they threaten a Communist revolution after the war. If space permitted, quotations could be given showing the prevailing habit of "squeeze," or graft, among the more selfish officials, not only on the downfall of each dynasty in degenerate times, but also during the most successful administrations—from the early days of the illustrious Han dynasty, beginning in 206 B.C., through the feudal period at the time of Confucius, during the decline of the Manchus, and under the Republic from 1911 to 1945.

The war has brought conditions in China to a crisis. As the world conflict comes to a close, China will be left standing at the parting of two ways. Everything is ready for her to choose either path. On the one hand, there is the path already being followed by some of the reactionary cliques of the party in power. We may heavily discount the glowing pictures painted of conditions in the Communist-controlled areas; but these Communist leaders will have before them not only China's agelong right and duty of revolution from the time of Mencius but also the example of successful Soviet Russia, its sympathy, and perhaps its tacit or active support. This powerful nation will be just over the border—a boundary of nearly five thousand miles, far longer than the thirty-five hundred miles between Canada and the United States.

Every Christian who believes in prayer should pray for

Chiang Kai-shek that he may have the courage to back the needed reforms wholeheartedly, and that he may not compromise nor stand on the sidelines to arbitrate between all the power groups and selfish interests on the one hand and the exploited peasants on the other. Things are far too desperate to wait for decades while the officials continue to profess to be loyal to the three "people's principles," including the livelihood of the peasants, who continue to be exploited and robbed. If Chiang does not have the courage to do this, the Communists will certainly undertake it. They have a powerful army that Chiang himself could not conquer in a decade, an army that has successfuly fought the Japanese by guerrilla warfare. They have able, sacrificial leaders and the sympathy of giant Russia behind them; and they demand justice for the peasants without hypocrisy or delay. I believe, however, that Dr. Yen as a Christian has the solution that China needs—the only solution. Based on the teaching of Amos and that of Jesus Christ, the solution of James Yen demands justice for all.

Before the Japanese invasion had destroyed his work, Dr. Yen had called for ten thousand Chinese students as leaders in a national crusade to go out in sacrificial service to meet these four great needs of China. In every evangelistic campaign his fellow evangelists could point to James Yen as a living example of the love of Christ that constrained him. They could point to his work for the Chinese coolies in France when he first taught them to read, and to his literacy campaign which, if backed by the government and public opinion, could make China literate in a generation, just as Japan and then Soviet Russia had become literate. They could show the practical nature of the Ting Hsien experiment, with a hundred returned Chinese students, in making the first model county where China's four problems could be solved and her four evils corrected. Finally, in every audience they could point Chinese students who were without the motivation of religion to those eleven graves in the churchyard in Foochow; to those five Stuart children who had given their lives in sacrificial devotion to the land that had killed their parents; to James Stuart's laying down of his life in France; and, more especially, to the courageous, selfless work of Jimmie Yen and his fellow workers in their program designed to meet the four deepest needs of China.

I close this section by showing how I actually used the illustration of James Yen in one typical evangelistic campaign in Foochow in 1914. The night before we were to begin the meetings, the Chinese interpreter—who was a great Christian and a member of the provincial parliament—and I went to the churchyard for a time of prayer beside those eleven graves of martyred missionaries, including four of the Stuart family who are buried there. Then with Professor Robertson we went up to the great guild hall where five thousand a day—students, officials, and representative businessmen of the ancient guilds— were pouring out to the meetings, admitted by ticket only. Professor Robertson and I had visited this province in response to a telegram of invitation received from the governor, the chamber of commerce, the minister of education, and the Confucian principals of the government colleges. Each student attended two successive meetings on science and religion—the two subjects China most needed and that her students most wanted to hear about. And the Christian message was always presented as a challenge for the whole of life, personal and social, individual and national.

In preparation for a campaign in the entire province, three hundred and fifty Chinese workers, including the strongest leaders from ten neighboring cities, were gathered in Foochow for a week of special training for the meetings in their own cities. Professor Robertson had prepared and equipped with apparatus five science lecturers, Chinese and foreign, to repeat his lecture on science, while another group had been prepared as evangelists. These men were now sent out two by two—an evangelist and a scientist—to speak to students and leaders throughout the whole province, with a population larger than New York State. The Confucian governor sent letters to the officials of the province to co-operate in arranging for the meetings, and to help gather picked audiences in the cities and secondary towns. Thirteen central and two hundred smaller cities and towns were visited. Many thousands attended the meetings, and over nine thousand inquirers were enrolled in that one province. One can recall no similar campaign or movement in any land in which Christians and non-Christians united to hear and to broadcast a message on both science and religion, and in which the Christian message included both individual and social aspects of life for the whole man, for a whole nation, and for the whole world.

To illustrate the meaning of the cross of Christ, I pointed to the sacrifice of my classmate Horace Pitkin, to the eleven martyrs' graves in the churchyard of their own city, and to the living sacrifice of James Yen. I asked every student audience this question: "Where did this man, Dr. Yen, get his dynamic motivation? Why should he give his life in sacrificial service when so many selfish, corrupt officials—even when they know Confucius' teaching by heart and can recite his moral precepts—are robbing China and letting her sink to her doom?"

I believe that such pioneers as Timothy Richard, Bishop Schereschewsky, Francis Hawks Pott, Hudson Taylor, Fletcher Brockman, and Karl Reichelt have laid strong foundations in China, but that it is the great pathfinders among the Chinese themselves, like Chang Po-ling, Wu Yi-fang, and James Yen, who must in the end save their country.

5

PATHFINDERS IN AFRICA AND THE MOSLEM WORLD

Africa has not the clear features of India with its scientific census, or of China with its massive unity. Not yet knit together by a system of communications, it is still the neglected continent, partly unknown, largely uncivilized, unchristianized—still a challenge to the Christian world. We can only estimate its population—about 157 million, compared to 400 million for India and an approximate 450 million for China. The pathfinder David Livingstone (1813-73), missionary and explorer, opened up the continent to the knowledge and sympathy of the Christian world. He had offered himself to the London Missionary Society for service in China, but providentially he was sent to Africa. Arriving at the station founded by Robert Moffat twenty years before, Livingstone became convinced that the success of the white missionary would consist not in reporting doubtful converts to the home society but in pioneering to open up new territory. And he also believed that new regions could best be evangelized by Africans themselves, as was done later in the highly successful work of the Church Missionary Society in Uganda.

After Livingstone's mission work north of the Orange, in 1851-56, he traversed the continent from west to east. From 1858 to 1864 he explored the lower Zambezi and Lake Nyasa. In thirty years he made possible African geography; as Britain's and the world's greatest explorer, he revealed the brutality of the Arab slave market in the heart of this neediest continent. Seeing Moslem Arabs shoot down helpless African women in the markets and villages that they might enslave the men for commercial profit, Livingstone realized the evils of Islam and the meaning of Christ for Africa and the Negro. His iron constitution finally broken by malaria and dysentery, he was slowly

239

crucified; but his lonely death in the heart of Africa created a keener desire on the part of Christendom to open up, civilize, and Christianize the Dark Continent than a hundred published volumes on exploration could have done. It was the pure and tenderhearted pathfinder Livingstone who dealt the deathblow to the slave trade and who raised up a thousand followers determined to evangelize Africa and the Moslem world. It was not science, nor exploration, but Christian missions, which undertook the long process of the saving of backward and neglected Africa, as they had begun the evangelization of Asia and Europe nineteen centuries before.

SAMUEL ZWEMER

Samuel Marinus Zwemer was a flaming crusader, given the unique call to arouse the student movement and a complacent world church to the evangelization of the Moslem world. He carried the whole Moslem world on his heart: he studied it, he knew it, he loved it, he preached it from the housetops, and he would have proclaimed it from every Moslem minaret and mosque could he have done so. It was fortunate that he "kept smiling," for this fact often saved him with Moslems from whom his life was at times in danger. I remember a tight spot on the upper Nile, when we were distributing New Testaments to Moslems in an after meeting, and Sam said, "Keep smiling, Sherwood." There was a broad grin of indomitable good humor upon his own face. He was a wonderful "mixer" and was equally friendly with the poorest coolie or the sheiks of Islam. When I saw him, still smiling, handing out tracts in the famous El Azhar Mohammedan University, which was the intellectual and bigoted center of Islam for all Africa, I had an idea that Sam would have coveted nothing on earth so much as to be martyred on that very spot—as Raymond Lull had been in Algeria, North Africa. Indeed, Zwemer was the Protestant Raymond Lull of the nineteenth century, trying to arouse the Christian world for a united mission to Moslems.

The simple Dutch-American boy, Samuel Marinus Zwemer,

was born in Vriesland, Michigan, April 12, 1867. Here his father, Adriaan Zwemer, was the godly Dutch pastor serving in the first of his seven long pastorates. Even before his birth, and again when he was laid in his cradle, this child Samuel was consecrated to mission service by his devout Dutch father and mother. Not only did Sam and his younger brother, Peter, become missionaries, but five of the thirteen brothers and sisters gave a combined hundred and fifty years of service to the Christian ministry and the missionary cause. Sam's daughter is now in missionary service and one of his grandchildren is training as a medical missionary. It did not affect this smiling little Dutch baby in his cradle that later there was to be added almost a whole alphabet of degrees and titles to his name—D.D., LL.D., Litt.D., F.R.G.S., M.R.A.C., Hon. Phi Beta Kappa, and so forth. What mattered more than his degrees was the inheritance of his solid Dutch and Huguenot ancestors. When the Huguenot Sur-Mer brothers fled from France after the revocation of the Edict of Nantes, they finally became Zwemers in Holland. From these ancestors, Samuel Zwemer derived his linguistic ability. He was fluent in Dutch, German, English, and Arabic, and could read literature on Islam in ten languages. And also from these orthodox ancestors he derived his rock-ribbed faith. Zwemer was further grounded in the truth about the Word and the world in Hope College, Holland, Michigan, and in the New Brunswick Dutch Reformed Seminary.

When John Forman came to Hope College during the very first year of the volunteer movement, in 1886, Zwemer and five out of his class of seven volunteered among the first thousand who entered upon this new crusade of evangelism. And nothing would satisfy this young crusader but an "unoccupied" field. He first thought of Tibet, but when his brilliant professor of Arabic and Hebrew, Dr. John Lansing, constantly talked Arabia, that became Zwemer's goal. When the two young enthusiasts Samuel Zwemer and James Cantine offered themselves for Arabia to the Reformed Board, this new field was not accepted by the society. Nevertheless the young pathfinders went to the field, with or without any human agency, and four years later, after they had put Arabia on the missionary map, the mission was permanently adopted by the board. Lowell Thomas tells in his introduction to Zwemer's *The Golden Milestone*— which gives the history of Zwemer's early twenty-five years in Arabia with James Cantine and others that followed them— that to this day, along the Persian Gulf, the sheiks of Araby still talk of these two young pioneer missionaries who had the courage to tell the story of Christianity to the fanatical Moslems, who believed that to kill "a dog of a Christian" was one sure way of earning admission to paradise.

Those first years in isolated Arabia are a romantic story in themselves, but from 1890 to 1912 Zwemer was always working consciously for the 250 million Moslems of the world, with the prayer of Abraham on his heart: "Oh that Ishmael might live before thee!" As a pioneer Zwemer crossed the Oman peninsula, and was able twice to make the dangerous journey to Sana'a, the old capital of Yemen, for he longed to witness for Christ everywhere in Arabia. He later visited the chief Moslem centers of North Africa, India, China, Turkey, Persia, and Malaysia. Once, when I was speaking with Zwemer in Denver, Colorado, at a Laymen's Missionary Movement conference, the Christian laymen carried a motorcycle to the pulpit and presented it to me for my station in South India, and they gave Samuel Zwemer the promise of a fleet camel, which was better suited for the sands of Arabia than a motorcycle!

Zwemer was a pioneer organizer and promoter. Chairman of the first general missionary conference on Islam, held in Cairo in 1906, he also attended the second conference in Lucknow in 1911. As a result of these conferences he pleaded the cause of Moslem missions in Great Britain, Scandinavia, Germany, and America. The result was the formation of the Fellowship of Faith for Moslems and, indirectly, the Christian Literature Society for Moslems in New York City. To endeavor to knit together as far as it was humanly possible the work of all the individualistic missionaries to Moslems and to co-ordinate the efforts of their scattered denominations was in itself a herculean world task. But the impossible always appealed to Zwemer more than the possible. The Mohammedan religion is the only one which has met Christianity on a major scale and conquered wide areas, including the Holy Land itself. Few Moslems have left their faith to become open and avowed members of the Christian Church. Many thousands of Moslems have become Christians in the East Indies, and in Iran there are more than a thousand former Mohammedans who have become open members of the church; but, apart from these, there have never been great numerical results in winning Moslems to Christianity. Islam is a tightly knit system which determines just how every act in life shall be performed from morning till night and from the cradle to the grave. There is a strong group solidarity among Moslems that is welded by a fanatical devotion into one system which combines faith and patriotism. No one of us would lightly become a traitor to his country, an apostate to his religion, and a disgrace to his race, as a Moslem convert must become. Neither Zwemer, nor Gairdner, nor any other worker for Moslems that I know has ever won a dozen baptized converts who became permanent Christians. But that very fact constituted the supreme attraction of this calling for Zwemer, because it was the very hardest work in the world. Although the mission of the Reformed Church has occupied Arabia for a little more than half a century, the number of converts is still somewhat less than the number of years the mission has been at work.

Among many scores in American colleges, the greatest volunteer Zwemer ever won was Dr. Paul Harrison, the brilliant medical missionary of Arabia. While Zwemer and Harrison were literally running from one meeting to another in Baltimore, Harrison then being a student in Johns Hopkins presiding at the meetings where Zwemer spoke, Zwemer asked him if he would go to Arabia. As they ran, Harrison replied: "If you could prove that Arabia is the hardest field in the world I would go." Zwemer said: "Just let me get my breath, and tomorrow I'll prove that it is the hardest country, the hardest climate, the hardest language, the hardest everything on earth." The next day, Zwemer proved it to Paul's satisfaction, and Harrison went to Arabia. When Harrison was asked why the Reformed Mission is the only American society at work in Arabia, he replied: "I believe that God has given only to Dutchmen that divine stubbornness that it takes to work with Moslems on their own home soil of Arabia." In his moving challenge to the crowded audience in the great tent at Keswick, Zwemer showed that the whole of Christendom now faces the Mohammedan world in the open and now knows the dimensions of this colossal problem. Mohammed permitted his followers to inflict utter brutalities on conquered nations in the taking of slaves. The Mohammedan press has said harder things against their religion than missionaries have ever said. We are witnessing the disintegration of Islam under the acids of modernity and the impact of Western civilization. The whole Moslem world is in deep spiritual need, and throughout it, the Bible is the best-selling book next the Koran. Zwemer urges the whole Christian Church to "go up and possess the land" that now lies before it. The whole story is told in Zwemer's *Arabia the Cradle of Islam,* written in 1902 in the grilling heat of that malaria-infested peninsula, in a small rented house at Bahrein without fountain pen or typewriter, a book of over four hundred pages, which went through four editions.

After working for twenty-three years in and from his base in Arabia, Zwemer moved to Cairo as the strategic center where missionaries could best be trained and literature could best be produced—from the Nile Mission Press, which Zwemer founded —for the whole world of Islam. Here Zwemer gained access to the leaders of the proud and influential Moslem University of El Azhar, and to larger audiences of Moslems than was possible in more bigoted and backward Arabia. I remember the masterly arrangements made by the daring Zwemer and Canon Gairdner for great meetings in Cairo, where we spoke each night to some two thousand Moslem men, in another theater to a thousand Moslem women, and in a church of the United Presbyterian Mission to several hundred interested students who came to ask questions in an after meeting. One night when we were delayed in going from the women's theater to the men's meeting, an Egyptian Christian read with impressive Arabic oratory the whole Sermon on the Mount to hold the audience quiet. Zwemer had two thousand copies of this sermon distributed to the Moslem audience, and they were taken home—not left to be trampled underfoot in the theater. The great Sheik Mitry Dewairy was the brilliant interpreter, and many of the Moslem students of the El Azhar through his impassioned interpretation were moved to tears as he spoke of the crucifixion.

In the breaks in his service abroad, when his health gave way in Arabia and he was for a time apparently going blind, Zwemer served for three years as candidate secretary of the Student Volunteer Movement in America. If he had never set foot in Arabia or Egypt, if his service had been confined to the colleges and churches of America as a secretary at the home base, his work would have been monumental. Zwemer was the blazing prophet on every platform, summoning the church to its most difficult task. He was perhaps a useful thorn in the side of missionaries and Copts who might be tempted to settle down to easier work among the members of the Eastern churches instead of having the daring faith to seek to win Moslems.

After twenty-five years of service in Arabia, seventeen in Egypt at the theological seminary and the Nile Mission Press and in traveling work throughout the Moslem world, and ten years as professor of missions and the history of religion at Princeton Theological Seminary, Zwemer at seventy-eight is still unbelievably young, and going strong. He is still active and virile as a teacher, speaker, and writer. He was the founder and for thirty-four years the editor of *The Moslem World* magazine. His publications are numerous, several of the more recent being *The Cross Above the Crescent*, 1941; *Into All the World*, 1943; and *Evangelism Today*, 1944. Some of his books have had wide circulation in several languages. He has been a prophet, a preacher, and a promoter. He has been a linguist, a writer, a publicist, and a money raiser for his cause. Any measure of success he has had he attributes to his adamantine, orthodox faith, to his passionate zeal as a crusader, to his ability to love men, to mix with them freely and to make friends, but most of all, he says, to prayer. In one of his devotional books he called prayer "taking hold of God."

The danger for any crusader is that a fanatical element may accompany his zeal. Though strictly orthodox himself, Zwemer has been on the whole tolerant of more liberal men who differ from him. A second danger in dealing with a fanatical religion like Islam is that one may easily fall into the Moslem's own habit of debate and controversy. Though apologetic and negative criticism has its place at a more advanced stage, there is a growing feeling against the old purely controversial method of approach. The very winning of an argument that you have a better religion and that Christ is superior to Mohammed usually repels, angers, and loses the Moslem. We have not been sent to win arguments but to win men. Paul contended in fierce controversy with the Jews, but he never learned to win men in large numbers until at Corinth he determined to know nothing but Jesus Christ and him crucified. His message Zwemer wrote in a series of twenty Arabic tracts which were translated into Urdu, Persian, and other languages.

Loyalty to Christ does not require a purely negative attitude to Islam. If Christ came to fulfill, our interest in truth does not demand a denial of all the moral and spiritual values in Islam. The Christian Church should conserve all that is of spiritual worth in that religion, such as its spirit of reverence in worship, its demand for complete surrender to God, the Moslem's lack of self-consciousness in worship and in witnessing, his loyalty to the only religion that he knows, and the sense of brotherhood, including racial brotherhood, in which Anglo-Saxon Christians have often so lamentably failed in comparison to Mohammedans, Buddhists, and even Communists.

Medical missions now hold the key to opening the doors of the Arabian peninsula which were closed for many centuries. Womanhood and childhood have suffered immeasurably under the blight of Islam. We have the unsearchable riches of Christ that can meet their need. We have kinship with Moslems in the realm of theistic faith. Zwemer points out that Arabia is the cradle of the greatest of the non-Christian religions, and that

Islam has much in common with Judaism and Christianity. Moslems hold that Jesus was the sinless prophet; some of them believe that he alone was sinless. They accept the Christian Scriptures as sacred books, though they believe that we now have corrupted Scriptures. Zwemer holds that historic criticism fights on our side in this matter. If the lonely missionaries in Arabia can still say that "there is a grandeur about God's work" and that God himself is their sufficient reward, then the future is bright with the hope for the whole world of Islam that the farsighted faith of men like Samuel Zwemer has claimed for us all. Unique in our generation, he has been a voice in the wilderness calling for the evangelization of Islam.

W. TEMPLE GAIRDNER

Canon Gairdner (1873-1928) seemed to me to be perhaps the most loving and most lovable character of all the pathfinders included in this book.[1] Like Daniel, he was "a man greatly beloved." Whether as a playwright or poet in English or Arabic, as a musician, as a scholar and linguist, as a saint, or, like Albert Schweitzer, as a versatile young Christian Leonardo, Gairdner was nothing less than a genius. And he had the absentminded carelessness of genius. It was a sight to see him riding in the heat, through the streets of Cairo on his bike, without collar or tie, reading an Arabic newspaper while spurting to be on time at a committee meeting. Who but Gairdner, leaving for Scotland, would have checked his bicycle in Cairo with the station porter, taking according to custom the porter's metal armband as a receipt, gone down to Alexandria to his ship and home to Scotland for several months' furlough, completely forgetting his bicycle? It was more remarkable to his friends that he remembered to claim the bicycle on his return!

William Henry Temple Gairdner was born in Ayrshire in 1873. His father was Sir William Gairdner, professor of medicine in Glasgow University; and from him the son inherited his passion for beauty, for music, and for truth in science and

[1] For the basic facts in Gairdner's life I am indebted to Constance Padwick's excellent *Temple Gairdner of Cairo*, Macmillan, 1929.

philosophy. From Gairdner's English mother came his reserve, his sense of humor, and the passionate love of his emotional nature. After a happy boyhood and school career, in 1892 Gairdner entered Trinity College, Oxford. Here he reveled alike in his college crew, in his music, and in philosophy and the Greek classics, saying, "I believe half my soul is Greek." While at Oxford, Gairdner gave an address on "The First Duty of Students," in which he said: "If once a man goes down from college without having acquired the habit of study, he will never acquire it. These years at college are our one chance. . . . Why should Christians have narrow minds? What grace is there in them? . . . These are characteristics of the warped mind. And such minds are often produced by failure to study while at college. Let us be broad-minded in the true sense of that much misused, much abused word."

In the evening Gairdner, Oldham, and a group of fellow students discussed Homer, Ibsen, Wordsworth, Carlyle, Burns, and Emerson. On Gairdner's first college vacation he sat at the bedside of his dying younger brother. He later wrote about that experience: "I felt the necessity of putting Christ first and the rest nowhere. . . . I went back to Oxford having tasted eternity firsthand." During his second term at Oxford the last glow of the evangelical revival leaped to flame in this group of friends, with their out-and-out passionate soul-saving, Bible reading, daily prayer meetings, and Puritan separateness from the world. It tore Gairdner's sensitive, poetic soul, however, to speak on the streets in open-air evangelistic services at the Martyr's Memorial, or to go down High Street with a group of Christian students singing hymns. Because of a text on the wall of his room, "Behold I make all things new," a group of students smashed Gairdner's furniture and ornaments, and as he entered the college gate one day, one of the "bloods" of the varsity football team stepped forward and struck him in the face. Gairdner walked on without a word, his face white, but rejoicing that he was counted worthy to suffer for his Lord.

When Gairdner was president of the Student Christian Movement, the daily prayer meeting was sometimes crowded out.

Quite unconsciously he prayed as he walked the streets, for like Paul he did "everything by prayer." The next year when he was a traveling secretary of the Student Christian Movement, he wrote: "Our purpose must be to enter every college in the kingdom, and having entered it win it wholly for Christ." At the summer conference of the Student Christian Movement held at Keswick in 1893, after hearing Robert Speer speak on the watchword, "The Evangelization of the World in This Generation," Gairdner and Joe Oldham walked out by the lake and yielded themselves to God, as did ten Oxford and Cambridge men who later became leaders of the British Student Movement. From that time Gairdner was a spiritual leader.

After studying Arabic, he sailed for Cairo under the Church Missionary Society to work for educated Moslems with his inseparable, lifelong friend, Douglas Thornton, of Cambridge. The practical organizer, Thornton, who, Gairdner said, thought "in continents and archbishops," supplemented the poetic genius, Gairdner. On October 16, 1902, Gairdner went to Nazareth to be married. Later, his home with its five children, in whom Gairdner simply reveled, was a place of beauty and a joy forever. His musical evenings, with as many as fifty present, when he "demonstrated" *Die Meistersinger* or *The Apostles*, were unique events. Gairdner had not the technique of Schweitzer to interpret Bach on the grand organs of Europe, but he might have been a great conductor like Toscanini had he not been so great a saint and scholar. He was an evangelist to Moslems, a pastor shepherding his Christian flock, secretary of the mission, attending—or perhaps failing to attend—to a hundred details, the joyous father of a family, friend to all the needy souls he knew in Cairo, an able apologist and theologian, "a philosopher on fire," and a prolific writer. Gairdner's Arabic publications cover many fields of literature and include eleven tracts and books on Islam and Christianity. He also wrote twelve books on Bible study and Bible biography, and six on prayer and the devotional life, for Oriental Christians. In the English language we have from his pen *The Life of D. L. Thornton; Edinburgh, 1910; The Rebuke of Islam; Notes on the Epistle to the Romans;* and three important works on the Arabic lan-guage. In addition, he founded a Christian monthly magazine in Arabic and English and was its chief editor for twenty-one years. In *The Rebuke of Islam* he stated that Islam was "the impossible-possible problem. For it is the only one of the great religions to come after Christianity; the only one that definitely claims to correct, complete, and supersede Christianity; the only one that categorically denies the truth of Christianity; the only one that has in the past signally defeated Christianity; the only one that seriously disputes the world with Christianity; the only one which, in several parts of the world, is today fore-stalling and gaining on Christianity."

In the only full six months' furlough he ever took in eighteen years, Gairdner further mastered Arabic with the three greatest Arabic scholars of the world—in America, in Holland, and in Germany. He was the only Westerner of whom the Arabic literary review of Cairo wrote that he "must be accounted an Arabic poet of genius." The circulation of his Arabic maga-zine climbed to three thousand, and his English *Orient and Occident* had readers in fourteen Moslem countries. For a time Gairdner concentrated on the nineteen-centuries-old Coptic Church to rouse it to work for Islam. When in Britain, he reveled in the Edinburgh Conference, and interpreted it bril-liantly in his *Edinburgh, 1910.* His last paper, written in weari-ness, was for the Jerusalem Conference in 1924. Gairdner's published letters are used by the British Broadcasting Corpora-tion in their radio religious services as among the finest pieces of Christian literature of the last fifty years.

In 1927 Gairdner for seven months fought a losing battle with pneumonia and tuberculosis. Instead of asking that his sickness be removed, he wrote: "I am resting on the ocean of God's love, borne there by the prayers of friends." Friends of many nationalities wept at his passing, for Cairo and Egypt, Islam and Africa were poorer for his loss. Zwemer said:

On May 22, 1928, there entered into rest and the glorious life of the triumphant faithful, one of the most distinguished leaders of missionary work in the Near East. From Cairo, as the center of his life activities, that wonderful spirit influenced wide circles far beyond Egypt, while in the great intellectual capital of the Moslem world his soul burned with the ardor of a star of the first magnitude in its intellectual brilliancy and the versatility of his genius. . . . Here was a missionary who gave one short lifetime of service, in one place, to one great idea—the evangelization of Moslems. He found his lever and fulcrum in Cairo and set out to move a world.

ALBERT SCHWEITZER

I give the last place in this section to the brilliant Albert Schweitzer—philosopher, theologian, musician, interpreter of Bach, and medical missionary in French Equatorial Africa.[2] Schweitzer is a modern rationalist who trusts more fully to the processes of human reason—not unaided, but aided reason— than does any other in this book. He does not, as do those under the nightmare of the Nazis, scorn reason in favor of the more instinctive, primitive, and brutal tendencies of fallen humanity. He says: "I acknowledge myself to be one who places all his confidence in rational thinking. Renunciation of thinking is a declaration of spiritual bankruptcy, in the expectation that men will end by accepting as truth what is forced upon them by authority."

A native of Alsace, Schweitzer's life has been crucified between Germany and France, and all his days seem to have been marked for suffering. He was born in 1875, the son of an evangelical Protestant clergyman, educated at the village school, the town gymnasium, and the University of Strassburg. After winning a traveling scholarship for postgraduate study in Paris and Berlin, he was ordained curate at St. Nicholas, and was a lecturer at the university and principal of the theological school at Strassburg.

Like Charlie Andrews, even as a boy Schweitzer was a dreamer and one who with poignant sympathy shared the pain of the animal world. In manhood he incorporated this sentiment in

[2] I have in this biographical sketch quoted and adapted paragraphs from my *Man Discovers God*, 1942, pp. 231-41, with the permission of the publishers, Harper & Brothers.

his system of philosophy, which centered in his reverence for life. Schweitzer developed first as a saint and an artist, and only later as a thinker, theologian, and historian. In his *Memoirs of Childhood and Youth* he writes:

I was born in the little town of Kaysersberg, in Upper Alsace, in 1875. My father lived there as pastor and teacher of the little evangelical congregation. I was a very sickly child. . . .

When I was eight, my father gave me a New Testament which I read eagerly. I was a quiet and dreamy scholar with a horror of studies and letter writing which lasted for years. A savior appeared in the person of a new master. Experience of his self-disciplined activity had a distinct effect upon me. He became my model. That a deep sense of duty, manifested in even the smallest matters, is the great educative influence has, thanks to him, become with me a firm conviction in all that I have had to do as an educator. My passion for reading finally became unlimited. Once I have begun a book, I can never put it down. I would rather sit up all night over it.

As far back as I can remember I was saddened by the amount of misery I saw in the world around me, especially for the unfortunate animals. In my evening prayers, I used to add silently a prayer that I had composed myself for all living creatures: "O, heavenly Father, protect and bless all things that have breath; guard them from all evil, and let them sleep in peace."

After telling of protecting the birds from the other boys who wanted to kill them, Schweitzer says:

From that day onward I took courage to emancipate myself from the fear of men. There slowly grew up within me an unshakable conviction that we have no right to inflict suffering and death on another living creature unless there is some unavoidable necessity for it. . . .

Out of the depth of my feeling of happiness there grew up gradually within me an understanding of the saying of Jesus that we must not treat our lives as being for ourselves alone; we must all carry our share of the misery which lies upon the world. When I was twenty-one, while still a student, I resolved to devote my life till I was thirty to the office of preacher, to science, and to music; I would then take a path of immediate service as man to my fellow men. Finally a chain of circumstances pointed out to me the road which led to the sufferers from leprosy and sleeping sickness in Africa.[3]

Schweitzer early became famous for his theological writings on Jesus and Paul—*The Quest of the Historical Jesus,* 1911, and *Paul and His Interpreters,* 1912—which immediately gave him a place among the most brilliant theologians of our generation. *The Mysticism of Paul the Apostle,* 1931, made secure his eminence in the field of theology. His two volumes on the philosophy of civilization, *The Decay and Restoration of Civilization* and *Civilization and Ethics,* in 1923, rank him as a philosopher and social thinker. Schweitzer's Bach organ recitals are famous in eight European capitals, he is an expert and consultant on organ construction, and he is the author of the most scholarly and understanding interpretation of Johann Sebastian Bach. Other books, telling of his life and thought and his experiences in Africa, are widely known.

Schweitzer is unique in that at the early age of twenty-one he made the deliberate resolve to follow the intellectual pursuits of theology, philosophy, and music until he was thirty, and then to take a path of immediate sacrificial service to his fellow men. When he reached the age of thirty, he read the magazine of the Paris Evangelical Missionary Society calling for a doctor at Lambaréné on the Ogowe River, in what is now French Equatorial Africa. He decided at once that he would go: "The article finished, I quietly began my work. My search was over." After a full medical course, specializing in tropical medicine, on Good Friday, 1913, he set out for Africa without the support of a missionary society. He had only some seven thousand dollars of his own money to build a little hospital and to provide for his work for two years, a royalty income of a thousand dollars a year, and the good will of a widening circle of friends who were to support him. On his own resources

---

[3] Schweitzer, *Memoirs of Childhood and Youth,* pp. 7-8. Used by permission of the publishers, The Macmillan Company.

Schweitzer traveled to Africa, built his own hospital, and rendered heroic sacrificial service for more than three decades.

Anyone who will read between the lines of Schweitzer's *On the Edge of the Primeval Forest*, the four books about his experience in his hospital in Africa, and his *Out of My Life and Thought*, will see that he himself was the silent Suffering Servant in the whole mission to Africa. Whether consciously or unconsciously, he relived in darkest Africa the fifty-third chapter of Isaiah. He wrote:

I had read about the physical miseries of the natives in the virgin forests, and the parable of Dives and Lazarus seemed to me to have been spoken directly to us. I resolved when thirty years old to study medicine and put my ideas to the test. I started with my wife, who had qualified as a nurse, for Equatorial Africa because Alsatian missionaries of the Paris Evangelical Mission told me that a doctor was badly needed there, on account of the rapidly spreading sleeping sickness. My work was undenominational and international; for humanitarian work should be done by us as men, not as members of any particular nation or religious body. After a year's residence, fatigue and anemia begin. At the end of two or three years, one becomes incapable of real work and must return to Europe for at least eight months to recruit. I treated and bandaged the sick in the open air before the hospital was built. The heat is intolerable. The poor creatures have rowed themselves two hundred and fifty miles upstream to visit the doctor and can hardly stand from exhaustion.

In the first nine months, two thousand patients were examined and treated for malaria, sleeping sickness, heart disease, rheumatism, pneumonia, tumors and a long catalogue of diseases with their misery and pain:

A poor fellow is brought to me for an operation. I am the only person within hundreds of miles who can help him. When the moaning creature comes, I lay my hand on his forehead and say to him: "Don't be afraid! In an hour's time you shall be put to sleep, and when you wake you won't feel any more pain." Scarcely has he recovered consciousness when he ejaculates, "I've no more pain! I've no more pain!" His hand feels for mine and will not let it go. Then I begin to tell him and the others who are in the room that it is the Lord Jesus who has told the doctor and his wife to come to the Ogowe. The African sun is shining through the coffee bushes but we, black and white, sit side by side and feel that we know by experience the meaning of the words, "And all ye are brethren." Would that my generous friends in Europe could come out here and live through one such hour! And who will make this work possible? The fellowship of those who bear the marks of pain. Those who have learned by experience what physical pain and bodily anguish mean, belong together all the world over: they are united by a secret bond. He who has been delivered from pain and anguish must help to overcome those two enemies and bring to others the deliverance he has himself enjoyed. This is the "Fellowship of Suffering."

Christianity is for the African the light that shines amid the darkness of his fears; it assures him that he is not in the power of the spirits, and that no human being has any sinister power over another, since the will of God really controls everything that goes on in the world. That thought fills my mind when I take part in a service in the mission station. In proportion as the Negro becomes familiar with the higher moral ideas of the religion of Jesus, he finds utterance for something in himself that has hitherto been dumb, and something that has been tightly bound up finds release. The feeling of never being safe from the stupidest piece of theft, however, brings one sometimes almost to despair. My copy of Bach's *Passion Music* into which I had written the organ accompaniment was taken. As the natives say, "It goes for a walk." [4]

Three hospitals had to be built in turn, and a hut erected for the treatment of sleeping sickness, which had reduced the inhabitants of Uganda from 300,000 to 100,000. In the midst of a journey in the jungle, there suddenly leaped to Schweitzer's mind the theme of his philosophy upon which he had long meditated in the African jungle, which he was to expand in his lectures in Oxford and other centers of Europe:

[4] Condensed from *On the Edge of the Primeval Forest*, Macmillan, 1924, *passim*, and p. 64.

At sunset, as we were making our way through a herd of hippopotamuses, there flashed upon my mind, unforeseen and unsought, the phrase "Reverence for Life." The iron door had yielded: the path in the thicket had become visible. Now I had found my way to the idea in which world- and life-affirmation and ethics are contained side by side! Now I knew that the world-view of ethical world- and life-affirmation, together with its ideals of civilization, is founded in thought.[5]

The first World War, from 1916 to 1918, was for Schweitzer the "Crucifixion Chorus" in Bach's *Mass in B Minor*. After four years in tropical Africa, his wife ill, his money and health gone, in debt for his hospital, at a day's notice, because of war hysteria Schweitzer was arrested and brought to prison in France. He was barely able to save his surgical instruments and the manuscript of the first part of his *Civilization and Ethics*. He continued to think out and write his philosophy in the prison in France, as he had done in the African jungle. He wrote from his prison experiences of the need of forgiveness: "It was part of the madness of the world. We must forget that time of hatred and fear." He felt that the war was raging as a result of the downfall of civilization. Lack of proper food, African malaria, anemia, and prison confinement led to his serious illness and to the necessity of two dangerous operations. Easter, 1920, however, brought Schweitzer spiritual renewal and resurrection. Bach's trumpets were sounding in his soul again. He traveled and lectured in England and Sweden, gave organ recitals in Spain and over Europe, and wrote another book. Europe had received him with open arms and still offered him a distinguished career; yet he heroically decided, like Livingstone, to return again to Africa, even though he had to go alone, without his sick wife.

With all his genius, Schweitzer is very human; and he is as tender and humane to the animal kingdom as was St. Francis. When my friend Alec Fraser met Schweitzer at a station in England, they had to climb a high hill. Schweitzer had a huge trunk weighing at least a hundred pounds, which Fraser of-

[5] *Out of My Life and Thought*, Henry Holt, 1933, p. 185.

fered to have transported. Schweitzer said, "I would not be fit to be a missionary in Africa if I could not carry my own trunk." He thereupon swung it onto his shoulder and started up the hill. When he came to a poor worm crossing the road, down went the trunk while he lifted the worm lest it should be crushed. Then they came upon a beetle; down went the box again while the beetle was rescued. After that Fraser walked in front to see that nothing further impeded his pilgrim's progress. Schweitzer's every act reveals the habits of a physical, mental, and spiritual giant, who is yet as gentle as Francis of Assisi.

In 1924 Schweitzer returned to Lambaréné with a European helper. In 1925 a third doctor came, and a second nurse to serve in his enlarged hospital. During the present war the Free French have spoken highly of the excellent work being done by Schweitzer, especially the scientific work of his institute. Both Africans and Europeans working in the timber mills and mines of the region share in the benefits of the hospital. General de Gaulle sent the following message to Schweitzer: "I know your merits and your reputation. I thank you for giving your services as you do to aid French science. I shall be pleased to see you when I make my next voyage to Africa."

In a unique way Schweitzer is a representative man. The Hebraist and Hellenist are as well balanced in him as are the mystic and the rationalist. He is at once, like Plato, an idealist and, like Aristotle, a realistic scientist. In some respects like the sensitive "pessimist" Jeremiah, he more closely resembles the great anonymous Prophet of the Exile, or his Suffering Servant of humanity. Refusing to go to Africa as German, French, Alsatian, or Protestant evangelical, he went only as "man"—an untitled son of man. He is a sympathetic scholar of the New Testament. But he is such a prophetic critic that his one passion is truth and his enemies are error and superstition. He is orthodox to the extent that he is a humble Christian, minister, and missionary; but he was so frankly "heretical" that he declined to submit to a theological cross-examination by the committee of the Paris Missionary Society which had just rejected a previous candidate because he did not believe that the author of the Fourth Gospel was John, the son of Zebedee.

Schweitzer was glad to meet every member of the committee individually with regard to his personal religious experience, and to submit to the most searching examination on tropical medicine, for he was going to Africa not to talk but to act and silently to heal the sick in what Livingstone called "the Dark Continent, the open sore of the world." Yet preaching to his patients was sheer joy when he was trusted enough to take the religious services. He passionately sought and admired the good in all men and systems. During a single month while in prison in World War I, Schweitzer acted as a physician for his fellow prisoners, finished his *Civilization and Ethics,* and practiced on the table and floor in lieu of a musical instrument to prepare for his organ recitals in the eight European cities, from Madrid to Stockholm, which were again clamoring for him as the great interpreter of Bach.

We give heed to Socrates before he drinks the hemlock, to Jesus in the Garden, and to Schweitzer as he thus concludes his philosophy of life in the epilogue of his autobiography, *Out of My Life and Thought:* "Two perceptions cast their shadows over my existence. One consists in my realization that the world is inexplicably mysterious and full of suffering; the other in the fact that I have been born into a period of spiritual decadence in mankind."

Schweitzer is not so much a pessimist as he is a cross-bearer for our suffering humanity. He considers Africa worth saving, for there is found "the brother for whom Christ died." Would those who do not believe in missions recall from the Gold Coast the little handful of missionaries and leave it to the mercies of several thousand traders, raiders, and rulers, with the old traditions of slaves and gold? Would they begrudge Albert Schweitzer's going out to share his life with the Dark Continent as he writes: "Physical misery is great everywhere out here. . . . Millions and millions are living without help or hope of it. . . . Sooner or later this idea [of sharing] will conquer the world."

6

WORLD STATESMEN AND EVANGELISTS

ROBERT E. SPEER

IN MY student generation there were two young giants who towered head and shoulders above the rest of us—John Mott and Robert Speer.[1] Both were men of large stature—physically, mentally, and spiritually. Together with Robert Wilder they were the leaders of the missionary crusade, of the student movement, and to a certain extent of the mission boards and the churches. In some respects they were alike; in others they were in striking contrast and supplemented each other.

Both were tall and distinguished in appearance. Both were of strong physique, with a titanic capacity for work; and both have preserved this capacity, almost unimpaired, for well-nigh fourscore years. The frail Descartes could work but two or three hours a day; for decades Mott and Speer could work twelve to fourteen hours a day without weariness. Both had keen and disciplined intellects and stood at the very top of the best students in college. Both formed the priceless habit of wide and rapid reading and retained it all their lives; they were never too busy or too tired to read. Both learned to debate well in college; they spoke with power in public address and were in great demand on a hundred platforms. Both were writers who produced scores of books and pamphlets and hundreds of articles.

Speer and Mott were sound and loyal in the Christian faith. Both were conservative in mind, theologically, economically, and politically; both emphasized very strongly and almost ex-

[1] This brief biographical sketch is written without the help or approval of Robert Speer. My only book of reference has been *Who's Who*, a cold, brief, impersonal record; but I am indebted to his friends, who have been generous in their assistance.

clusively the individual and personal side of religion. Both of them, despite the fact that they were powerful figures in the religious world, remained laymen. Counting religion the vital center of life, they were concerned chiefly with spiritual issues. Both kept the "morning watch," or quiet time of Bible study and private prayer, as faithfully as did John Wesley two centuries before them; and both, like Wesley, kept it methodically, intellectually, and with deep spiritual devotion. I remember once, at the Kansas City Student Volunteer Convention, the old Methodist bishop had taken from his safe his chief treasure —the original diary kept by John Wesley when in Georgia. I watched Mott and Speer bending over those pages now yellow with age. It seemed to me that both men had to an unusual degree learned the secret of John Wesley and, like him, in their hidden lives were paying the price of spiritual power.

There were also differences between the two men: Speer was the prophet and Mott the statesman. Speer saw every problem from a vitalizing, spiritual center, *sub specie æternitatis,* in its bearing upon the Kingdom of God. Mott organized everything he touched. The two made a great team. In the quadrennial student volunteer conventions, which were the high-water mark in the spiritual life of North America throughout the generation, Mott, with his colleagues, planned each convention to the last detail; and he was the masterly presiding officer, while Speer gave the addresses of the deepest spiritual power.

Robert Elliott Speer was born at Huntington, Pennsylvania, September 10, 1867. With his clear, ringing voice, he retained his moving Pennsylvania accent throughout his life. He was the son of the Honorable Robert Milton Speer, who probably had ambitions for his obviously gifted son at the bar; for Speer would have made a great lawyer. He was educated at Phillips Andover Academy, 1883-85; Princeton, 1885-89; and Princeton Theological Seminary, 1890-91. Though always deeply reserved, he was a born leader throughout his four years in Princeton, in the Class of 1889. Like Mott, but unlike Wilder in this respect, he was not prominent in religious work at the beginning of his course in college. When the religious men of his class got together in freshman year at college, Speer was the only one who was not a church member. He was apparently the only member of his family who devoted his life to religion.

During his sophomore year, when Robert Wilder and John Forman visited Princeton, Speer was challenged to the very depths of his being and had to fight out his hardest battle on the question of his life work. He could not be unmindful of his intellectual gifts, of ambitions in the law, and of other worldly allurements that came before him with almost the force of his Master's three temptations. It took not forty days in the wilderness but hours of thought and prayer before Speer finally yielded his life once for all as the willing bond servant of his Lord. Though made in the quiet of his own heart, the decision was as clear-cut as when Ignatius Loyola laid his warrior's sword and dagger upon the altar, to take the vows of poverty, chastity, and obedience and the pledge to found the Society of Jesus. There was no blare of knightly trumpets, no public dedication; but from that hour Speer was a different man.

For hundreds of student volunteers the signing of the volunteer declaration marked a spiritual epoch in their lives. Foreign mission service in Protestantism took the place of the monastic life in Catholicism. Like Mackay of Uganda and like Horace Pitkin of China, Speer felt he must be more terribly in earnest where he was, expecting that he must soon go elsewhere; but Speer was a man of ten talents, far more gifted than Mackay or Pitkin.

Almost from the day of his decision Speer became a religious leader in his class and college. He was on fire; but it was a smoldering fire shut up in his being. Gentle though he was, Wilder blazed without; he was a flame thrower; he tackled every man he met. But that was not Speer's gift. From his sophomore year, in 1887, Speer was constantly called upon to speak on religious or missionary themes, far beyond the walls of Princeton. He could concentrate and read or study on a train as well as in the quiet of his own room. Both Mott and Speer from student days were "redeeming the time," wasting no hour, no moment of the day. This habit, coupled with their attainment of what Mott called "conclusive thinking," enabled both men to achieve titantic results for many decades.

Speer played three years on the varsity football team. I watched Bob Speer play at tackle opposite Yale's greatest player, Charlie Gill, who was an all-round athlete and physically the strongest man I ever knew. Speer was universally admired in college by students and faculty for his character and ability. In his senior year he was president of the Student Christian Association and managing editor of the daily *Princetonian,* besides having many other duties. And with all this work inside and outside of the college he was the valedictorian of his class. When Bob Speer graduated, at the age of twenty-one, he was mature for his years and strangely conservative. At the same age Wordsworth had been swept by the fire and dreams of the French Revolution; but Speer at his graduation, in his valedictory address, attacked the liberalistic temper of the time. Being mortal and human, of course Mott and Speer both have their limitations. Speer's deep-ingrained conservatism and his yet deeper reserve were two of the strong points of his character, but they placed some limitations upon him all his life. As he shrank from the invasion by anyone of the sacredness of his own personality, he could not aggressively invade the privacy of another. In consequence he could not deal with men in direct personal work as easily as could Robert Wilder, or Speer's great friend Henry Clay Trumbull, nor could he be an exuberant evangelist like Dwight Moody or John Wesley.

The year after graduation, 1889-90, Speer became the traveling secretary of the Student Volunteer Movement and enrolled over a thousand volunteers for the foreign mission field. In those early days, when cards were signed more easily than now, none could know how few would pass all the hurdles and obstacles and actually reach the foreign field. Yet many of the detained volunteers, like Speer and Mott, became world missionaries in places where God wanted them, and did more for the cause of God's Kingdom than they could have done overseas.

In 1890 and 1891 Speer studied in Princeton Theological Seminary. During the second year of his course he was unexpectedly called by the Presbyterian Board of Foreign Missions to become a secretary of the board. Many felt that his brilliant gifts, his fresh contact with youth, and his experience in the student missionary uprising would make a great contribution to a mission board led by members of the older generation. This call upset Speer's equilibrium, and he fought hard against it. He certainly did not want to stay at home when he had asked a thousand volunteers who had signed the declaration to undergo the hardships of the foreign field. When he consulted his friends, however, practically all advised him to accept the responsibility as the call of God. So Speer decided to try it for a time and then reconsider his future work. The result was that for forty-six years, from 1891 to 1937, Speer was a secretary of the Presbyterian Board of Foreign Missions. He magnified his calling and enlarged the possibilities of his office. For years Wilder, Speer, and Mott were the three great champions of the foreign missionary cause among the colleges and churches—and what champions they were! Together they put foreign missions on the map and widened the horizon of thousands. Whatever the imperfections of every human cause, missions became, as they should be, the chief task and the vital life of the church, the center of church history, the advancing front of the partially realized Kingdom of God on earth.

In 1891, when Speer and I had both left college to enter Christian work in New York City, he lived in bachelor's quarters in University Place. I remember going to his room one night to talk over spiritual problems. As my eyes were troubling me, I lay on his couch and closed them while he read aloud from F. B. Meyers' *Seven Rules for Daily Living*. It breathed the spirit of the "Cambridge seven" who had just gone to China and the new spiritual life that was then quickening the student and church world through the missionary movement. Before I had closed my eyes, I had seen a striking photograph of a college girl on Speer's roller-top desk. When I opened my eyes, the picture was gone, and I saw that Speer did not wish to have any questions asked about it. It was the picture of Emma Bailey of Harrisburg. When Emma Bailey was a student and leader at

Bryn Mawr, she had asked Speer to come there to speak to the girls in the college. Obviously meant for each other, Robert Speer and Emma Bailey were engaged in a few weeks. They were married on April 20, 1893. These two remarkable people, so rarely and well mated, have been blessed to many through their beautiful home. Their four children have been fine and useful world citizens.

Speer was a great board secretary. He was brilliant in debate, an art that he had learned in the marble hall of Clio at Princeton. His mind worked rapidly. In a board meeting, or in a missionary conference, he was often the last to speak. He could balance four clear arguments for, and four against, any proposition, or state five convincing reasons for his conclusion on an issue. He sometimes carried the day against men of equally sound judgment who could not so brilliantly expound their position. His capacity for hard work, his wide reading, and his prolific correspondence enabled him to grasp the intricate problems of his world mission field, and he was in certain respects the strongest board secretary of his day.

In preparation for speaking he wrote out his propositions clearly and logically, and without effort indelibly photographed them in his mind. His verbal memory was prodigious. On occasion, long paragraphs and poems—such as, for example, a piece on David Livingstone in *Punch*—would flow without a flaw from his tongue. Men seldom saw him refer to a note; yet he would speak for an hour, rolling off quotations, statistics, and references from his wide reading without a mistake. His messages were not only keenly intellectual but deeply spiritual. When not in forensic debate as a defender of the faith, there was a deep tenderness in his strong masculine nature. I could use this word more truly of Speer than of almost any of the score of characters described in this book.

Of all the speakers at Northfield and the student conventions —and I heard them all: Moody, Drummond, and the leading lights of the religious world—Speer always struck the clearest spiritual note, and moved me more deeply than any other. I remember one Sunday morning in 1896, when in Princeton

Theological Seminary, he spoke to our student volunteer band, many of whom were about to sail for the foreign field. There were tears in his voice as he prayed; yet he was at the farthest antipodes from an "emotional" speaker. Speer appealed to mind and heart and will—the whole man in due proportion.

Speer's work as secretary of a mission board took him on many long missionary journeys over the world fields. These carried his messages of spiritual inspiration to the missionaries, the workers, and the churches in many lands. They enabled him to share with the missionaries their unsolved perennial problems and to apply whatever gifts he had of statesmanship in seeking to meet them. The contact with the field furnished dynamic material for the great messages which he brought back to the home churches; and the journeys usually resulted in printed volumes on the different countries and world problems. In 1896-97 his first tour in Asia included a visitation of the missions in Persia, India, China, Korea, and Japan, and a long bout with typhoid fever. In 1909, and again in 1916 and 1925, he visited South America and interpreted it to us on his return. Mexico was visited in 1894 and 1906. In 1915 Japan, Korea, China, the Philippines, and Siam were covered. In 1921-22 the fields of India, Iraq, and Persia, and in 1926, Japan and China, were revisited.

Most men when traveling work best by thoroughly preparing a limited number of addresses, using them repeatedly with ever-fresh audiences in the different countries; but Speer's mind was such that he seldom needed to repeat himself. A man is not a hero to his valet, but Speer was both respected and loved by the younger men who worked with him, who rejoiced in his great gifts and his glowing personality. Guthrie Speers, pastor of the Brown Memorial Presbyterian Church of Baltimore, had the priceless privilege of accompanying Speer on one of his world tours. In answer to my request to tell me his impressions of Speer and of his work on that journey, Guthrie Speers writes:

When I went to the Hill School he was one of the regular preachers. Often on Sunday evenings when the whole school used to sing hymns together he would read us something. I think my love for Kipling's *Soldiers Three* started with hearing him read some of those stories. Then, like so many thousands of fellows, I heard him speak at student conferences at Northfield and Silver Bay and Eaglesmere, where he was always tremendously stimulating and challenging. We used to say that he put our Christian responsibilities up to us butt end first, without being the least bit hesitant about making it a hard challenge.

Just before the end of my last year in Seminary, I had the great opportunity of being invited to go with him on one of his missionary trips in the capacity of secretary. I am sure I was a poor secretary, but he was a great companion. Having known him mostly as a speaker and preacher, I was a little frightened when contemplating that trip; but I soon discovered that he was a prophet with a great sense of humor and the most amazing fund of knowledge. Nobody could have been a better traveling companion. Just being with him was as good as a college education. Nobody could miss his singlehearted devotion to Christ. He told me once that when he waked up in the night and couldn't sleep he would take some incident from the life of Christ and simply think about it and try to make it vivid to himself—which always impressed me as a very effective way to handle sleeplessness. I was tremendously impressed by his methods of work. He never wasted any minute. If there were ten minutes free before lunch time, he would use those ten minutes to get something done. He used to carry a book with him so if there were time on a trolley or a subway he would get a few minutes reading done. As for his addresses and sermons, I have never ceased to marvel at his ability in that field. He would make out outlines of his addresses and put them in a looseleaf notebook, but I never saw him refer to any notes when he was speaking. During that trip of nearly nine months in the Orient, he spoke from three to five times a day when we were ashore, and I never heard him repeat himself once. He has a phenomenal memory. Months after we had visited the churches in Thailand, he was dictating his report. He would start to write about some church and give its membership without referring to any records. Then he would say we had better check that to be sure it was correct. But when I checked, he had always given the correct figure. I have seen him take a financial report, go over it before entering a meeting, and then give the report without looking at the paper.

I was greatly impressed also by his way of getting others to work. He never drove any of us, nor did he lay any heavy burden on us; but he created an atmosphere in which all of us wanted to do everything we possibly could. Wherever we went, not only the missionaries, but business people and government officials, respected him and loved him. He has a great ability to get information from all sorts of people. Nobody could be around him even for a few minutes without knowing that he was a grand Christian.

There are no Christian "virtues" resembling the four cardinal virtues of the Greeks, but on every one of the four cardinal attitudes and relationships which characterize the life and teaching of Jesus—humility, faith, moral purity, and love—Speer ranks high indeed. Like any true Christian, he could not bear fulsome praise; it gave him real pain. Nor did he ever seek honors or recognition; but they came to him unsought and well deserved. When he was fittingly given an honorary D.D. at the University of Edinburgh, and spoke all over Scotland, Scotsmen were reminded of their own great and well-beloved Alexander Duff. Speer's honorary M.A. from Yale, his LL.D's from Rutgers, Otterbein, and Washington and Jefferson, and his Litt.D. from Princeton, meant more than perfunctory acknowledgment of his work. Speer was wisely chosen president of the Federal Council of the Churches of Christ in America (1920-24) and moderator of the Presbyterian Church, the latter by acclamation on the first vote. He was chairman of the Wartime Commission of the Churches, 1916-18; chairman of the Committee on Co-operation in Latin America, 1916-36; and president of the board of trustees of Nanking University. His addresses will be found in the reports of all the student volunteer conventions —from Cleveland in 1890 to Indianapolis in 1935, including London, England, in 1900.

With his wide interests, Speer reads from a hundred to a hundred and fifty books a year; and he has written some fifty books, among the more recent of which are *Christian Realities*, 1935, and *When Christianity Was New*, 1939.

At the students' conference at Keswick in the summer of

267

1894 the student leaders of Britain—Donald Fraser, Joe Oldham, Temple Gairdner, and Douglas Thornton—were simply bowled over. After hearing Speer speak on the watchword, Gairdner wrote in his diary: "Speer simply God-inspired. Evangelization of the World in This Generation. Never heard anything like it. Oldham and I walk up the road and give ourselves to God."

After a night spent alone on the neighboring mountain, the Druids' Circle, Donald Fraser—who was to lead the Student Volunteer Movement for Great Britain and Ireland before he became the David Livingstone of Livingstonia, British Central Africa, and later a leader in the reawakening of Scotland—returned quietly to the Glasgow University tent the next morning. A fellow student in that tent wrote: "After that we all felt a prophetic touch of leadership was on Donald Fraser. . . . That night was a turning point of crisis not only for that one soul but for hundreds who followed in Africa, in Scotland, and in the Student Movement."

Gairdner wrote of Douglas Thornton, who was his fellow missionary in Cairo, concerning his experience on that night: "The whole inner man suddenly expanded; new visions floated before his astonished eyes; horizon opened out on horizon; deep called to deep. His flaring zeal settled down into a clear burning flame." And Thornton himself wrote in his diary: "For the first time some ten of us at least began to realize that we individually were responsible for the Evangelization of the World in This Generation. B. and I had to get away quietly three miles out on the hills, from 9 to 12 P.M., to let God speak to us face to face. It was an awful time."

A watchword that thus commanded Wilder, Mott, and Speer, and then hundreds of leaders of the British Student Christian Movement—including the four remarkable men Donald Fraser, Joe Oldham, Temple Gairdner, and Douglas Thornton—had both meaning and power for the men of that day. On a single night the veil is lifted for a moment to let us catch a glimpse of the working of God's spirit through Robert Speer in the hearts of these ten leaders as revealed in their diaries and in their biographies written long afterward.[2] Yet this night was only one of thousands of nights in which human hearts were touched and often moved for life by this man of God, Robert Speer.

When Speer retired automatically on account of age from the Board of Foreign Missions in 1937, he left it completely and passed on the work, unencumbered, to younger hands. He now resides at Lakeville, Connecticut, where he loves to study, to write, and to work in his garden on his ten-acre place. Both in 1943 and in 1944 he was asked to speak in more than thirty states of the union as a loyal defender of the faith who still has a vital spiritual message.

Robert Speer was in some respects a missionary statesman, but he was primarily a spiritual prophet. There are many who thank God that they knew him, there are more who were quickened by his message. His work was prodigious; but far greater than his work was his character. What he was, was more important than what he did. In the face of the deepest personal tragedy and sorrow his character, mellowed with a deeper tenderness, rose to nobler heights.

Though Speer's mind has never aged and his arteries have never hardened, no one can say more fearlessly or more joyously, with Browning: "Grow old along with me!" I once heard him quote with approval a professor in Princeton who wanted to "live with a vengeance and die with a snap." But for him there is no death, only a wide portal into a light too bright for human eyes to bear, and an abundant entrance into an ever-enlarging life beyond. His faith, founded on what he believes are divine absolutes, holds firmly to eternal verities. His mind seems never to have been assailed by the doubts that distract some of his friends. One almost envies the simple, childlike faith

[2] See Constance Padwick's *Temple Gairdner of Cairo*, Society for Promoting Christian Knowledge, London, 1929, p. 48; W. H. T. Gairdner's *D. M. Thornton*, Hodder & Stoughton, 1908, p. 30; Agnes R. Fraser's *Donald Fraser of Livingstonia*, Hodder & Stoughton, 1934, p. 27. This remarkable result of one man's influence on four of these ten lives—and we must remember that there were always others of whom we know nothing—was discovered and is traced by Miss Ruth Rouse in her forthcoming *History of the World's Student Christian Federation*.

that can use words that are to him of tender meaning, words that Paul himself could have used. Robert Speer can still say, as he could say in his buoyant youth:

And so I am watching quietly every day.
Whenever the sun shines brightly I rise and say,
"Surely it is the shining of His face,"
And I look unto the gates of His high place beyond the sea,
For I know He is coming shortly to summon me.
And when a shadow falls across the window of my room,
Where I am working my appointed task,
I lift my head to watch the door, and ask
If He is come.
And the angel answers sweetly in my home—
"Only a few more shadows, and He will come."

E. STANLEY JONES

No one can more appropriately be called a world evangelist, no one has more consistently maintained his evangelistic work —for over forty years—in the spirit of a crusader, than E. Stanley Jones. Born in Baltimore, Maryland, January 3, 1884, he worked as an earnest Christian student in Asbury College, in Wilmore, Kentucky, spending his summers as a student evangelist. At the age of fifteen he passed through the normal process of conversion, but this implied merely a change in name, not in nature. Two years later, however, when the evangelist Robert J. Bateman was conducting an old-fashioned revival, Stanley Jones came under real conviction. One day in his own room he prayed fervently, "Lord save me tonight." That evening he ran all the way to the meeting, a mile distant, and took a front seat there. He was the first to reach the altar; and as he knelt he knew that something had happened to him at last, and he spoke to the man next to him, saying, "I've got it!"

Stanley Jones for a short time had studied law in Baltimore, but in college he became a student volunteer. At one time Asbury College had a hundred volunteers out of the five hundred students enrolled, Bishop Pickett of India being among the volunteers. When Jones went to speak at a meeting on Africa, he prayed that a missionary for the Dark Continent should come from that gathering, saying confidently to the audience, "Someone will go as a missionary from this meeting." Unconsciously he was praying himself into it, but he did not yet realize that he was the man who must go to a foreign field.

While he was continuing in Asbury College as a teacher, the Methodist Mission Board wrote to ask Jones if he would go to India; and he laid the matter before the Lord in prayer. Ordinarily, Stanley Jones is guided—through a heightened moral intelligence that comes from a study of the life of Christ —in the full exercise of his own best thought to discover general principles that may be applied to situations. But where there are, in a situation, too many unknown factors, factors beyond his own experience and the competence of human wisdom, then he looks for immediate divine guidance. In a case like this, where no man could tell whether he could do more good in India, in Africa, or in America, Jones felt he was utterly dependent on the direction of God's spirit. As he prayed on and on, until he had eliminated self-interest and lower motives, he believed he heard the Inner Voice guiding him to India, as he has heard it more than a score of times at the great crises of his life, saying, "This is the way, walk ye in it."

As an evangelist, Stanley Jones obviously owes much to John Wesley. Like Wesley he has the spirit of burning evangelism, the emphasis upon conversion, personal responsibility, and free will; upon conviction of sin, repentance, faith, and the grace of God. Jones feels he owes much to Wesley in his doctrine of perfection, though, like Wesley, he never thinks for a moment that he even approaches sinless perfection in his own life. He believes in a "second blessing," in an experience for the normal Christian of the receiving of the Spirit, similar to what the early disciples knew at Pentecost. He knows that men differ in temperament and training, in their religious background and vocabulary; but he believes also that basically men are very much alike. Most men are exhausted as they face their unsolved problems and fight their inner battles between the conscious and the subconscious mind. Most need to go through a second crisis, or series of crises, when they can no longer live superficially but must go deeper; when they must take a further step in complete consecration, or utter surrender, ready to go the whole way and enter upon the life of faith, the victorious, the abundant, the overflowing life, that bears much fruit and realizes abiding spiritual results. Most men live habitually on a natural level, far below their best. It is Stanley Jones's special gift and call to see men through these two steps or crises in life: conversion and consecration.

In 1907 Stanley Jones went to India under the Methodist Board. For three years he was the pastor of an English-speaking church in Lucknow, where he sought conversions each Sunday, while he studied Urdu and Hindi during the week. He was then transferred to Sitapur for work in a district which contained several hundred Indian workers and several thousand Christians. Here he preached chiefly to the outcastes, for few of the high castes, like the rich young ruler, would seriously consider leaving all and losing all to follow Christ. In the cities, however, occasional audiences of educated people gathered, and he acquired a taste for this work. The educated always preferred meetings in English, with the prestige and interest of a foreign language.

After eight and a half years of strenuous work, Stanley had a nervous breakdown and took a year's furlough in America, but without fully recovering his health. On his return to India he asked his board to assign him to special work among the educated classes. When he was called to enter interdenominational work, with full freedom to use his special gifts, it is to the credit of Frank Mason North and the statesmanship of the Methodist Board that he was left free and untrammeled, wherever the Spirit might lead him. He now began his work in India among the educated classes, but with frequent breakdowns. In 1917 he came to the end of his tether. He faced the alternative of a final breakdown, or of throwing himself upon the infinite resources of God, sufficient for spirit, mind, and body, to enter the triumphant life of faith. As he knelt in a church in Lucknow, he asked himself, "Can you continue this difficult work among the educated classes?" He had to reply, "No, Lord, I'm done." Once again in a crisis came the Divine Voice, which seemed to say to him clearly: "If you turn this matter of your illness over to me and do not worry about it, I will take care of it." Jones replied: "Lord, I accept the terms; I close the bargain." In the twenty-eight years since that day, many who have received blessing through him can testify that the abundant life has been flowing in Stanley Jones at high tide. He makes mistakes, as every man does; he needs daily to say the Lord's Prayer, "Forgive us our trespasses"; but he confesses his sin and gets immediate forgiveness without letting it rankle and become a center of infection.

For the next twenty-three years, from 1917 to 1940, Dr. Jones worked for the educated classes in India and abroad. During this time he had two furloughs in America, where he usually spent a week in a city or college. In 1928 he was elected a Methodist bishop, but he immediately—and wisely—resigned to keep to his divine calling. There are a thousand bishops all over the world, but bold evangelists in the spirit of John Wesley, who can rise above narrow orthodoxy, who can reach educated people in many lands, are few indeed. Stanley Jones was the greatest English-speaking evangelist in all India. During some two decades in that country he had the largest hearing among the educated that any man ever had, a hearing that the great Alexander Duff himself might well have envied. Among the least of the results of this work, there were a score or more of converts who underwent the ordeal of baptism, which severed them from their homes and from their roots in the soil of India. Much more important than the statistics of baptism, there were thousands who received blessing—blessing that cannot be measured or tabulated. Many Hindus tried to follow Christ in their homes despite great obstacles. Many because of this effort became better Hindus.

At the close of a public meeting where he had discussed "The What and the Why of Christianity," Dr. Jones would invite to stay to an after meeting all who desired to know how they could find God and live their lives with his aid. In this meeting he would describe briefly the ten steps up the ladder that each must take who desired to find God:

1. Review your own life.
2. Reverse whatever is wrong in it.
3. Return to God, who is revealed in Christ.
4. Renounce yourself and your sin.
5. Restore, wherever restitution is necessary.
6. Receive God's grace and his Spirit in your heart.
7. Relate the new Christian truth to your whole life, in your own home and daily work.
8. Replenish your life by a daily quiet time of communion with God.
9. Seek release of your personality from all the manacles and graveclothes of the dead past, to free it for service for your fellow men.
10. Rejoice in God as your heavenly Father and thank him daily for his unspeakable gift of Jesus Christ.

In India, Burma, Ceylon, and Singapore, Dr. Jones was equally effective. Students, professional men, government officials, and all classes among the four millions who speak English in this portion of Southern Asia have welcomed him. He is uncompromising and outspoken in his claims for the supremacy of Christ, but in all else he meets Hindus and Mohammedans halfway. He does not emphasize baptism, as Paul did not, though he still looks upon it as necessary to the best Christian life. He knows that there are many non-Christians leading truly Christian lives today, people who are not baptized and are not members of the Christian Church. He leaves his meetings open to questions, and usually has a round-table group in which the freest discussion is welcomed. Although it involves a tremendous physical strain, he makes as many personal contacts as possible in order to know people and their intellectual and moral difficulties.

Stanley Jones reads widely and continuously; and he has come to grips with the social, political, and economic problems of the people of Asia. Those who have known him intimately in the Orient have watched him grow. When he began, his message was fervent but narrow, academic, and somewhat painfully orthodox. It did not take in the wide sweep of modern or social problems, nor did it link itself with the everyday human difficulties and perplexities of those he was trying to help. But as he has come into close contact with thousands of people he has seen the working of the spirit of Christ outside the so-called Christian community, he has seen "the light that lighteth every man" who is made in the image of God, and he has come to love the "other sheep" which are not of his orthodox fold.

Stanley Jones can say as truly as could his spiritual progenitor, John Wesley, "I look on all the world as my parish." He has been preaching the gospel over the length and breadth of India for several decades; four times he has conducted fruitful evangelistic campaigns in China, four times in the Philippines, six or eight in Malaya, once in South Africa and Kenya, once in South America, and several times in Mexico. But he regards the United States as one of the greatest and neediest mission fields in the world—great in its potentialities and great in the depths of its spiritual need. He does not offer men a selfish, personal, possessive salvation as an escape from life. He tries rather to present them with the challenge of a whole gospel, with both personal and social implications and obligations. His social message includes economic justice, racial brotherhood, and just and lasting peace among all nations. He recognizes that nations have been heretofore all too selfish, proudly "sovereign," and isolationist, often pharisaically proud of their own merits and suspicious of their fellow nations and of any adequate world authority which could stop war.

For eight years now Dr. Jones has participated in various missions in America: in 1936 in the Preaching Mission; in 1938 in the University Mission; in 1940-41 in the Christian Mission. For the last three years he has been conducting "one man" missions under the sponsorship of the Department of Evangelism of the Federal Council of Churches, of which Jesse M. Bader is secretary. These missions are held from Sunday to Friday in cities, for the most part, of a hundred thousand or less in population. The Department of Evangelism selects the cities, directs the preparation, and gives guidance in the promotion and publicity work. In these missions Dr. Jones speaks to luncheon clubs, high schools, colleges, labor unions, to public school teachers and to ministers, he speaks on the radio and in evening mass meetings. During the closing part of each evening service of the mission Dr. Jones asks those to remain who would like to realize the experience he has been talking about. As a rule about three fourths of his audience remains for the after service.

In 1940 in Los Angeles, when Dr. Jones already had his ticket to return to India and his baggage was on the steamer, he again heard the Inner Voice: "I want you here in this country." He fought against this call for two hours, and then ordered his baggage taken from the ship. Each summer he participates in four ashrams of two weeks each in four quarters of the country; on the Pacific Coast; at Green Lakes, Wisconsin; at Lake Winnepesaukee, New Hampshire; and at Blue Ridge, North Carolina. During the rest of the year he conducts Christian missions of a week each in various cities, speaking from three to five times a day in meetings arranged by the Department of Evangelism, with numerous personal interviews. The printed page carries his message far beyond the range of the human voice. Over six hundred thousand copies of his book *The Christ of the Indian Road* have been sold, and it has been published in twelve languages. Of his more recent books, *Abundant Living* (1942) has sold over four hundred thousand copies and has been translated into Spanish and Chinese, and transcribed in Braille, and *The Christ of the American Road* (1944) has sold over a hundred thousand copies.

Stanley Jones is a real Christian. He gets not only daily spiritual refreshment but hourly energizing to meet all his physical needs in the enormous drain upon his nervous energy required in this delicate and difficult and continuous work. He has learned to draw upon the illimitable divine resources, not only for his mind and spirit, but for his body, in the way that Moody and Spurgeon did in their day, and that Gandhi and Kagawa do today. And with it all, he keeps smiling in his old boyish way. Any man entrusted with so much power is in grave danger of suffering from a messianic complex; yet he is unspoiled, he is diverted to no tangent or fanatical fixation, he has no dogmatic hobby. He tries to put first things first and to keep his feet on the earth. With a fine sense of balance he combines the rational and the mystical and, to a considerable degree, the individual and the social gospel in one living blend. He has prophetic courage and he is first and foremost a consistent and passionate evangelist, blessed to many. His whole life seems a fulfillment of the promise made to those who had first given themselves to the Lord. "My God shall supply all your need."

J. H. OLDHAM

Joe Oldham, to those who know him, is a great Christian, a spiritual statesman, a creative thinker and planner who, keeping himself always in the background, has helped to unify, organize, and lead the Christian forces of Great Britain and their missionary outreach over the world. He and his late associate William Paton played a part in Great Britain similar to that of Mott and Speer in America. Oldham and Paton were men of intellectual and spiritual stature. They were not limited to the individual and personal aspects of Christianity but were possessed by a whole gospel that laid on them the equal imperative for the building of a new man within and of a new world without. Both had the unlimited vision of the Kingdom of God in the whole earth. Both had a wider theological, economic, and political vision than most of their American contemporaries. With William Temple, the late Archbishop of Canterbury, Oldham and Paton made a great triumvirate who, themselves profoundly influenced by the Student Christian Movement, in turn deeply influenced the Christian churches and their world-wide missions. Though smaller than the American movement, this British student movement was both deeply spiritual and passionately social.

During the dark days of the present war Oldham's *Christian News-Letter* has carried its spiritual message to the leaders of the Christian forces of Britain. This awful conflict, ravaging the whole continent of Europe, has been an incalculably greater ordeal than anything the safe and isolated American continent has known. The very hell of war has subjected the people of Britain to an experience not wholly unlike the persecution suffered by Christians in the first century. Oldham's unshaken faith and contagious courage throughout the deep suffering of this crucifixionlike experience has done for British Christians something of what the great Epistle to the Hebrews did for the Christians of the first century. In the language of that epistle, it has lifted up the hands that hang down and the palsied knees, it has made straight paths to walk in. It has helped believers to know that they have received a spiritual kingdom which cannot be shaken, and that Jesus Christ is the same yesterday, today, and forever.

Joseph Houldsworth Oldham was born on October 20, 1874, and has now passed the age of seventy. When I landed in Bombay in 1896, I used to hear much of his godly father, Lieutenant Colonel G. W. Oldham of the Royal Engineers. He was one of "the good colonels" who count for so much in British life, and his home was a warm center of Christian influence, with a strongly evangelical atmosphere. Joe's two younger brothers, Harry and Jack, were both secretaries of the Student Christian Movement and later missionaries. In fact, the pioneers of the student movement in Britain and America were almost without exception volunteers, and the student movement in both countries had a passion to win the world for Christ.

Joe Oldham was educated in Edinburgh Acadamy and at Trinity College, Oxford, where he acquired the habits of wide reading and of thinking. Here also he formed deep Christian friendships with other leaders of the student movement who were later leaders of the world mission of Christianity. At Oxford, Oldham, Gairdner, and A. G. Fraser, whom Oldham had won to the Christian life, were the leading spirits of the Oxford Christian Union. From student days, in every movement Oldham entered, he became the philosopher, the creative thinker, the adviser in chief, and the spiritual guide. As an earnest Christian student and a capable leader in the Student Christian Movement, in 1896 Joe Oldham became one of its first general secretaries. As a secretary he was strong in his emphasis upon Bible study, and he produced several textbooks on this subject. His *The Teaching of Jesus* had a large circulation and was used in other movements. His *Devotional Diary*, written much later, has passed through a number of editions and has been of untold help to many, including myself.

Oldham did not linger at home, but as an ardent missionary pressed on to India. In 1897 he accepted the call of the Scottish National Council of Y.M.C.A. to become its general secretary in Lahore, the Punjab, North India. In January, 1898, a reception was given by the young men of Madras to two young secretaries of the association recently arrived in India—Joe Oldham and myself. I was a young bachelor centering in Madras in my traveling student work, and I recall the practical and theological problems I discussed with Joe Oldham at that time. I remember my impression of his spiritual consecration and the drive of his strong will—stubborn in the best sense, for all his quiet manner—and his mental maturity and well-balanced judgment.

In 1898 Oldham married Mary Fraser, the daughter of Sir Andrew Fraser, governor of Bengal, and sister of A. G. Fraser, formerly of Achimota, Africa. From 1898 to 1900 he was secretary of the Y.M.C.A. in Lahore; and, though his stay in India was brief, he left there a lasting spiritual impression. Oldham's health had never been good, and he was compelled to return to Great Britain after a severe attack of enteric, or typhoid, fever. One of the leaders whom Oldham reached in India was a young student who became the brilliant educator and writer S. K. Datta. When Datta was a medical student in Edinburgh, he said of Oldham: "Two or three years may seem a short time in the life of a man like Oldham, who was so soon invalided home never to return. He left no organization, no bricks, nor mortar, nor monument, to perpetuate his name. But he builded greatly for time and eternity in the hearts of a few men. Joe Oldham, a young Y.M.C.A. secretary, will live forever in the life of the Punjab." And the same was true in ever-larger measure for seventy years of his life. Oldham, always seemingly silent and obscure, lived himself into the thought and life of his time, just as his Master had done in Galilee.

When ill-health brought Oldham home, he studied theology in New College, Edinburgh, and for a time at Halle in Germany, in 1904. He then became mission study secretary of the Student Christian Movement. Oldham was engaged at the home base of British foreign missions for the next four decades. Here he was to play a formative role in more than one ecumenical movement, working out in it ideas which had first laid hold of him in the Student Christian Movement.

Several years before Edinburgh, in 1910, Oldham began making preparations for this first world conference, winning British leaders, especially Anglican High-Church bishops and board secretaries. They had already been won loyally to support the interdenominational Student Christian Movement and its conferences, but they had to be convinced of the potentialities and of the imperative necessity of this meeting of the world missionary leaders of all the churches. As early as 1805 the prophetic William Carey had proposed the first of a series of decennial missionary conferences to meet at Capetown, but it was fifty years before this dream was fulfilled. From then on, British and American missionary societies held so-called Ecumenical Missionary Conferences at intervals, until the conference held in New York in 1900. Several years before 1910, Oldham and others saw the possibility of focusing, formulating, and then broadcasting to the Church of Christ the thought of her worldwide mission. Canon Gairdner brilliantly tells the story in his *Edinburgh, 1910*. Eight carefully selected commissions working for two years had prepared the reports on which the discussions and recommendations of the conference were based. Here, only one man was thought of as chairman of the conference—John R. Mott, the "master of assemblies." Always on the lookout for leaders of the new day, Mott had arranged that the "stewards," or ushers, of the conference should be carefully selected, promising students. These included such future bishops, archbishops, and student leaders as William Temple, Kenneth Kirk, now Bishop of Oxford, Neville Talbot, and William Paton.

Canon W. H. T. Gairdner speaks of Oldham, as secretary of the Edinburgh Conference, as "small of stature, and of unassuming face and mien"; yet "the first time he rose to give out a notice, the whole conference applauded as though it would never cease." Christian Britain now knew his worth. Some wanted to show their appreciation of this triumph of organization: "But those that knew were aware that, more than any other, the spirit that was in this very unobtrusive exterior had been at the back of that great conference, not merely in respect of its organization and its methods, but also of its ideals, its aspirations, and its hopes."

At Northfield at the old quadrennial student volunteer conventions, at Liverpool in 1896, and at Edinburgh in 1910, we were all on a common level; we were all at the bottom. As in Isaiah's vision, God was all in all. The Edinburgh convention revealed not only a world of desperate human need and the Christian forces striving toward unity to meet that need but also the baleful effects of the chaotic disunion of Christendom. Men like Oldham felt this deeply, and the following year Bishop Brent set in motion forces that brought into existence the Faith and Order Movement.

Oldham from 1908 to 1910 was the highly efficient general secretary of the World Missionary Conference at Edinburgh, and then from 1910 to 1921 the secretary of its Continuation Committee. John R. Mott as chairman and Oldham as secretary made a wonderful team, in their differing gifts supplementing each other. The Edinburgh Conference marked the first milestone of a *world* missionary movement. Hitherto there had been no unified mission policy, no one Church of Christ with its mission to one world-wide field. That began at Edinburgh. It was perhaps conceived first in the hearts of Joe Oldham and John Mott and a widening group of their fellow workers. In the judgment of Tissington Tatlow, Edinburgh owed its success to Oldham more than to any one person. The Edinburgh Conference did not just happen. Years before its public achivement, this conference was conceived in thought and prayer. There were many, many months of preparation. There was thorough and thoughtful and creative work done by its eight commissions, before and after the conference. The Edinburgh Conference as a widely representative body came to grips for the first time as a unit with world problems. It left a unified Continuation Committee, and then a united world organization to carry on the growingly integrated work of the mission of Christianity. This was in the early part of the same decade in which Woodrow Wilson, Lord Cecil, and General Smutts were struggling in the secular sphere, in the midst of a war-torn world, to realize one world organized for peace.

The Edinburgh Conference did not stand alone; it was not an isolated event. It was based upon a great past and it was linked to a continuing future. Even within the last decade there have been five great world-wide and truly ecumenical gatherings. From the time of the meeting in Edinburgh the international leaders began not only to hold other conferences but to organize the Christian world. The Apostle Paul had appointed spiritual "bishops and deacons" in every local church, and had seen the church universal as the body of Christ functioning in the world. But these twentieth-century leaders, recovering Paul's vision, now began to link up scattered churches, nations, and continents. Under the Continuation Committee, Mott and Oldham, working together with men like the Archbishop of Canterbury, Robert Speer, and the more farsighted board secretaries and Christian leaders, began to co-ordinate the policy and work of the various mission boards and denominations. Out of Edinburgh grew the British Conference of Missionary Societies, centering in Edinburgh House, the *International Review of Missions,* and the International Missionary Council. The unifying spirit and message and organization of the Edinburgh Conference was carried to all the scattered and isolated mission fields, like China and India, until some thirty of these national or regional councils were organized. The fruit of this work in developing co-operation, working toward unity and, in some cases, toward organic union of hitherto isolated and competing bodies, will show in all the centuries to come.

Both Mott and Oldham had the Apostle Paul's highly multiplying gift of raising up great fellow workers. There were leaders like Miss Ruth Rouse and men like William Paton in Britain and A. L. Warnshuis of America. I had seen Warnshuis doing great work in Amoy, China, and from 1920, for five years he was associated with Oldham, and part of the time with Paton, in London. Oldham and Warnshuis were both general secretaries of the permanent International Missionary Council and Oldham remained on its staff until 1939. No one man could lead all the work of the world or be everywhere at once. Before the meeting at Edinburgh, there had been two national missionary organizations, the North American Foreign Missionary Conference and the organization in Germany. Geographical considerations made necessary two or more bases or centers of the international missionary movement. As North America was supporting about two thirds of the foreign missionary movement, there had to be a center in New York as well as in London and on the continent of Europe.

When the Germans were embittered and felt left outside the world movement, while Mott was temporarily under their suspicion because he had served on President Wilson's special mission to Russia, Oldham was a great Christian conciliator, with genuine humility, tact, and Christian love. He visited Germany and again brought the Christians of the land of Luther into the heart of the world movement. Oldham also showed great ability when through his efforts provisions were made in the Versailles Treaty for the safeguarding of German missionary property under trustees, and its ultimate return to the German missions. Oldham reads extensively in German theology and philosophy and has been much influenced by German thinkers. I know of no man who so radiantly fulfills Christ's command to love his enemies, to pray for them, and to do them good.

Oldham became editor of the influential *International Review of Missions* and held this post until he passed it on to Paton. K. S. Latourette was the editorial correspondent for America. This periodical proved to be a shuttle to bind together the scattered mission fields and their home bases. The annual January feature of the review was a masterpiece by Oldham—a balanced survey of world-wide missions. He had wide knowledge of Roman Catholic missions and their publications and had many friends among Roman missionary leaders. Oldham's genius, tactful and unobtrusive, helped to organize the British Missionary Conference as it began to take the first cautious and conservative steps in co-operation and growing unity. It had to span wider gulfs between some of the Anglican societies and those of the Free Churches than existed in North America. As soon as the conference of the British missionary societies was organized and working smoothly, Oldham passed on the leadership to his lieutenant, Kenneth Maclennan, and devoted himself to international problems and organization.

Oldham not only had great gifts but like all the rest of us, he also had his limitations and peculiarities. Though his interests were world wide, he had in a sense a single-track mind. With burning interest and terrific absorption, he concentrated on one great issue at a time. This was one secret of his success —concentration rather than superficial or scattering diffusion. He dealt with "one world at a time." I remember seeing him in England when he had just been reading William Ernest Hocking. Not only did he read Hocking but also he personally met Hocking, he thought Hocking, he talked Hocking—until it became a joke among us. Whichever child was upon Luther's knee at any time was his favorite child; so Oldham had in turn many favorite brain children. The International Missionary Council would have fared badly at times had it not been that both Mott and Paton possessed the Pauline power of being interested in a dozen questions at once, and of bearing always on their hearts "the care of all the churches."

Oldham became concerned and absorbed about Germany and German missions until he had done all he could possibly do for them; then he turned the Germans over to his fellow workers Warnshuis and Miss Gibson. Next he took India to his heart. He lived, he thought, he prayed, he planned and organized, for India, enlisting able lieutenants and fellow workers, Indians and foreigners, on behalf of the land that was his first love.

He visited India twice and never rested until the Continuation Committee of India was reorganized into the permanent National Christian Council of India, Burma, and Ceylon, and until William Paton was secured as its able general secretary.

Oldham's next obsession was race. Because of his burning interest, he was asked by the International Missionary Council to devote part of his time to a study of Christianity and racial relations. Racial brotherhood now became his evangel; and this resulted in multiform activities, until in 1922 it bore fruit in his *Christianity and the Race Problem,* which is still a classic. Then Africa, and in particular African education, was laid upon his heart, and absorbed his thought, prayer, and planning. He was never content to beat the air, but gathered influential groups for study; and these, always under Oldham's patient and persistent leadership, resulted in effective action and organization. He studied the contribution which Christian education might make to the solution of Africa's burning problems. Then he turned from the church to the state. He moved heaven and earth and the British Colonial Office to undertake a far-reaching plan of research and reform in their colonial possessions. He then induced the Carnegie and Rockefeller foundations to support these projects. He got the colonial offices of all Europe interested and concerned not only for the Belgian Congo and German East Africa but for the whole continent. He planned and achieved an all-Africa conference of the great powers, which met in Belgium, and then organized the Institute of African Languages and Literature. Oldham was appointed one of three members on a British Royal Commission on East Africa, Tanganyika, and Kenya. Always behind the scenes, never in the limelight, Oldham was nevertheless the commanding general or field marshal for all the Christian forces and government agencies working on behalf of the Dark Continent.

For a time Oldham considered a call to government service connected with Africa, but fortunately he turned back to his major interest in the Kingdom of God. When he wrote *The Remaking of Man in Africa,* published by the Oxford Press in 1931, he was aiming to mold the work of the Christian

Church in Africa; and his aim was high enough to embrace "the *whole* good of African peoples." His book influenced both missions and governments. Oldham felt deeply that the wrongs which Western civilization had committed and was continuing to commit against Africa were such that nothing but the Christian gospel could save that continent. He believed, with Albert Schweitzer, that "we are not free to confer benefits on these men, or not, as we please; it is our duty. Anything we give them is not benevolence but atonement."

Oldham has been at the very heart and soul of the world mission of the Church of Christ. He has the power to see where the next emphasis in the world mission is due. He thinks in continents, he thinks of world problems in world terms. He concentrates upon them one at a time; he gets the Christian Church thinking, until it acts, and then something happens. This was illustrated in the readmission of German missionaries to their fields, and in the Oxford Conference on Church, Community, and State in 1937, where he was the unseen but moving spirit. He is a spiritual world statesman at the heart of the world mission of Christianity.

WILLIAM PATON

William Paton, or Bill Paton as he was affectionately called, was for well-nigh four decades a fellow worker of Oldham and Mott, from the time of his student days at Oxford until he died in 1943 at the early age of fifty-seven. He was both a world statesman and, in a broad sense, an evangelist of a whole gospel, in which its individual and social aspects were vitally integrated. He was both deeply devout and completely modern. At the time of his death he was the secretary of the International Missionary Council, he had been editor of the *International Review of Missions* since 1927, and he had been joint general secretary of the Provisional Committee of the World Council of Churches since 1938.

William Paton was born in London, November 13, 1886. He was educated at Whitgift School, Croydon, and Pembroke College, Oxford. He entered heart and soul into the evangelistic meetings at the university conducted by John R. Mott and William Temple, then a young Oxford don, and was one of the moving spirits of the Christian life of the students. He read "Greats" at Oxford and took honors in "Classical Moderations." He pursued his theological studies at Westminster College, Cambridge. From 1911 to 1921 he was central secretary for volunteers and missionaries and later assistant general secretary of the Student Christian Movement of Great Britain and Ireland. Here he followed in the great succession of Donald Fraser, Joe Oldham, and Tissington Tatlow. In Tatlow's opinion Paton was "the best qualified missionary secretary the movement ever had." He was a sound theologian, of vigorous churchmanship and good judgment, who always kept his theology related to actual life.

While Paton was an influential factor in shaping and furthering the entire comprehensive program of the Student Christian Movement, his most distinctive contribution was in the development of its missionary life and action. In outlining the plans for mission study, in ensuring the preparation of suitable missionary textbooks, including some of his own authorship, in organizing the bands of student missionary volunteers and stimulating their recruiting activities, in his countless intensive visits among the colleges and universities, and in helping to ensure the success of annual Swanwick student conferences and the great missionary quadrennial gatherings, he accomplished a work of far-reaching importance.

Paton was an effective promoter of the World's Student Christian Federation and worked in collaboration with other leaders in three of its conferences—at Constantinople in 1911, at Lake Mohonk in 1913, and at St. Beatenberg, Switzerland, in 1920. Throughout his ever-growing intellectual development, he never lost touch with the student life of the world. His words to the students of Britain just after World War I reveal his attitude and his own knowledge of the world situation:

Knowledge of the actual facts of the world situation is the first essential. We ought to know something of the meaning of the race problem—that urgent and perplexing question which greets us wherever we look around the fringes of the Pacific, in India, in Africa, in America, and in Great Britain. We ought all of us to know something, and some of us to know a great deal, about the industrial and economic linking up of the world, and the far-reaching effects it has had upon the lives of the peoples of Africa and Asia. Confronted as we are by the great venture which is now being made in Indian government, we ought to know the major issues which are at stake, and have some idea of the spirit and attitude needed in Britishers who are to be of any real service to the new India. We ought to know something, and some of us to know a great deal, about the great religions which maintain sway over Asia and Africa and enter into the very fibre of the life of millions of our fellow human beings. I do not pretend that, within limits of our college careers, we can all expect, or should expect, to know very much about these things, but we ought to have enough knowledge to gain the right point of view.

A short period of Paton's life was devoted to India. At the call of K. T. Paul, who became his intimate friend and fellow worker, Paton began student work in India under the Y.M.C.A. He was soon called, however, to be the general secretary of the National Christian Council of India, Burma, and Ceylon, during its formative and important period of foundation laying, from 1922 to 1927. This was one of the most important posts in connection with the world mission. Paton helped to perfect this organization, which was soon recognized as one of the four or five most efficient and fruitful of the thirty or more national Christian councils of the world. In his frequent tours of visitation throughout his great field, he also fostered the development of agencies and plans in different provinces of the country. In addition to his work of organization and visitation, he made a great contribution in launching and editing the *National Christian Council Review,* possibly the most ably conducted organ among the various national councils. Paton's editorials throughout the period of his editorship are remarkable and have done much to influence missionary policy and practice.

After his invaluable experience in India, in 1926 Paton was called back to the home base in London as secretary of the International Missionary Council. As the work of the council gathered momentum and the demands for its service multiplied, it became necessary to add him as a third secretary to the two remarkably effective men already on the staff, J. H. Oldham and A. L. Warnshuis. From that time down to the day of his death, Paton carried forward his great trust from strength to strength. It would be difficult to decide where he rendered his most important service, whether at his London office or out in the field —and his field was literally the world. Much could be written of his different visits to India, of his brief round-the-world journey, of his many visits to North America, and of his errands to the Continent. On the other hand, one cannot overstate the value of his ably conducted office, with its countless ministries, not only to the network of national councils throughout the world but also to his well-maintained relationships with governments and with various ecumenical organizations. His ability, knowledge, and experience will be missed by the entire world mission.

The careful and wise planning of Oldham, Paton, and Warnshuis made possible the important gatherings at Jerusalem in 1928 and Tambaram in 1938. And the work of these men was furthered by their able editorial colleagues, the Misses Gollock, Underhill, and Sinclair. Paton's last years became increasingly concerned and occupied with the great ecumenical development connected with the World Council of Churches, now in process of formation. He took part in the significant sequence of preparatory meetings—at Westfield College, London; Oxford; Edinburgh; and Utrecht. He was then called to become an associate with W. A. Visser't Hooft as one of the two general secretaries of the provisional committee for bringing into being the World Council of Churches. Attention should be called to Paton's large and influential part during the last two years of his life in bringing into being the important and most promising British Council of Churches. Fortunately he has left on record the results of much of his researches, experience, and reflections. There were notable articles and editorials in the periodicals to which he was related, many reports and forecasts of conferences and commissions, and pamphlets and leaflets bearing on opportunities and preparation for life service, and also various printed volumes. Among the more recent of his books are *The Church and the New Order*, 1941, and *Continental Christianity in War Time*, 1942.

A few pages of cold print cannot tell the story of this great soul, who was a fearless pathfinder and a sane as well as a burning crusader. Upon the news of Paton's untimely death, at the height of his powers in the midst of his growingly fruitful work, John R. Mott wrote in the *International Review of Missions* in January, 1944, this tribute to Paton's memory:

He devoted his whole life and all his powers to serving great causes. One of the finest things about him was his selflessness. He thought in large dimensions: international, interracial, inter-confessional, oecumenical. He comprehended great issues. He had developed a great tolerance. Recall his aggressive attacks on anti-semitism. Think of his identification with the cause of the untouchables. He believed that the only path of progress lay in the fearless facing of difficulties and in believing in a Truth which transcends them. He had an unerring sense of what really mattered. He had the ability to command the confidence of men of large affairs and great influence. We think at once of such men as the Metropolitan of India, the Viceroy of India, the Archbishop of Canterbury, Ambassador Winant and leaders of various departments of the Government.

He was sane, balanced and never went off at tangents. One recalls the discerning remark of Tissington Tatlow: "The Student Christian Movement has had few leaders who possessed such absolute 'horse sense'—to use his own phrase—as did Bill Paton."

He had a first-rate mind. . . . In his reading he was reflective and covered a wide range. He richly deserved the honorary D.D. conferred upon him by Edinburgh University. He had an amazing capacity for work. He took on too much, but he insisted on doing it all well and he never allowed himself to be harassed. His work was characterized by conscientious thoroughness in dealing with every trust. . . .

In all his dealings with men he was downright, frank and courageous. He never failed to take issue with men advocating or supporting wrong or questionable positions and practices.

At the base of his character and of all his constructive action was unshakable religious conviction. He had a firm grasp of essential Christianity and triumphant trust (to use his own language) in "the Incarnate Word, Jesus Christ, and the Body in which that Word still speaks." His was a deeply devotional spirit. It did not express itself so much in words as in attitudes and actions, again, in resisting the sins of the tongue and, above all, in silences unto God. . . .

One cannot understand Paton without thinking of him in relation to his family. One hesitates about entering into this sacred circle, but I must bear testimony. In all my wide acquaintance I recall no one who furnishes a better example of maintaining throughout all their years, from their tender childhood right up into the years of entering upon the serious burden-bearing and conflicts of life, such constant, unhurried and helpful relations to each of his six children. . . .

As we reflect on the career and contribution of our friend, so abounding in helpfulness, and remind ourselves that he is now in the land of large dimensions and occupied with the high activities of the heavenly host (are they not all ministering spirits?) let us, with vivid appreciation of the great gap in our ranks occasioned by his translation, close up the gap by multiplying our number, by fighting the harder and, above all, by reliance upon superhuman wisdom, love and power.

JOHN R. MOTT

In bringing to a close this series of brief biographical sketches, I give the final place to John R. Mott because he, possibly more than any other, was used of God to draw together and organize the Christian forces of our generation.[3] Just as the Apostle Paul had to organize little groups of believers as churches, appointing "bishops and deacons" in every place, so the crusading student movement of our generation had to be organized and integrated. Organization to Mott was not an end in itself. The

[3] In this sketch I am indebted for various quotations and facts to Basil Mathews' well-written *John R. Mott, World Citizen*, Harper, 1934.

essential thing was spiritual life. But in our earthly existence the human spirit animates a body "fitly framed and knit together" which enables it to function. Mott knew that the spirit must come first, but like Wesley he did not ignore the body. As a Christian statesman he was the chief organizer used of God to weave together in five great movements many of the spiritual forces of the modern world.

John Raleigh Mott was born in Livingston Manor, New York, May 25, 1865. The Daughters of the American Revolution have placed a tablet by the roadside which reads: "This marker overlooks the farm in the valley on which was born John R. Mott." When John was two years old his father, John Stitt Mott, moved with his family to Postville, Iowa, a village of some five hundred inhabitants, where he entered the lumber business, hoping that later his son would succeed him in the enterprise. Mott's mother was an earnest Christian; three magazines which came into the home were typical of her interest: *The Christian Advocate, The Guide to Holiness,* and *The Heathen Woman's Friend.* Thus Mott all but imbibed Methodism, holiness, and missions with his mother's milk!

When John was thirteen, the Iowa Quaker evangelist J. W. Dean held evangelistic meetings in the town, and not only the boy himself but also his father and one of his sisters professed conversion and joined the Methodist Church. The unusually earnest and able pastor, Reverend Horace Warner, spent many hours with John and kindled in the boy the habit of good reading and an ambition for a college education. Accordingly, John entered the financially poor and struggling Upper Iowa University at Fayette and spent four profitable years there. There was little of outward promise in this tall, gangling, freckled youth, whose stubborn crop of reddish-brown hair was worn aggressively pompadour, standing straight up when I first knew him. In those early days and all his life, I can testify to his human qualities. He had a normal though hidden sense of humor, which appeared especially when he was tired. I have sat up till after midnight reading detective thrillers aloud with him on shipboard—books which he had taken for rough weather,

292

for he was a bad sailor. These found their place in his habitual trunkload of books. And he was full of pranks and practical jokes. But he was, even in the early days, terribly in earnest— he must have been born so. He found his major interest in college not in athletics but in his studies, especially in English literature, history, and philosophy. He joined one of the two rival literary and debating societies, the Philomathean, whose constitution proclaimed its members' purpose to develop their "moral, social and intellectual faculties, . . . to become active participants in the great battle of life."

Lacking the ripe culture that Mott's younger contemporary John Buchan was enjoying at Oxford, the college on that Western prairie was rawboned and efficient. Mott early familiarized himself with the state papers of the early presidents and statesmen of the United States, and secured copies of many of them for the Philomathean library. His enthusiasm was "for high politics through the convincing power of logical oratory." He won prizes in debates and orations on the questions of Chinese immigration thirty years before Woodrow Wilson was to urge him to become United States Minister to China; and he also debated successfully "Our Debt to the Twentieth Century," on which occasion he waxed eloquent against "the red flag of Communism" and "the blighting curse of the liquor traffic."

As a raw college boy of seventeen, Mott had mastered *Robert's Rules of Order* and was showing a deep interest in politics, constitutional law, historical analysis, and logical reasoning. Professor Chauncey Colegrave speaks of his early interest in these things and in English literature, in which he showed dramatic talents in his acting of *Macbeth*. His paper on English literature was marked "perfect," and was kept by the professor for thirty years as a prized possession. Even then Professor Colegrave considered Mott a prodigious worker, "destined for greatness." Mott's 385-page account book, kept through Upper Iowa and Cornell, is a marvel of accuracy, and contains his systematic rules, drawn up at the early age of nineteen for the regulation of his life. Governor Larrabee of Iowa proposed to Mott the ambitious vocation of the law as leading to a political career.

In 1885 Mott entered the Sophomore Class of Cornell University at the mature age of twenty. He had joined the Methodist Church and the Y.M.C.A. immediately upon entering college, but he was assailed by agnostic doubts during this early stage of his college course. On January 14, 1886, the Cambridge cricketer J. Kynaston Studd—later knighted, and Lord Mayor of London—came to Cornell on his visit to the American colleges at D. L. Moody's invitation. Mott said concerning this visit: "As I entered the hall I heard the speaker give three short sentences which proved to be the turning point in my life: 'Seekest thou great things for thyself? Seek them not. Seek ye first the Kingdom of God.' . . . On these few words hinged my life-investment decision. I went back to my room that night not to sleep but to fight."

After an interview with Studd the following day Mott, under deep conviction of sin, began in earnest to study his Bible, spending an hour a day in his morning devotional period. His coming out into a clear faith in the following months was greatly facilitated by his helpful service among prisoners in the county jail. Whatever his own doubts, he found that nothing less than Christ could save these criminals, some of whom were completely changed in character by their new faith.

After Mott was chosen president of the Christian Association of Cornell the membership of the association increased from slightly more than a hundred to three hundred and thirty out of a total of eight hundred students in the university. At this time C. K. Ober twice visited Cornell to try to persuade Mott to become one of the two national student secretaries of the North American Student Associational Movement. After Mott, at Ober's request, had prayed—behind an old coal shed opposite the station—for guidance in the matter of his entering the secretaryship, he decided to try for one year this form of Christian work, instead of preparing for the legal profession or of entering the lumber business as he had formerly planned. He was chosen as a delegate to represent Cornell at the first Christian Student Conference for the States and Canada, held in 1886 at Mount Hermon, where 251 men from eighty-nine colleges spent a month with Mr. Moody and other eminent Bible teachers. By the last day of the conference exactly 100 delegates, including Mott, had volunteered for the foreign field, pledging: "We are willing and desirous, God permitting, to become foreign missionaries."

As in the case of Robert Speer, the terrific wrench of turning his back forever on his ambition for business, law, and politics and the signing of that volunteer declaration changed and focused Mott's whole life. He now confronted the humanly impossible task of the evangelization of a whole world "in *this* generation." One world at a time was enough even for Mott; but great tasks, grappled with in earnest, make great men.

In many ways Mott was the Wesley of the nineteenth century. Both men had a titanic capacity for work, both took a high stand in scholarship in the university, and both were proficient in debate there; both formed an inner circle, or "holy club," in student days; both were voracious readers; both were preeminently rational men with a horror of emotionalism; both had iron wills; both, though somewhat autocratic, learned to be supremely tactful in working with men; both became great evangelists—though Wesley had not Whitefield's natural gift and Mott lacked Moody's human touch—both were prolific speakers and writers and incessant travelers; but above all, both were great organizers.

Of his organizing ability Wesley wrote in his *Journal:* "I know this is the peculiar talent God has given me"; Mott did not even need to write it. If either faced a church or a state, a mob or a world, he must organize it. Successively Mott helped to organize five great movements:

1. First was the fervid crusade of students volunteering to evangelize a whole world within their lifetime. Over two thousand had felt impelled to sign cards indicating their desire of becoming missionaries, but there were indications of reaction and the disintegration of this impulsive movement, which lacked supervision and continuity. Mott's first task as a college Y.M.C.A. secretary, assigned by his chairman, Cleveland H. Dodge, was to organize and save this movement. Mott formed

a small permanent committee with official representatives of the Intercollegiate Y.M.C.A., the Y.W.C.A., and the Interseminary Missionary Alliance, as the executive committee of the Student Volunteer Movement for Foreign Missions for the States and Canada. Then, at the invitation of Donald Fraser and the British leaders, Mott placed his experience at the disposal of the movement in Great Britain. Without Mott's talents the volunteer movement would have been almost as evanescent as the crusade under Peter the Hermit. But under Mott's leadership as chairman for nearly forty years, from 1888 to 1920, it became a disciplined, dependable movement related to the colleges, the churches, and the mission boards, which sent out sixteen thousand student volunteers, three fourths of whom were from North America, in the one-world mission of the Church of Christ. By 1940 eighteen thousand volunteers had reached their fields. This was something beyond the dreams of William Carey, or of the Williams haystack band, or even of the Apostle Paul, made possible only in the nineteenth century with its genius for organization.

2. The second movement with which Mott was identified was the Young Men's Christian Association. Here he followed McBurney, Morse, and Wishard; but he became the master organizer of them all. He was in turn student secretary (1888-1915), foreign secretary (1898-1915), and general secretary (1915-31) of the International Committee of the Young Men's Christian Association, and then chairman of the World's Committee of the association at Geneva from 1926 to the present. When Mott gave up the leadership of the student work in 1915 there were 778 student associations with 75,000 members, 120 employed secretaries, and a voluntary enrolment of 38,000 engaged in Bible study. That meant that the association then occupied nearly all of the accessible liberal arts colleges and universities of that day, when the chief emphasis was upon personal religion and personal evangelism. There were three thousand students in attendance annually at summer conferences, such as Northfield, Lake Geneva, and Blue Ridge.

Through Mott and his associates the habit of the "morning

JOHN R. MOTT

watch" of Bible study and prayer became for fifty years the practice of a multitude of students, ministers, and missionaries of that generation. As foreign and then general secretary, Mott with his fellow workers sent out nearly six hundred men to foreign fields, for long or short periods, he organized hundreds of local associations, and helped to plant the association movement with its modern developments in thirty-two countries. He quietly helped to raise a fund of some twelve million dollars for over a hundred of the finest modern association buildings in the teeming cities of the Orient, Latin America, and Europe—cities which were rife with temptation for young men—and saw the membership of the associations throughout the world rise to some two million.

In the first World War a wonderful ministry for soldiers and prisoners of war was launched by Mott and his associates. As soon as the United States joined in the conflict, the program of the American associations rapidly expanded, until by the end of the war, in 1918, it was not only serving 4,600,000 men in the American Army and Navy at home and abroad but also carrying forward a program of service on behalf of over five million prisoners of war and many millions of men in certain of the Allied armies and navies. In the United War Work Campaign, President Wilson asked the seven organizations raising funds to unite their appeals and requested that Mott direct the campaign. Although conducted against unparalleled obstacles, such as the raging epidemic of influenza, this campaign, which appealed for $170,000,000, finally raised $192,000,000 for the seven agencies—a sum which was characterized later as the largest voluntary offering in history.

In addition to the warm commendation of the association war work by presidents Woodrow Wilson and Theodore Roosevelt, President Taft wrote:

The American Young Men's Christian Association in its welfare work served between four and five millions of soldiers and sailors, at home and overseas. As General Pershing has said, it conducted nine tenths of the welfare work among the American forces in Europe. Moreover, alone among American welfare societies, this or-

297

ganization, first and last, ministered to not less than nineteen millions of the soldiers of the Allied Armies, and extended its helpful activities to over five millions of prisoners of war. Its operations were conducted on western, southern, and eastern fronts in Europe; in northern and eastern Africa; in western, southern, and eastern Asia; in North and South America; and in different parts of the island world. It may be questioned whether in all time a human society has ever brought its helpful ministry to such vast numbers of men over such wide areas, under such varying conditions, and in so short time. . . . It would be difficult to overstate the value of the unselfish action of the association in the war, viewing it from a military point of view.[4]

Most tragic and inspiring was the opportunity for work among the millions of men in the prisoner-of-war camps in World War I, as it has been also for a yet larger number of prisoners in World War II. Although physically alive, many of these men were spiritually dead or hopeless. For these prisoners, many of whom would otherwise rot in despair, both mentally and morally, to have the benefit of a recreational program, to study and take correspondence courses under the direction of their own national educators, and even in many cases to be permitted to take their examinations and degrees, has been an unimaginable privilege; and to those who have directed this noble work in both wars the words of Jesus truly apply: "I was in prison, and ye came unto me."

3. Always reaching out toward the one world, Mott and his associate, Karl Fries of Sweden, next helped to organize, in 1895, the World's Student Christian Federation in the old medieval castle at Vadstena in Sweden. During his twenty-five years as general secretary of the federation, Mott helped organize and then draw into this world fellowship nearly a score of national Christian student movements and fostered their spiritual growth. The World's Student Christian Federation united Christian student societies in approximately three thousand universities and colleges, with a total membership of some three

[4] *Service with Fighting Men*, Association Press, 1922, I, 246.

hundred thousand men and women students spread over forty countries on all continents.

The federation began at Vadstena with five movements representing ten countries. Before 1897 it doubled the number of movements included largely as the result of Mott's first world tour as general secretary of the federation, which tour took over twenty-one months, from 1895 to 1897, and covered some sixty thousand miles. Mott visited 144 universities and colleges in twenty-four countries, he established 70 local Christian unions, and organized national student movements in India, China, Japan, Australia, New Zealand, and in some areas of Europe and the Near East. The Bishop of Ely called Mott the "Ulysses among modern missionaries." Wesley in fifty years had traveled the amazing total of a quarter of a million miles in an age when railways and steamships were unknown. The total of Mott's journeys by land and sea now reaches some two million miles, or the equivalent of over seventy times round the globe. This is probably a world's record. This traveling work forced Mott to write in order to meet the needs of the colleges and churches he sought to serve. When he wrote his first Christian pamphlet in his student work, there was only one other devotional pamphlet of its kind that had been published. This period of travel led to the publishing of a long list of books, among the more recent of which are *Five Decades and a Forward View*, 1939, and *The Larger Evangelism*, 1944.

4. Mott sought to co-operate with mission board secretaries in organizing on January 12, 1893, the Foreign Missions Conference of North America. He was elected repeatedly to serve as a member of the Committee of Reference and Council, the executive body of this conference, which unites the missionary forces of the United States and Canada. He was elected honorary life member of that committee at the Foreign Missions Conference in 1942.

At the fiftieth foreign missionary conference—1893-1943— Mott reviewed the progress of five decades that have culminated in the International Missionary Council. This council is, as he points out, composed of the missionary forces of North America united with similar bodies of all other parts of the world. This movement dates back to the Edinburgh Conference of 1910 and its Continuation Committee, which requested Mott to carry out a series of twenty-one regional conferences across Asia in 1912-13. The conduct of these conferences was a masterly piece of work. While working to the point of fatigue the best minds in Asia, Mott himself was doing two men's work—managing the conferences and speaking to huge audiences of students at night in evangelistic campaigns. These conferences in some countries brought into being national missionary councils, which later became national Christian councils in India, China, and Japan, uniting indigenous and foreign elements; and these national councils were linked in fellowship constitutionally with the central Continuation Committee of the Edinburgh Conference. Mott was chairman of this body and its successor, the International Missionary Council, for a period of thirty-one years. A series of world conferences, over all of which he presided, brought together carefully chosen representatives of all regions, races, and communions and marked the milestones of advance in the organization of the Christian forces of the world.

At Edinburgh in 1910 there had been fourteen hundred delegates, all from the older churches of Europe and North America except a score of nationals representing the younger churches. At the Jerusalem meeting of the International Missionary Council in 1928, a third of the delegates were from the churches of Asia, Africa, Latin America, and the Pacific islands; while a decade later at the World Meeting of the International Missionary Council at Tambaram, Madras, fully half the delegates were from the younger churches. Under Mott's leadership, aggressive Anglo-Saxon foreign imperialism was taking a back seat and nationals of the younger churches were brought forward in leadership and developed in initiative.

Within the last decade there have been five great world-wide and truly ecumenical gatherings: the World Conference of the Young Men's Christian Association held at Mysore, India, January, 1937; the World Conference of the Universal Christian Council for Life and Work at Oxford in July, 1937; the World

Conference on Faith and Order at Edinburgh in August, 1937; the World Meeting of the International Missionary Council at Tambaram, near Madras, India, in 1938; and the World Christian Youth Conference at Amsterdam in 1939. Mott is the only person who attended all of these creative gatherings. They all revealed world-wide interest and concern on the part of the Christians of all lands; world-wide recognition of the fact that the problems of the day which most burden us can be solved only in a world-wide context, and a world-wide desire and purpose on the part of Christians to come together for united fellowship, thinking, planning, and action. This is a phenomenon of the twentieth century foreseen and made possible at the epoch-making conference in Edinburgh.

5. The fifth great unity into which Mott, working with other Christian leaders, has been trying to organize the world, is the World Council of Churches, now in process of formation. This movement has been arrested, of course, and held in abeyance by World War II. How can we realize "one world" when we now have to enumerate our world wars serially and when, like the poor, isolationists are always with us, seeming blindly intent on national "security" and national advantage in World War III, making all but impossible a just and durable peace? These men do not see what Thomas Carlyle saw in 1850 and what is more true today than it was a century ago: "There must be a new world if there is any world at all. These days of universal death must be days of universal rebirth if ruin is not to be total and final."

The Protestant world had been shattered into two hundred and more sects in the divisions of the nineteenth century. Even in 1816 there was organized the American Bible Society, which was followed by the Sunday School Union; in 1846 the Evangelical Alliance was formed, and then the World's Y.M.C.A. and the World's Y.W.C.A. But it was only the twentieth century that marked a real turn of the tide at Edinburgh, in 1910. Mott had taken a vital part in the movement for "faith and order" launched by Bishop Brent and other great catholic souls. In the first conference, at Lausanne, Switzerland, in 1927, many of us heard Bishop Brent sorrowfully admit: "In our breasts most of us are devotees of the cult of the incomplete—sectarianism."

The second conference, the World Conference on Faith and Order, held at Edinburgh in August, 1937, marked a great advance over Lausanne. The ideals of the Conference on Life and Work, held at Stockholm in 1925 and promoted by Bishop Söderblom, the primate of Sweden, were realized much more fully in the next conference, the Conference on Life and Work at Oxford, in July, 1937, where 119 churches from forty-five nations were represented. The realists at Oxford said: "We have tried to look without illusion at the chaos and disintegration of the world."

It marked another advance when the leaders of the two movements on "Life and Work" and "Faith and Order" met at Utrecht, Holland, in May, 1938, with seven representatives from each conference serving on a committee of fourteen. At the same time that the representatives of the secular League of Nations were meeting at Geneva in a "council of despair" on the issue of Ethiopia, eighty leaders of world Christianity were meeting at Utrecht as a council of hope. The report of the first conference on Christian unity, which met in Jerusalem, is preserved in the fifteenth chapter of Acts. In the last conference on Christian unity, held at Utrecht, May 9-13, 1938, the Provisional Committee adopted, without a single dissenting voice, a constitution and plan of organization for the World Council of Churches. They say that this council is "a fellowship of churches which accept our Lord Jesus Christ as God and Saviour."

The World Council of Churches is in no sense intended to be a superchurch. Mr. Visser't Hooft, the general secretary of the Provisional Committee, who presided at the youth conference of fifteen hundred delegates at Amsterdam, shows that the leaders who are ready at the close of the war to bring into being the World Council of Churches can even now engage in study, in planning, and in mutual aid for the distressed countries and churches. All men of vision and good will can even now work in co-operation, in a spirit of unity, looking toward ultimate union, when we may fulfill the prayer of our Lord that we may all be one. The new quarterly review, *Christendom,* may be a symbol and prophecy that we may realize a great ideal more perfectly than it was realized during the Middle Ages.

In all these movements it is generally recognized that John R. Mott has been indeed a world leader. As truly as John Wesley, Mott can repeat the words of the great Augustine: "I take a whole Christ for my Saviour; I take the whole Bible for my staff; I take the whole Church for my fellowship." That is what we all want to do, not in the letter, but in spirit and in truth. Even though no formal organizational meeting can be held in a war-torn world, we look for unity not in words, creeds, or definitions but as founded in Jesus Christ himself. Unfortunately, all are not yet ready to enter into full communion with each other and to act as one undivided body. Most of us, however, are ready to give up all policies of sectarian isolationism and enter at least into Christian conversation and fellowship with each other. We should all seek *Una Sancta,* and enter into this spiritual holy of holies with our Lord.

All his life Mott has been seeking to bring together Christians, and then, as far as may be possible without any loss of Christian loyalty, men of all faiths. It seems paradoxical that a little village on the prairies of Iowa should have provided a leader for a world mission of the Church of Christ which, with the seeds of international understanding that have already been planted, may some day, without leaving God out, be instrumental in organizing the world for peace. Mott was not only the Christian leader in Cornell but was also one of a small group who took the initiative in forming the Religious Association, which included not only Protestant, Catholic, and Eastern Orthodox Christians but also Jews, Buddhists, and—at times—Mormons. Even while Pundita Ramabai was a Hindu, Mott formed at Cornell a Ramabai Circle to support her work. Mott, who has worked with Roman Catholics as far as they themselves would permit, has a greater knowledge of the working of the Roman Catholic Church throughout the world than almost any other Protestant. And his deep interest in the Jews and their welfare is well known. In speaking to students of non-Christian faiths in Asia he boldly said: "I beg of you to hold on to everything in your own faith which reason, conscience, and experience show you to be the truth; but do not let that keep you from entering upon an ever-deepening acquaintance with Christ, who made the stupendous claim, 'I am the way, the truth, and the life.' "

The former Archbishop of Canterbury, Dr. Davidson, on August 6, 1912, gave Mott a letter of introduction commending his work to Anglican bishops in Eastern lands. No other man has had such access to or influence with the Eastern Orthodox Church all over the world. In 1917 Mott was asked to address the Great Sobor of the Russian Orthodox Church, then in session at Moscow. The bishops of the divided Syrian churches in Travancore journeyed a thousand miles to Carey's college in Serampore, to permit Mott to endeavor to reconcile their differences. I can remember E. C. Carter's little boy climbing into the laps of these venerable patriarchs and to their great delight pulling their long beards, calling one a "white pussy" and the other a "black pussy"—which even Mott would not have dared to do! A thousand things has Mott done in his nearly fourscore years, on the public platform and more especially behind the scenes, in striving for co-operation, for sympathy, for understanding, and for the unity of the divided hosts that cannot yet say:

> Like a mighty army
> Moves the Church of God.

In some ways more remarkable than Mott's work of organization was his ministry as a world evangelist to students. I can remember the days before he developed this gift. When he spoke to the students in the University of Virginia on their temptations, he had to throw himself upon God for a bold evangelistic message—and it was given him. Mott addressed himself to the reason, the conscience, and the will—not to the emotions. He could not touch the heart of the man in the street, as Moody could. But Mott's method appealed to critical students.

When in 1889 the students of the University of Tennessee were so moved that men came out publicly for Christ, President Dabney said: "You have at last touched the men of the state university, which has never been done before." All regular Monday classes and lectures were canceled in order that the students might hear Mott's message, and "a spiritual wave swept the meeting" as some thirty men publicly accepted Christ. This broke the ice in other colleges of the South, and finally this work of evangelism was carried over the world among students of sixty nations. To the amazement of academic circles, the universities of Oxford, Cambridge, and conservative Edinburgh fell like the walls of Jericho. The often flippant and cynical student magazine, the Oxford *Isis,* wrote:

Dr. Mott is in the true sense a great statesman. . . . It is his wonderful intellectual power (it will be remembered that he was nominated to fill the post rendered vacant by Mr. Woodrow Wilson, at Princeton University, but he declined it), his amazing sympathy, and above all the intense devotion of his whole being to his work of bringing home to university and college students a fuller sense of the meaning of their life that stamp Dr. Mott as indubitably one of the greatest men alive today.

This experience was repeated in the university cities of the world: Paris, Milan, Naples, Rome, Budapest, Athens, Moscow, Cairo, Calcutta, Canton, Peiping, and Tokyo. One or two thousand students a night would listen in hushed conviction as Mott spoke on "Be Sure Your Sins Will Find You Out." This was true whether the students were Moslems, Hindus, Buddhists, or Christians. In Moscow the heart-hungry students followed Mott about day and night. In Cairo the Abbas Theater was overcrowded with two thousand students. In Mukden five thousand students and teachers attended. In Canton the audience would not leave, and Mott had to give three addresses in succession—for three hours.

Not only was Mott a great evangelist but he was also, as he was often called, "a master of assemblies," the outstanding Christian presiding officer of his day. At Edinburgh he held the most distinguished speakers to time and called them down on the second, yet without offense to them or to the audience. He was equally adept at chairmaning a conference or committee: he could draw out the maximum contribution of each veteran or specialist, or of each more timid representative of the younger churches. And he was a great financier and a master money-raiser. Here I have never seen his equal. I remember a half-hour luncheon with a New York multimillionaire. As we waited for the rich man's arrival, Mott got up his faith and raised his sights to ask him for a million dollars. The multimillionaire was profuse in apology and begged off with half a million! I remember an unhurried interview with an industrial magnate and his wife in their home, when they cheerfully responded with a quarter of a million. The greatest giver of them all was the late A. A. Hyde of Wichita, Kansas. He was one of three American laymen who, decade after decade, gave regularly nine tenths of their income to the cause of the Kingdom, sometimes cutting into capital, and gladly ready to die relatively poor.

With deep concern Mott watched the giving of the churches and strove to develop the full consecration of Christian stewardship. He fostered the Laymen's Missionary Movement, which was one agency that helped to lift the giving of the Protestant churches in two decades from nine to forty-five million dollars. The high tide of giving and of mission work was reached before the Wall Street crash of October 29, 1929, and the world depression of that decade. The *World Missionary Atlas* records that in 1925 the annual income for foreign missions of 380 Protestant missionary societies—139 in America—was $70,051,-617. Of this sum, $45,272,793 was from the United States, $3,357,739 from Canada, and $12,821,406 from Great Britain. At that time there were some thirty thousand Protestant foreign missionaries and about the same number of Roman Catholics. Mission work was severely crippled by World War I, by the world depression following, and then again by World War II. American giving to Christian causes fell to pitiful depths, and half the missionaries were recalled by some boards. Even today, when the net national income in the present war boom is approximately twice what it was at the crest of the Coolidge capitalist boom, our giving to foreign missions has never recovered. The total income for foreign missions for the boards and societies for the last year, according to the *Fiftieth Foreign Missions Conference Report* of 1944, is only $22,380,045. Few of the sons of the great Christian stewards who, on Christian principle, were giving one tenth to nine tenths (in exceptional cases) of their annual incomes, have learned sacrificial giving. Although permitted to deduct from their income-tax returns amounts given for charity or benevolence up to 15 per cent of their total incomes, American Christians as a whole have never exceeded 2 per cent of their incomes in giving to churches, missions, and philanthropies.

It would probably be agreed that no man of our time has so stimulated Christian giving as has John R. Mott. Within a period of fifty years he has been in a position of major responsibility toward raising some $300,000,000 for Christian and philanthropic work in war and in peace. And his first concern has always been the adequate support of the world mission of Christianity. In this connection, although I have never known or cared to inquire, I have always suspected that the presence of many of the poor Oriental delegates at the Jerusalem Conference—or the several thousand other delegates from the younger churches at world student or church conferences during the last three decades—was due not only to sacrificial giving by churches, students, and student movements, but especially to John R. Mott and that truly humble Christian, John D. Rockefeller, Jr. At a distance I have watched the latter—who never willingly allowed his left hand to know what his generous right hand was doing—give wisely year after year to Christian causes, especially if they were missionary projects that could in time become self-supporting, self-governing, and self-propagating.

I have not space to carry up to date the story of the life and work of John R. Mott. It was inevitable that honors should be heaped upon him. He was made a Knight of the French Legion of Honor; he was awarded the Distinguished Service Medal by his own country in the last war; he was given the Order of the Sacred Treasure in Japan, where a life-sized bronze bust was made by his admirers. As a world traveler he was a fellow of the Royal Geographical Society. He was appointed a member of the Mexican commission by President Wilson in 1916, and with Elihu Root was on the special diplomatic mission to Russia in 1917. He was offered and declined all kinds of academic and worldly honors and offices. His work was privately and publicly praised by every president from Theodore Roosevelt to Herbert Hoover.

If some student of a later day should read in a musty library this account of John R. Mott, he would probably think it an exaggeration; but it is not. It is only fair, however, to add that Mott, like other men, has his limitations. For one thing he suffers from the extreme individualism that was rampant in the nineteenth century, especially in America. In my own personal view it is a strange psychological phenomenon that neither Mott nor Speer ever adequately saw, or felt, or preached a social gospel—that neither ever realized the full social implications of the whole Christian message. They never seemed to see what Walter Rauschenbusch, Francis McConnell, or Reinhold Niebuhr so clearly envisioned. They never realized the whole individual-social, organically unified message of William Temple, Joe Oldham, and William Paton. Mott, as no other man, fought courageously for my individual right to preach the social gospel, even when the income of the foreign work inevitably suffered thereby. But he never preached it himself. Perhaps he was too close to and too deeply involved in our economic order of capitalism to realize or to expose its evils. I do not say that Mott was *called* to proclaim a radical social message, and I realize that if he had done so he could not have led the united forces of Christendom. I realize also that there are many who will not agree with me in this matter; some of them have, perhaps, never themselves realized the full social implications of the gospel. Mott himself dealt constantly with international issues; he realized the social evils connected with race and war more deeply than he realized economic injustice. In this connection I quote from the *Decennial Review* of the World's Student Christian Federation at the Zeist Conference, 1905, where he says: "The movements should take up the study of social questions, seriously, earnestly and thoroughly. . . . Students must be influenced to stand for bringing the Christian religion into every department and relationship of life—. . . the world of thought, family and social life, commercial and industrial life, municipal affairs, national problems and international relations."

Mott has always been highly sensitive to criticism. He suffers somewhat from the effects of having worked for fifty years in the limelight and almost constantly on the public platform. He is not the greatest character mentioned in this book; but, judged by any standard, religious or secular, he is a great man— and the ablest man I have ever worked with.

He has not only the plodding, rational processes of a statesman but also the swift intuition of a woman. He knows exactly what is going on at the back of the mind of the man to whom he is speaking. He can size up his strength and weakness, and call him to say or do just what needs to be said or done on the occasion. He has always been discovering, developing, and training leaders for the future. His central passion has always been to win the world for Christ.

Mott has been a great friend—as Miss Ruth Rouse, after working with him for forty years, shows in *John R. Mott, an Appreciation*. His friends mean much to him, and he has craved and returned the affection of men like Canon Gairdner. He has had unique contact with the famous personages of the world. After meeting Lord Kitchener in 1910 he wrote: "We talked of affairs in Egypt, the Sudan, South Africa, Australia, and New Zealand, India, Ceylon, China, Japan, Russia, the United States, and Great Britain. We roamed over the fields of war, politics, and education, especially of the backward races."

There is a certain massive and colossal quality about Mott. Dr. Davidson, a former archbishop of Canterbury, who knew all the leaders of Britain of his day, thought Mott had the most impressive presence of any man he had ever seen. Professor Wieman of the University of Chicago describes Mott's presiding at a modernist student conference where "bright young men said smart things, keen things. When occasionally Mott himself spoke they showed him where he was wrong. He never argued. Never once did the slightest note of irritation come into his voice or manner." At the end Mott briefly summarized the situation and stated the simple faith by which he lived. "Then he went away with that calm, unhasty step, with that manner that seemed never ruffled, never excited, never anxious. There is something like the mountains and the sea in John R. Mott. He will always be the same, very simple and a bit sublime."

EPILOGUE

At first glance it may appear that the brief biographical sketches included in this volume lack unity. In a sense this is true. No two individuals were alike. They had all the varying gifts of the diverse members of one body described by the Apostle Paul, but there was a deep unity in their diversity—the unity of the one Kingdom of God on earth and in heaven, of one Church of Christ, militant and triumphant. Their lesson is written large in history.

The three great veterans who laid the foundations for the work of modern missions in Asia—Carey, the cobbler, Morrison, the farmer's boy, and the brilliant Judson—were builders of a new age and of a new world.

The work of Samuel Mills and of Robert Wilder was of obvious historic significance in the awakening of the American churches and colleges and for the evangelization of the world. I chose the members of the first Yale band, not one of whom was in any way remarkable, to show what a small group of consecrated men could do toward the building of a new China and in transforming Korea. Among the pathfinders in India, every life mentioned from Carey to Dr. Ida Scudder shows the abysmal need of that vast subcontinent—physically, mentally, and spiritually—and reveals what a few carefully chosen missionaries in the work of evangelism, education, and modern medicine can do to meet that need. The account of Bishop Thoburn's life is a vindication of mass movements at their best, in spite of the difficulties and obvious dangers in these movements, while the grand pioneering of Dr. Miller and his "boys," so many of whom led in almost every reform movement in India, brings out the complementary and equally necessary agency of educational missions. The work of William Miller was typical of that of a score of great missionary educators I could have described.

The great Dane, Larsen, the beloved Charlie Andrews, and

311

the saintly Miss Carmichael were similar in only one respect—they were all Christlike. Larsen was a rational modernist, Andrews was heterodox, and Amy Carmichael was frankly fundamentalist. Yet I can find no difference between liberals and conservatives in their consecration or in the spiritual results of their work. I believe both are needed provided they are each loyal to Christ and will work with others who differ from them. It seems to me that the lives of men like Bishop Azariah, Bishop Abraham, and K. T. Paul are the obvious fruitage and splendid vindication of foreign missions and missionaries. Azariah would have been a tree climber and devil worshiper, Abraham a nominal member of an almost dead Oriental church, and Paul a pagan worshiper of Krishna, had it not been for God's unspeakable gift through foreign missions.

The nine pathfinders in China herein discussed could no more convert that once proud Middle Kingdom than could Robert Morrison, but with him they believed that God could do it. Timothy Richard was a farsighted pioneer in the discovery of the "worthy"—of all that was good or potentially good in this sinful but most deeply moral country. Bishop Schereschewsky and Dr. Pott were among the noble educators of the leaders of the once illiterate masses of China. Hudson Taylor had laid upon his soul the evangelization of the eleven neglected inland provinces, and fittingly crowned his life as a pathfinder in the last citadel of Changsha. Fletcher Brockman did a unique work for the awakening students of China in the greatest crisis of her history, and boldly claimed every provincial capital and metropolis for Christ.

Karl Reichelt's unique ministry to Buddhists speaks for itself and reminds us, together with the ministries of Schwartz and Larsen, of the mighty contribution that continental Europeans, both Lutheran and Reformed, have made in Asia. The three splendid products of Christian education in China—Chang Po-ling, Wu Yi-fang, and James Y. C. Yen—were all the result not only of educational missions but also of the personal contact or personal work of three great Christians.

The lives of Samuel Zwemer, Canon Gairdner, and Albert

Schweitzer—three brilliant but utterly different men—show at once the dire need of the "dark continent" of Africa and the whole Moslem world and what three men can do to meet it. Zwemer was a prophet to challenge Christendom to confront Islam; the Christlike Gairdner carried the Moslem world upon his heart; and Schweitzer was—and is—not only an individual but also a symbol, like David Livingstone, calling us to heal "this open sore of the world."

I have briefly told the story of the American and British world statesmen and evangelists. Each was a pathfinder in his own way. Each had his faults and limitations; but each of these, as well as each of the others mentioned in this book, had his place and did his work for God. These world statesmen and evangelists were giants, not in any mythical or heroic past, but in our own day; and they have a message for our time.

Is it not possible to draw a single lesson from the widely differing lives recorded in this volume? By life and word, do they not all proclaim with one voice: *Christianity in its very essence is missionary?* God so loved the world that he gave himself in his Son—to the world and for the world. Jesus Christ so loved that he gave himself and sent his apostles and missionaries into all the world with the good news of the Kingdom of God. Not only the early Christians but all true followers of Christ in every age, whenever the vision of one world is recovered and especially at every high tide of abundant life, have felt called, as were the pathfinders and crusaders in this volume, to follow in his steps. We as Christians are called—as truly as the early Twelve, or the later twoscore mentioned in this volume—to give our time, our money, yea, our lives, to the one cause of the Kingdom of God on earth, which we are to seek first, last, and always.

Yesterday I wrote of William Temple as "now" the Archbishop of Canterbury; today I must write of the "late" Archbishop, when, alas, there is no one in sight to take his place. This very morning, as the book goes to press, comes the word of the passing of Fletcher Brockman. One by one the leaders of our generation are passing on. The student movement in

EPILOGUE

America in fifty years has not raised up the like of Mott or
Speer. When these men join "the great majority," when they
pass from the ranks of the church militant to those of the
church triumphant—when, with Wilder and Paton and Temple,
who have already passed over, Oldham and Speer and Mott and
the other living pioneers discussed in this book have entered
the Great Beyond—we shall all sing with deeper meaning: "For
all the saints who from their labor rest." We shall say with
Tennyson, in his *Passing of Arthur:*

> Then from the dawn it seemed there came, but faint
> As from beyond the limit of the world,
> Like the last echo born of a great cry,
> Sounds, as if some fair city were one voice
> Around a king returning from his wars.

STATISTICS OF RELIGIONS AND DENOMINATIONS

We may take the estimated population of the world in 1945 as 2,200,000,000, and the population of Asia as 1,117,221,353, according to the *Lutheran World Almanac,* 1934-37, Volume VIII. I estimate the approximate constituency of the principal religions, and their percentage of the world population, as follows:

RELIGIONS	MILLIONS IN WORLD	PER CENT OF POPULATION
Christians	737	33.5%
Hindus	255	11.6
Mohammedans	250	11.4
Buddhists	150	6.8
Jews	16	0.8

The apportionment of the Christian denominations, based on figures from the *Lutheran Almanac,* is as follows:

CHRISTIAN DENOMINATIONS	MILLIONS IN WORLD	PER CENT OF CHRISTIANS
Roman Catholics	375	50.8%
Eastern Orthodox Catholics	165	22.4
Protestants and other Christians	197	26.8
Lutherans	84	11.4
Methodists	25	3.4
Presbyterians	25	3.4
Episcopalians	20	2.7
Baptists	20	2.7
Congregationalists	5	0.7
Disciples of Christ	2	0.3

INDEX

317

INDEX

INDEX

Roman Empire, 12
Rome, 14
Rouse, Ruth, 7
Russia, 5, 19

Sailer, T. H. P., 7
Sanskrit, 27
Santiago, 154
Saracens, 20
Saxons, 12
Scandinavians, 12, 18, 87, 299
Schereschewsky, Bishop, 189-93, 312
Schwartz, C. F., 21, 87, 106-08
Schweitzer, Albert, 251-58, 312
Scotland, 12, 17
Scriptures, 22
Scudder, Ida, 69, 128-38
Sepulcher, 11
Serampore, 22, 27
Servant of the Lord, 254
Slavic missions, 19
Smith, George, 25
Spain, 12
Speer, Robert, 259-70
Stowe, Harriet Beecher, 48
Student Volunteer Movement, 40-48
Syrian Church, 155-60

Tagore, 114, 118
Tamil language, 5, 105, 125
Taylor, Hudson, 60, 194-99
Temple, William, 308, 313
Tennyson, Alfred, Lord, 314
Tertullian, 114
Thessalonica, 14
Thoburn, Bishop, 84-94
Thoburn, Isabella, 93-95
Tinnevelly, 89, 125, 143
Trajan, 14
Tranquebar, 87, 106

Travancore, 87, 88, 155-60
Twelve Apostles, 14

Uganda, 255
Ulfilas, 16
Union Theological Seminary, 48, 50, 54
United Church of South India, 5
Unity and union, 152

Virginia, 21, 200

Ward, William, 22, 30
Wesley, John, 21, 49, 295
Western civilization, 12, 13
Whitefield, George, 21
Whitehead, Bishop, 152
Whittemore, Norman, 50, 70-76
Wilder, Robert, 38, 40-48, 311
Williams haystack, 30, 37, 43
Williams, S. Wells, 35, 179
Wodin, 15
World's Student Christian Federation, 46, 75, 298
Wu Yi-fang, 7, 220-28, 312
Wycliffe, John, 20

Xavier, Francis, 20, 177

Yale, 37, 38, 48, 76
Yale band, 12, 48
Yale-in-China, 56, 62-68, 76
Yen, James Y. C., 7, 199, 227-38, 312
Yenching University, 56, 80
Y.M.C.A., 40, 45, 75, 139, 170-75, 206-10, 295-97
Yun, Tchi Ho, 75

Ziegenbalg, 105
Zwemer, Samuel, 240-47, 312

319